NO CASH,
NO FEAR

NO CASH, NO FEAR

ENTREPRENEURIAL SECRETS TO STARTING ANY BUSINESS WITH NO MONEY

Terry Allen

John Wiley & Sons, Inc.
New York • Chichester • Weinheim • Brisbane • Singapore • Toronto

Published by John Wiley & Sons, Inc.

Published simultaneously in Canada.

This publication is designed to provide accurate and authoritative information in regard to the subject
matter covered. It is sold with the understanding that the publisher is not engaged in rendering professional services. If professional advice or other expert assistance is required, the services of a com-
petent professional person should be sought.

Designations used by companies to distinguish their products are often claimed as trademarks. In all
instances where John Wiley & Sons, Inc., is aware of a claim, the product names appear in initial
capital or all capital letters. Readers, however, should contact the appropriate companies for more
complete information regarding trademarks and registration.

Library of Congress Cataloging-in-Publication Data:

Allen, Terry F.
   No cash, no fear : entrepreneurial secrets to starting any business with no
money / Terry F. Allen.
     p.   cm.
   Includes index.
   ISBN 0-471-41532-4 (pbk. : alk. paper)
   1. Entrepreneurship.   2. New business enterprises—Finance.   3. Small business—
Finance.   4. Allen, Terry F.   I. Title.
HB615 .A67 2001
658.1'1—dc 21

                                       2001023752

Printed in the United States of America.
10 9 8 7 6 5 4 3 2 1

To my parents, Archie and Lucile
To my wife, Debbie
To my sons, Seth, Andrew, and Jared
And to Debbie's daughters, Floery, Heather, Heidi, and Shannon

Who are the true wealth of my life.

CONTENTS

■ Contents ■

PREFACE

In the early 1970s, Harvard Business School published a case study that chronicled my business activities to that time. I was invited to sit in on the first class discussion of the case. My presence was not announced to the class.

The first student who spoke prefaced his analysis with "This is a story of a chronic entrepreneur." It sounded to me like I had been diagnosed as having some terminal disease.

Nearly 30 years have now elapsed, each one filled with new entrepreneurial activities. Clearly, that student had made an astute observation.

I am hopelessly addicted to starting new businesses, and will continue to bet the farm on the next venture until I run out of money. If I do run out of money, I am confident that I can convince someone else to fund the next deal.

I hope my story will make you smile. Perhaps you can benefit from hearing about some of the stumbles. Or be inspired by some of the successes. I did manage to get an awful lot of things going without any money. Starting businesses has been a magnificent rollercoaster ride for me, and I look forward to having you join me for the ride. If you would like to check up on my latest ventures, you can find me at **www.terrystips.com**.

ACKNOWLEDGMENTS

Since this is a story of my life, there are hundreds or thousands of people who influenced or inspired me. I wish I could thank them all.

First, thanks go to my parents, Archie, coach extraordinaire, and Lucile, my lifelong cheerleader. Without them, there would have been no story, at least this one.

Thanks to my best friend, soul mate, and wife, Debbie, for bringing her zest, enthusiasm, and love into my life. I have never known the happiness I now enjoy every day at Muddy Creek Farm.

Thanks to my three sons, Seth, Andrew, and Jared, for being the unique, spirited individuals that they have become. They are constant reminders that no matter how influential parents might be, each child ultimately chooses his or her own path.

Thanks to Debbie's four daughters, Floery, Heather, Heidi, and Shannon—each in a business of her own—for bringing new excitement into my life.

Thanks also to my sister, Christa, and my brother, Jeff, fellow siblings and entrepreneurs, and to my extended family—Charlie, though I still can't beat him at poker; Leslie, mother of my sons, their primary upbringer, and who was loyal throughout; and Winston and her children, Peggy, Brian, Tim, and Amanda, who endured the stormiest years.

Andrew Tobias gave me the idea for the book and encouraged me to write it—he is its true godfather.

A thousand students over the years taught me more than I taught them and provided a wonderful window on their refreshing younger worlds.

■ Acknowledgments ■

Thanks are also due to the entire crew at County Data, who proved that hard work can also be play. Without their contributions, I would still be scrambling to meet payroll.

And finally, thanks go to Beth Diamond, who deciphered my illegible handwriting, encouraged me to keep at it, and edited out the more blatant assaults on grammar and sentence construction.

INTRODUCTION

This is a book about starting businesses with no capital. It is also a manual on how to run any business profitably. Almost everyone gets an idea for a new business sometime in his or her life. Yet, few people act on their idea. Most of the time, they think they don't have enough money to launch the business venture.

While there may be many legitimate reasons for not starting a business, the lack of capital should not be one of them. This book will show you why, using my life as an example.

Since I launched my first business (selling worms and frogs at the age of six), I have started, depending on how you count, about 20 different businesses (and learned at least 40 different lessons). These include everything from manufacturing electronic video games to retail toy stores, from data publishing companies to board game manufacturing, from ski lodges with 160 beds to pizza parlors in Russia.

You don't need a Harvard Business School degree to start a successful business of your own. I learned far more running part-time businesses on the side than I ever did in the classroom.

Having your own business is an accelerated learning experience. And what you learn most about is yourself. You learn what you like to do and what you do best. You also learn what you don't like to do and shouldn't do. You can't get these valuable lessons from a textbook, yet they determine how successful you will be.

You need four ingredients to cook up a business of your own, and only one of them is in short supply. First, you need an *idea*. Ideas are a dime a dozen. Everyone has ideas. All of our friends have ideas, and strangers have even more ideas. There are literally thousands of good business ideas out there, just waiting to be plucked off and used as the basis for a successful business.

For many years, I taught a course in entrepreneurship at Babson College in Wellesley, Massachusetts. I required each student to create a list of at least 10 unique ideas that were potential million-dollar businesses. Every semester, every student created a list, and there were very few duplicate ideas between lists. Good ideas are truly everywhere.

Second, you need some *money*. No matter how small the new business, at least a little hard cash will be required. Most people seem to think that money, or the lack thereof, is what's holding them back from having a business of their own. In reality, money is even more abundant and easier to get than the thousands of good ideas that are floating around.

For example, over 70 percent of Americans own a credit card with unused credit on it. Every one of them (over 200 million adults) is a potential source of capital for your business. Money is everywhere! It's just a matter of knowing where to look for it and how to get it. This book will show you how.

The third ingredient is a person—you, the *entrepreneur!* Once again, people are universally abundant, just like ideas and money. No special personality traits are required. Entrepreneurs come in every shape and size—some are extroverts and others introverts; some are educated and others not; some are rich and most start poor. For every entrepreneur you find with a certain personality trait, there will be another entrepreneur out there who has just the opposite.

All entrepreneurs share one common characteristic, however: At one point in time, they all felt enough confidence in themselves to at least try to start a business of their own. Entrepreneurship is an entirely self-selective process. You don't have to pass a test first. Everything you need to start a business of your own is abundantly available to anyone who can read this book.

Only one thing is in short supply, and that one is absolutely free! The fourth ingredient is the hardest of all to find. It's the only ingredient whose supply is absolutely fixed. If you use it up, you can't go out and buy, or rent, more of it. The mysterious, elusive, most critical of all ingredients for a successful business of your own is *time*—your time. It is absolutely inelastic and fixed.

Every minute that you consume—whether it be by watching television, eating or sleeping, reading a book, exercising, working at a paying job, washing the dishes, or any of the thousands of things that we do in our lives—subtracts from the precious hours you could use to start a business of your own. Every minute that you spend in your own business means a minute that is stolen from these other activities that are so important to you.

I have started many companies with little or no money of my own. When you see how easy it has been for me, maybe you'll choose to have some fun for yourself in your own business.

When I turned 40, I decided to give up the yo-yo-like life of an entrepreneur and invest the sizable nest egg that I had earned in the stock options market. Before heading west to the Chicago Board Options Exchange, I spent several weeks touring through Scotland and Ireland with my new wife. She had an interest in spiritual matters and wanted to spend some time on Iona, a small island off the coast of Mull, Scotland.

Iona is supposedly the most spiritual spot on earth. For thousands of years, religious leaders have visited Iona for inspiration. Saint Patrick meditated there. The Church of England was founded on this little island.

I did not go to Iona for inspiration. I didn't expect anything. However, in the middle of the night, I was awakened by some white light, and four messages were mysteriously sent down to me. I found a pencil and wrote down the commandments, which I assumed were the key to having a successful business of my own (that being the only thing I knew much of anything about).

Six months later, I had lost my entire nest egg in the options market. I lost so much money that I had to declare personal bankruptcy. Once again, I was given the opportunity to start over. It was time for me to pull out the four commandments and see if they were for real. And they were. It took me a few years to get going, but once I started really using the commandments as a guide, I earned an average of over $1 million a year for the rest of my life, *starting with no capi-*

tal whatsoever. Here are the four commandments for having a successful business of your own.

1. *Discover what you love.* It is absolutely imperative that you love the business you start. Many successful enterprises grow out of someone's favorite hobby. If you can come up with a unique product or service, it is easy to fall in love with it. Or you can appreciate something neat that someone else has invented. Emulation can be the highest form of creation.

   Whatever you do, you must have a passion for it. There are so many challenges to creating a successful business of your own, if you don't love what you do, you will give up long before the business ever reaches its potential.

   Many times, I have started businesses just to make a lot of money. If I didn't also love what I had to do to make those businesses successful, every one of them failed. If you don't love what you do, you will figure out some way not to have to do it any longer. The easiest way to accomplish this (subconsciously, perhaps) is to make your business fail.

2. *Do your homework.* Every industry has unique rules of thumb, ways of doing business, and secrets to success. Unless you understand these phenomena totally *before you start your business,* you will surely fail. The best way to discover these unique industry secrets is to get some real-life experience in that industry, even if you have to work for free for someone else to learn the rules.

   Doing your homework also involves checking out the competition and talking to prospective customers. This book will show you how to do the right kind of homework, quickly, without breaking the bank.

3. *Go for it!* Once you have figured out what you love and have done your homework, start your business, even if you don't have the money. This book will explain dozens of ways to substitute creativity for capital. I have started many businesses with less money than most people have available as a cash advance on their credit card. I have even started businesses when I was so broke that I couldn't even get a credit card.

Going for it takes guts. It means conquering your fear of failure. You might fail and lose all of the money that you invested or borrowed. If you follow the lessons of this book, you will be way ahead, no matter how much money you make or lose. To my way of thinking, there is no such thing as failure. There are only two possible outcomes to going for it. The first possible outcome is what most people call *success*—you accomplish what you set out to do. You feel satisfied. Perhaps you made some money. If you go for it enough times, this outcome will surely come at least once, and maybe several times.

The second possible outcome is probably the most common. You don't achieve *success* in the traditional sense—but it isn't failure, either. It is a learning experience. Every learning experience costs money and time. (Anyone who has paid a college tuition bill knows how expensive some learning experiences can be.)

Many learning experiences (even if you lose money) are ultimately more valuable than some of your successes. A good learning experience may be leveraged into a considerably larger success the next time you muster the courage to go for it.

While I believe that there is no such thing as failure, there most certainly is something called *fear of failure*. It is totally debilitating, and it robs you of any chance you might have of soaring with the eagles. As Winston Churchill once said, "The only thing we have to fear is fear itself." Stifle your fear and go for the gold!

4. *Ride with the tide.* This is also known as *go with the flow*. But Iona was an island, and there was a tide. Once you are truly in business, the universe (or more aptly, your customer) tells you what is working and what is not. Sometimes, it is difficult to see these lessons because we have preconceived notions of what *should* work.

If one part of your business is easy to sell, and another part seems like pulling teeth, channel your resources to the easy part. If one radio advertising program draws customers best, invest more in that program, even if you believe that no one in their right mind listens to that radio station.

Most successful companies do not start out with the product or service that makes them a big hit. The role of the first product (especially if you thought it up yourself) is to get you into business. As you try to sell this product, your customers tell you how you could change it to give them *exactly* what they want. If you ride with the tide, you will alter your product and create a marketing success by providing what your customer really wants.

Another way of saying *ride with the tide* is to ride the horse in the direction it is going. And remember—if the horse is dead, get off.

All four of these commandments must be followed if you hope to be successful. Ignore any one and you will have a three-legged table that will surely crash.

This book is full of stories in which I neglected one of the commandments and earned an expensive learning experience instead of success. There are a few stories in which I attended to all four of the commandments and prospered beyond my wildest dreams.

I am convinced that getting rich through your own business is a lot easier, more fun, more exciting, and more personally satisfying than making money in the stock market. In addition, you don't have to have a large nest egg to get going. I feel confident that my story will help you find the way.

Good luck! Remember, the worst thing that can happen is that you will have a wonderful learning experience that might lead to even greater riches in the future. Furthermore, you will have more fun than you ever could have working for someone else.

Chapter 1

The Early Years: Worms, Frogs, Turtles, and Snakes

How to Start a Business That Needs No Cash

I clearly remember my first commercial transaction. The year was 1946, and I was seven years old. My mother had suggested that I send my grandmother a letter (my first ever correspondence) and had given me a nickel to buy a postcard. I nervously entered the post office in bustling Red Creek, New York, secretly wondering if the nickel would be sufficient to buy both the postcard and a stamp.

When the postmistress gave me the postcard and 4 cents change, I said, "Is that all it is?" She kindly explained that it was called a *penny postcard* for a reason—it only cost a penny. "If there is one thing that you can count on in this world," she promised, "it is that a postcard will always cost a penny. It always has, and it always will."

Today, the penny postcard costs 25 times as much, and the post office complains about not being able to cover costs.

NOTHING IN BUSINESS EVER STAYS THE SAME

The lesson that I learned from my first commercial transaction is that nothing in business ever stays the same, no matter how much it seems that it will at the time. But what about the lessons? Are the lessons constant, or do they keep changing, just like everything else? I think that what makes life interesting is that it somehow becomes a perpetual learning experience. We have an experience, learn something from it, and then move on to do something else that may very well contradict what we have just learned.

BORROW A FLASHLIGHT AND START A BUSINESS

At the age of nine, in St. Albans, Vermont, there was a camp on Lake Champlain—every kid's ideal for the perfect summer vacation. My father was a player and a coach for a minor-league baseball team in the Northern League.

I was really proud of my father. How many kids have seen their father hit a home run in a professional baseball game? I saw him hit many home runs and slowly trot around the bases, enjoying the applause from the home-team fans. (Years later, I learned that my father didn't like to run fast, or couldn't, depending on who was telling the story, and hitting home runs was his way of taking a leisurely stroll around the bases.)

At the age of nine, however, I was most proud of how my father could catch night crawlers. In the middle of the night, in a driving rainstorm, no one was his equal (at least, no one I knew at the time). He was so quick that he often caught two worms with a single grab. It wasn't until I reached the 10th grade and was doing a science project on earthworms that I learned of the *why* of these "double catches." The poor worms were merely making love when snatched from their entanglement.

FIND BUSINESS OPPORTUNITIES IN THE INTERSTICES

The real trick to catching night crawlers was knowing where to shine the flashlight. Night crawlers never completely leave their hole, but keep their lower halves safely inside their burrow. If you shine the light directly on the unsuspecting worm, it will quickly withdraw to its hole. To be successful, you have to keep the main beam of the flashlight away from where you expect the worm to be, and look for it in the shadows.

For me, catching night crawlers served three purposes. First, it satisfied my father's enthusiasm. He really enjoyed the process (don't we all love to do the things we're especially good at?). Second, we got bait for our frequent fishing expeditions. And third, I was allowed to sell the excess worms, thus eliminating the need for my parents to give me an allowance.

Selling earthworms became my passion. I put up signs everywhere and accosted everyone I saw who carried a fishing pole. When a bass fisherman told me what he really wanted was some small frogs, I diversified my product offerings and spent countless hours wading through murky swamps in search of those quick little devils.

INCREASE THE PRICE AND INCREASE PROFITS

I remember thinking about what to charge for my catches. I never could understand how prices got set. How could the post office buy a piece of cardboard, print a stamp on it, and deliver it anywhere in the country for only a penny? That's what I got for a single night crawler, and it would be gone in a single gulp by some lucky (or not-so-lucky) finny creature.

I also couldn't understand why frogs fetched only 5 cents each, while they were at least 10 times as hard to catch as a worm. I charged 1 cent for worms because that's what other kids charged. I didn't know how much to charge for frogs because no one else seemed to be selling them. My first customer told me that 5 cents was the right price for a frog, so that became the price.

Prices have continued to confuse me. Forty years after the summer when I set 5 cents as the price for a frog, when I was nine, I sold my data compilation business, which charged 30 cents for each record we sold. After my company was sold, the new owners raised the price by 400 percent—to $1.20 per record. To my absolute astonishment, the customers continued to buy at these absurd prices. In retrospect, I think I could have gotten 10 cents for those frogs.

Halfway through the summer, I had amassed a small fortune of nearly $12, catching and selling 1,000 worms and 40 frogs. This was no easy feat for a nine-year-old.

BEWARE OF PARTNERSHIPS

It was at this time that I was offered my first business proposition—a partnership with two early-teenage girls who lived in the cottage that we shared with the Bob White family. These girls had bikes, and they promised to pedal up and down the lake selling my worms and frogs wherever they went. Sensing new markets and greater riches (even if we split the proceeds three ways), I agreed to the partnership. We formalized our arrangement in front of our parents at our regular Sunday night special treat of cold milk and crackers.

For a week or two, our new partnership prospered. Our inventory of worms almost disappeared, and I couldn't catch enough frogs to keep up with the demand from further down the lake. Then, nature took its course. My two young partners discovered some boys on one of their marketing trips (really cute ones, they assured me). All marketing efforts suddenly ceased. I think they decided that pedaling worms was not part of the cool image that they were trying to create.

Every Sunday night, over crackers and milk, Bob White would take down the coffee can that held the partnership's weekly receipts and dump it in the middle of the table. Tears would fill my eyes as two-thirds of my money was parceled out to my philandering partners.

PARTNERSHIPS ALWAYS FAIL, EVENTUALLY

Forty years later, I look back and realize that I have not encountered a single partnership that worked for all of the partners for any length of time. What generally happens is that, over time, partners' needs change. One partner inevitably remains more committed to the partnership's original mission. This partner ends up working longer hours and getting angry with the slacking partner.

SOME BUSINESSES SHOULD *NEVER* BE STARTED

Another third-grade business was perhaps the shortest of my entire career. Earlier Kool-Aid stands had lasted only until the ice cubes melted or thirst overtook me. This business, however, ended in less time than an ice cube could melt.

I had noticed that many well-dressed families walked by our house every Sunday on the way to church. Somehow, the idea of church made me think about charity, and I had a brainstorm. I took a large tin can from the trash, peeled off the outer wrapper, and found some bright red nail polish that my mother had foolishly left out in the open. I painted a large red cross on the tin can and dragged a barrel out to our front yard.

My parents, still in bed, heard my plaintive cry coming from the front of the house: "Donate to the Red Cross! Donate to the Red Cross!"

It's a miracle that my entrepreneurial zeal was not squelched when my mother closed down my operation before I even collected a nickel.

IF YOUR CHILD DEMONSTRATES ENTREPRENEURIAL INTERESTS, BE CAREFUL ABOUT WHAT YOU GIVE HIM OR HER

Christmas of my fourth-grade year, age 10, I received the most wonderful present I can ever remember getting. It was a loom for making potholders, complete with a bag of elastic cloth loops. I also got a flashlight (for catching night crawlers, I think). That was a bad combination, because I could stay up after being put to bed, weaving a potholder by flashlight. I stayed up almost all night weaving my first few potholders.

I fantasized about hiring all the kids in the neighborhood to make potholders using my wonderful loom, and I would go door to door selling the handiwork. I was certain I was closing in on my first million.

This business was also short-lived. When I found out how much the loops cost and what I could sell the potholders for, there wasn't enough margin to make it go. I still remember lying in bed, though, dreaming about my about-to-be-started business. It was a night like dozens of others that I later enjoyed, full of great hopes and fantasies of endless flows of money—better (at least safer) than falling in love.

BOUNDLESS OPPORTUNITIES IN VACANT LOTS

In fifth grade, my parents moved to the suburbs outside Springfield, Massachusetts. We lived in the last house on a new street in a subdivision. Next to our house was a vacant lot, and behind us were woods teeming with white birch trees. I saw opportunity everywhere.

The vacant lot served as the site for a kids' carnival I set up and ran every summer for several years. I enlisted my younger sister and her friends to run the booths. Apparently, I never paid them. To this day, my sister bristles every time anyone mentions the carnivals I ran.

What I remember most about the carnival was the popcorn. Popcorn is a most wonderful product. It takes up a lot of space, so you think you're getting something big. And it really tastes good. There are two other things about popcorn, however, that really make it great. First, it's really cheap. I sold a wax paper sandwich bag of it for 5 cents at the carnival, and it cost me less than a penny.

The second great thing about popcorn is that it's salty. Eating something salty seemed to cause my customers to buy lots of Kool-Aid and soda as well. I truly loved popcorn.

As long as you can come up with something—anything—that will attract a crowd, even if you offer something that is absolutely free, you can make a profit. The answer is popcorn. It is a truly magnificent invention.

NEVER DEAL WITH SNAKES

One of the biggest draws of my carnival was my collection of snakes. At one time, it consisted of 40 different varieties, almost every nonpoisonous snake found in New England.

I earned money by taking my snake collection to several day camps in the area and giving lectures about the snakes. There were other great things about collecting snakes, like the adventure of seeking them out and capturing them. I got most of my collection in a large dump where I could look for discarded but useful items at the same time.

THE BEST LEARNING TAKES PLACE AFTER SCHOOL

Snakes were also great for terrifying girls and disrupting classes at school. I released my favorite snake (whom I had affectionately named Hector the Hognose) in science class one day, much to the teacher's dismay. She put me in detention. In fact, I spent many nights after school with her, mostly because Hector often accompanied me to school (comfortably resting in my lunchbox).

I actually came to enjoy detention. Not at first, however, when she made me write 50 times, "I will not release a snake in science class." I told her that detention should be an opportunity to make me do some really difficult assignments relating to science. Much to my surprise, she agreed. I can remember being given the assignment of naming 20 reasons why it was a good thing that water expanded when it froze. That was fun. Detention was the only opportunity I can remember in junior high school where I could be creative.

I would have continued misbehaving (which was usually fun in itself) and earning detention as long as I got punishments like that. However, staying after school meant that I missed the school bus home and I was forced to take public transportation, which cost me hard-earned money. So, I eventually let Hector stay at home with his scaly friends.

IT IS ALWAYS HARDER TO SELL SOMETHING THAN IT IS TO MAKE IT

The white birch trees and wild princess pine in our backyard provided the materials that I needed for my next project. I cut the trees into 16-inch lengths, drilled three shallow holes in them, attached two cross-sticks as a base and added princess pine, a red ribbon, and three red candles—a perfect table decoration for Christmas.

As with most businesses, making the product was easy, and selling it was not. The biggest difference between making something and selling it is that you never encounter rejection in the manufacturing part.

I took my candleholders to all the houses in my neighborhood, and averaged one sale for every eight houses I visited. That meant that for every person who bought my product, seven people rejected it. I had never experienced this level of rejection before.

When I ran out of houses within walking distance, I asked my mother to drive me to a different part of town and leave me for an entire Saturday. I selected a more affluent area with large houses. I thought that perhaps the families in my neighborhood could not afford the candleholders.

That Saturday, I encountered an entirely new level of rejection. I stopped at over 50 houses, and did not sell a single candleholder. I was devastated. It was hard not to take it personally.

KNOW YOUR CUSTOMERS

Years later, I learned that the neighborhood that I visited that day was inhabited almost entirely by Jewish families who clearly weren't celebrating Christmas that year. It was my earliest reminder of how important it is to intimately know your customer.

In the summer of my 15th year, I was a virtual conglomerate. I felt that I owned the neighborhood (which was growing at the rate of about 40 houses a year). I knew which people would buy whatever I had for sale (in addition to Christmas decorations, I grew and sold vegetables from my garden, corn picked from other gardens, and much more).

I delivered newspapers to almost every house every day. Each week, I had to collect 28 cents from each customer (3 cents for six daily editions and 10 cents for Sunday). The difference between a mediocre business and a great newspaper business was getting a 2-cent tip on collection day. When my customers handed me a nickel and a quarter, as most of them did, I could count on most of them saying, "Keep the change." I always gave them a big smile and "thank you."

When those customers who generally did not tip gave me 30 cents, I would reach in my change pocket with hundreds of coins, and start searching for pennies. Of course, I had carefully removed all the pennies from that pocket. If I waited long enough, or asked if they might have three pennies for exact change, I usually got my tip.

Twice a week, I also delivered a free *Shopping News* to each of my customers. And once a month, I pulled out my wagon and went around to each house collecting newspapers. I got in on the recycling craze way ahead of my time.

A 3-foot-high stack of newspapers weighs 100 pounds. If I collected a ton of newspapers, or 20 stacks, the scrap paper dealer would come to my house to pick up my paper. I don't think my father was able to park his car in our garage again until I went away to prep school. When I had accumulated a ton of paper, I would call the dealer and get the current price, which ranged from 25 to 50 cents per hundred pounds. Sometimes, I waited months until the price went to 50 cents, or until my parents rebelled because there was no room in the garage for the lawnmower.

NEVER RENT ANYTHING TO A KID

I learned that there was a real demand for lawn mowing services while collecting on my paper route. Our only lawnmower was a hand-push reel type, however, and I figured I would break my back if I mowed everyone's lawn by hand.

Then I noticed a "Rent to Own" ad in the newspaper. A gasoline-powered reel lawnmower was available for $7 per month. I rode my bike to the hardware store advertising the deal. It was clearly a rental contract. There was no obligation to continue renting until the mower was paid for in full. I rented it with the intention of keeping it for the three summer months and then returning it.

I mowed over 20 lawns each week that summer. One was a full acre and earned me $10 per week, a small fortune at the time—enough to hire another kid to mow about half the lawns for me. While the arrangement meant giving up three-quarters of my income, I made a profit on his labor, and freed up time to make money on other businesses.

At the end of the summer, I returned the lawn mower to the hardware store. The owner was incensed. "This is a piece of junk!" he said. True, the two rubber tires were worn almost to the rim of the wheels. The mower really had been through a tough summer. "Let me speak to your mother!" he screamed at me. I replied, "My mother didn't rent this mower, I did." He vowed that he would never sign a contract with a minor again in his life.

If the hardware store owner learned his lesson about dealing with minors, and it only cost him what he lost by renting that mower to me, he got a great educational bargain. Many years later, a friend of mine sold an almost-new motorcycle to a minor (whose father was a physician) and financed the deal. The kid totaled the cycle and never had to pay my friend a cent.

While another kid in the neighborhood was mowing lawns for me, I embarked on a wonderfully successful project. I purchased Coca-Cola by the case for 2½ cents per bottle. The local Coke distributor delivered it free if I bought 10 cases.

I put two pails on the handlebars of my bike, filled each pail with Coke bottles and the contents of my mother's ice cube trays, and set off for the new house construction project on the next street. Every house under construction contained a painter, plumber, carpenter, or other worker, often working alone and almost always thirsty. I sold each Coke for 10 cents, netting a whopping 7½ cents on every bottle. Oftentimes, a worker, apparently lonely for companionship, bought me a Coke to enjoy with him. I had never encountered such riches!

DON'T FEEL PRIDE WHEN YOU'RE BEING STUPID

At the end of the summer, I had deposited almost $1,000 in a savings account at the local commercial bank. I was 15 years old and the branch manager told me I had one of the largest savings accounts at the bank. I was so proud of myself. Only later did I realize that it was stupidity, not pride, I should have been feeling. A savings account at the commercial bank was paying 1 percent interest, while a savings account at a savings bank paid 4½ percent. No wonder I had the largest savings account at the branch.

I will never forget that branch manager who would not tell me about a better deal elsewhere. He was one of only two snakes I ever encountered at a bank. I discovered that most bankers were like turtles—afraid to stick their necks out. Usually, I would have preferred to deal with snakes. I never minded paying an outrageous interest rate if only I could get the loan. Bankers, however, are generally turtles.

In September, after my summer of selling and drinking Coke, I went to the dentist for my annual checkup, and discovered that I had my very first cavity. In fact, I had eight cavities! My parents' dental bill surely exceeded my summer's profits from selling and drinking Coca-Cola.

THERE IS NOTHING AS INSPIRATIONAL
AS AN AUTOBIOGRAPHY

As a teenager, I was totally mesmerized by Andrew Carnegie's autobiography. For many years, I wished that I had been born a century sooner, in an earlier, simpler time period when opportunities were truly unlimited. I fantasized about building an American industry, much like Carnegie had done.

I still recall three vivid incidents in Carnegie's autobiography. The first was a minor episode in the book. Carnegie was walking down a street in New York City and saw a grand opening for a new bank. In the lobby window was a plaque listing the founding partners of the bank. Much to his surprise, he noticed his own name on the list. Upon returning to his office, he asked his assistant for an explanation. He reported that the bank had asked for a nominal contribution of capital and that they were willing to give up a large share of the ownership for the privilege of having Andrew Carnegie's name on their letterhead. Carnegie became quite angry and demanded that they remove his name immediately.

He understood that each partner, no matter how small his or her contribution, could be responsible for all of the debts of the business entity. In this particular instance, it made a huge difference. The bank declared bankruptcy after losing millions of dollars. Carnegie, even though he had made only a token investment, would have been held responsible for every nickel of the multi-million-dollar loss.

The second part of Carnegie's autobiography that has stayed with me was his decision to devote the second half of his life to giving away the fortune that he had accumulated in the first half. He said that giving money away was harder in many respects than making it in the first place. I liked his ideas, and I vowed to myself that someday I would make a million dollars and give it all away to deserving charities.

The third part that I remember was Carnegie's refutation of the adage "Don't put all your eggs in one basket." He believed that you should put all your eggs in a single basket and watch that basket as if you were the mother of all mother hens. Focusing all your energies on one business or one endeavor has always seemed to me to be a more promising formula for success than scattering your energies on a multitude of projects. Yet, I rarely focused on a single project until quite later in my life.

In my mid-20s, I was once again hooked by a book: this time, Ayn Rand's *Atlas Shrugged*. I totally identified with John Galt, just as I had earlier adopted Howard Roark of *The Fountainhead* as my idol. Empire builders doing it their own way. No compromise. Wow! I loved them both. Books can be a wonderful inspiration.

WHAT I LEARNED

■ *Since every partnership is destined to fail, a prenuptial agreement is essential.* Over time, one of the partners will become more committed to the original business plan than the other. It is important to create a mechanism for a fair transfer of the business to the committed partner.

■ *Snitch a niche.* The best business opportunities are found in the shadows, not in the bright lights where everyone else is looking. The secret to a successful business is to find a niche that no one (at least in your area) is serving, and to totally dominate that niche.

■ *Raise your prices.* Most entrepreneurs underprice their products or services, perhaps out of fear that they will lose business. Customers who buy because of low prices are disloyal—they will quickly leave you if someone else offers a lower price. The most successful businesses charge premium prices and offer superior service.

■ *Never execute a contract with a minor.* Ever! No more needs to be said. Period!

■ *There are thousands, probably millions, of ways to make money.* You can find riches by capturing wild worms, frogs, turtles, and snakes, or by finding a vacant lot and adding entrepreneurial skills.

■ *With enthusiasm, you can accomplish (or sell) anything.*

Chapter 2

Formal Education: Trying to Learn, Even While in School

How to Use Your Classmates as a Source of Capital

In my 16th year, I heard two men talking about Harvard Business School. Their tones were reverential. (I suppose they had both attended the school and were mutually congratulating themselves.) It sounded like the place I had to be, and I vowed to attend there someday.

I know I made this vow because I have it in writing. Almost every month since I was 16, I have written to myself what I call a progress report. It is sort of a diary, but it deals most of all with the issues with which I am wrestling at the time. My progress reports, now several volumes in size, are the basis for my life story that is unfolding here.

I turned down a full-tuition scholarship at Harvard because I did not want to spend six years at the same place (in my mind, Harvard Business School was already a certainty for me.) Cornell was too big, and Wesleyan seemed liked a good place to get a liberal arts education.

The first business in college was selling stationery. I went around to every dorm room in the freshman dorms and took orders. This was a very profitable business per hour of my time and required no capital to start. For some reason, only freshmen seemed to be interested in personal stationery—upper classmen just wrote on a sheet of plain paper or used the telephone when they needed to contact their parents about sending money.

I used profits from the stationery sales to invest in my next business—paperback books. When I went to the college bookstore to buy books for my freshman classes, I noticed that they offered only hardcover editions. I knew that paperback versions were available for many books, especially the classic novels. I spoke to the bookstore manager, and he said that their distributor only handled hardcover books.

I found a distributor about 10 miles away that handled paperback books. I gathered up a list of course syllabi, and hitchhiked to the distributor. He agreed to deliver the books to me if I paid cash in advance, and he gave me 30 percent off from the list price.

Each evening just before dinner, I would arrive at a different fraternity house, offering my selection of books. Many students bought my paperbacks, and returned their hardcover editions unread to the college bookstore.

CASH IN THE MAIL OFTEN DISAPPEARS

On one occasion, I mailed $60 in cash to my distributor with an order for more books. He never acknowledged receiving my letter. I learned a $60 lesson at a time when $60 was a lot of money. And I opened my first checking account.

After two months in business, I offered my remaining inventory to the college bookstore (at cost) if they would agree to carry paperback books in the future. They agreed, and I felt like a winner in two ways: (1) I had made a profit in my own business, and

(2) I got the bookstore to do what I wanted them to do in the first place.

YOU NEVER KNOW HOW MUCH YOU CAN DO UNTIL YOU DO IT

When I look back on my freshman year in college, I wonder at the energy level I had. I worked an average of 20 hours a week in the college library, and I washed dishes every lunch and dinner at my fraternity (in exchange for meals). I attended most of my classes and got on the honor roll. I ran my two businesses, and I earned letters in four sports.

In my sophomore year, the public school kids caught up and passed me by. I was put on academic probation and agreed with the dean to eliminate one sport (basketball) and not start any new businesses. I didn't play basketball, but a new business opportunity came along and I couldn't resist.

Once again, I found the opportunity in the bookstore. It was a bookbinding kit (made in England) that could convert three paperback books into hardcover books. I thought it was a wonderful way to fill your library with hardcover books at a fraction of the cost of regular hardcover books.

IF YOU WANT SOMEONE'S ATTENTION, TELL HIM OR HER THAT YOU CAN SELL HIS OR HER PRODUCT

I telephoned the importer in New York City and asked if he were interested in someone distributing his kits throughout New England. When I think back on my phone call, I wonder why I assumed that he didn't already have a distributor since he had somehow managed to get his kits on our college bookstore shelves.

I have since learned that if you contact anyone who has a product and say that you have an idea about how to sell more, he or she will be nice to you. This man was no exception, and he invited me to visit him at his home in Westchester County.

NEVER UNDERESTIMATE THE POWER
OF A BAD SMELL

I told him that I liked everything about the bookbinding kits except for one thing—the glue to adhere the cardboard binding smelled like a cross between ammonia and rotten eggs.

He told me that the manufacturer worked hard to get that smell in there—if it smelled like Elmer's glue, no one would believe it was strong enough to hold the cover in place. Attention to little details like this often makes the difference between a successful product and a failure.

I spent a lovely evening learning about the import business. He had become an American distributor for the bookbinding kits by contacting the manufacturer when he first saw the kits in England, much like I had contacted him.

He told me that I could have sole distribution rights in New England for the next summer if I purchased $1,000 worth of inventory in advance. That was only about $980 more than I had in spare cash.

I returned to college and sold four of my fraternity brothers on the idea of investing $250 each for one-fifth of the inventory. If they couldn't sell their kits, I agreed to buy them back from them. This plan gave me one-fifth of the kits to sell at no out-of-pocket cost.

Once the school term ended, I hit the road and started calling on bookstores and libraries in every town I visited. Within two weeks, I had sold all of my kits. I called my fraternity brothers to see how their sales were going, and learned that not one guy had sold one kit—and they never did. By the end of the summer, I had sold everyone's kits, much to their relief.

I experienced different levels of success at different kinds of prospects I called on. Public libraries were fairly easy to sell, but there were usually no decision makers in the library, and I had to come back or telephone to complete the sale. Independent bookstores were a pretty good bet, but they invariably asked me to try some on consignment. Fortunately, I was having enough success without resorting to giving them away without payment.

RIDE THE HORSE IN THE DIRECTION IT IS GOING

The easiest of all sales were to U.S. Veterans Hospital libraries. The hardest part was finding them. I looked in the Yellow Pages for these hospitals as soon as I got to each new city. It seems that people donate thousands of paperback books to these institutions, and binding them into hardcover books was a therapeutic activity for patients.

Shortly before the end of the summer, I used one of these kits to bind a paperback book for the first time. Up to this point, I was so enthralled with the idea of turning paperbacks into hardcovers that I had not actually tried it for real. I was extremely disappointed with the results. The finished product was a poor excuse for a hardcover book. I didn't feel like making one more sales call. If I don't believe in something, I can't sell it.

I had a problem, however. I still owned several dozen cases of kits. How could I sell them when my heart wasn't in it? I then remembered the Veterans Hospitals, where the therapeutic value of making hardcover books was more important than the quality of the end product.

I telephoned the U.S. Veterans Administration in Washington, D.C. and secured a list of their hospitals. I wrote and mimeographed a sales letter and mailed it to 10 hospital libraries as a test. I sold two of them, and believed I had discovered a perfect way to dispose of my remaining inventory. When I sent the same letter to the rest of the hospitals, I sold out my remaining inventory; I was forever hooked on the miracle of direct mail.

A LITTLE PLANNING CAN DOUBLE YOUR OUTPUT

I worked an average of 20 hours a week throughout college in the college library. I asked for late-night hours when I could work the front desk and get some homework done at the same time. It was during college that I realized that *time* was the single most important variable that ultimately determined how much I could accomplish. Doing two things at once is one way of minimizing the fixed nature of time.

I also washed dishes in my fraternity house for all four years in exchange for free food. I was actually one of several waiters, but the rule was that the last person to arrive to set tables had to wash the dishes. I was always the last person to arrive and believed that I was the real winner because I worked about half as much time as the other guys. It didn't bother me that my job was smelly and extremely hot, and often involved getting water burns on my arms. I was working fewer hours. To remind myself of my good deal, I kept two quotations over my desk:

Time is money

—Ben Franklin

Time is everything!

—Napoleon

ECONOMICS 101 ISN'T BUSINESS

I majored in economics, and I soon figured out that it was quite different from real business. Economics 101 was an eye-opener. I still find it hard to believe that the economics teacher confidently explained that in the long run, given free competition (like we have in the United States), a firm's profit becomes zero (new competition enters the market, driving down the other firm's short-run profits). I had spent many hours reading corporate income statements and knew that long-run profits were the norm rather than the exception for most public companies.

In microeconomics, I learned about balance sheets. A student asked if it were possible for a company to have a negative net worth, and the professor said that it was a mathematical impossibility. I brought him the annual reports of several companies that I had been following whose shares traded on the pink sheets. They all had negative net worths. Funny thing, my professor didn't seem to appreciate my pointing out his error. I guess I never was the most politically astute student.

I soon decided that I should stop going to economics classes. The lectures were boring, and I often felt compelled to point out the differences between economic theory and the real world. Fortunately for me, for upper-level economic classes, our entire grade was based on two 3-hour exams on two consecutive days at the end of the semester. Instead of going to class, I read every article and book on the required reading list as well as the recommended reading list. On my exam, I quoted freely from the recommended but not required readings. I am sure that I was the only one in the class who read every one of the recommended readings. I got the highest marks of all the economics majors, and for most of the courses, I only attended the first class to pick up the assignments and reading list.

BETTER TO DELEGATE THAN DO IT YOURSELF

As a senior, I was given the job of keeping up the periodical room in the economics lab. The job paid $20 a month, a princely sum at the time. Each week, I had to open all the periodicals that had arrived in the mail, check off that they had been received on a master list, and then place the most recent issue on the top of the pile for that periodical. The magazines were arranged alphabetically by title around four walls of a conference room.

One day I arrived to do my job after skipping a week. There was a large pile of unopened periodicals in the middle of the conference table. There was also a new janitor there—it was his second day on the job.

"Do you know what I am supposed to do with these magazines?" he asked me.

Without missing a beat, I answered that the last janitor used to open them, check them off on the master list, and find the right pile on which to put them. I even helped him do the job the first time, for which he expressed his sincere gratitude. Fortunately for me, this man stayed on the job for my entire senior year. I often wondered what happened the next year when some lucky economics major was given this salaried situation. Needless to say, it was about the best job I ever had, if you didn't count the guilty feelings. I justified them by remembering that the janitor had a lot of spare time on his hands and seemed to enjoy the work.

DON'T PROMISE WHAT YOU CAN'T DELIVER

The professor who taught Economics 101 and who gave me the library job also hired me to do mathematical calculations and research for a journal article that he was writing. I became extremely interested in this project and told him that I would not play football my senior year so I could spend more time on his project. As I walked by my teammates on the first day of fall practice, however, I suited up.

The economics professor was livid! He barely spoke to me for the rest of the semester. Then, I asked him to write a recommendation letter to Harvard Business School for me. He couldn't believe it. "You know what I think of how you run your life," he said, "and I will have to tell them the truth." I said that was fine with me.

I had gone home for a full week to concentrate on filling out my Harvard application. I figured my greatest shortcoming was my age. Only one out of four entering students came directly from college. The other 75 percent got full-time business experience first. My strategy was to convince Harvard that I was mature enough to really know myself. There was a required essay on my personal strengths and weaknesses, and I went to great lengths to explain that my greatest weakness was trying to do too many different things at once. I knew that my economics professor would totally corroborate this statement.

I have no idea why Harvard did accept me (my test scores were below my class average), but I have always believed my economics professor's damning "recommendation" helped me considerably. I can still remember seeing his jaw drop when I told him of my acceptance. It was one of my most joyous moments.

POKER CAN BE A GREAT LEARNING EXPERIENCE

Another way of supporting myself in college was by playing poker with my fraternity brothers. They all had a lot more money than I did and would rather play than win. In other words, you couldn't bluff them, no matter what kind of cards they held. I had two rules that guaranteed I would win. First, don't bluff—stay in only when I had a good hand. Second, drink half as much beer as anyone at the table. This rule was easy to follow, not because I didn't like beer, but because my fellow cardplayers seemed to like it more. My winning strategy did not require much poker skill, just discipline.

Every night after playing poker, I carefully recorded how much I had won and how many hours I had played. I had made a deal with myself that if I ever played poker for 10 consecutive hours and earned less than I could in the library ($1.25 per hour), I would quit playing poker. It never happened.

HAPPINESS COMES WHEN WORK
AND PLAY ARE THE SAME ACTIVITY

I enjoyed playing poker for all four years of college, even if it seemed a little more like business than play. My poker experience was a microcosm of my entire life: There was rarely a difference between work and play. I always seemed to love them both equally, and it was usually difficult to figure when one stopped and the other began. Business is really a game, after all—especially when it's your own.

In May of my senior year in college, already accepted to graduate school, I was hoping for a summer internship with some company, any company, so that I could bring a tiny bit of actual business experience to Harvard. I had applied at several large companies, including General Electric and New York Telephone. No word yet, and I was getting discouraged because many of my classmates had already received word of their acceptance.

When the phone finally rang from a potential employer, I got excited with hopeful anticipation. However, it was not a real company (at least in my mind); it was a summer camp. The camp director was a former student of my father's at Springfield College. They had had a chance meeting, and my father told him that I was looking for a job. I'm not sure what else my father told him, but it was enough to cause the camp director to call me.

It was a sailing camp on the Connecticut shore. I immediately thought about my one and only experience in a sailboat. The prior summer I had worked at the Lake George Club, a yacht club in upper New York State. I was a bar waiter. One night after work, several of us tumbled into a sailboat. We were perhaps a little too adventurous having sampled a large quantity of the various products we were serving at the bar. The boat sank, and we probably all would have drowned if two crazy guys who were water-skiing in the middle of the night hadn't saved us.

The camp director asked, "Can you teach sailing?" I sensed desperation in his voice. The camp season started in less than a month, and he was short one sailing instructor.

"You're in luck," I said, "matter of fact, I worked at a yacht club all summer last year." He hired me on the spot.

The following week, I went to the library, got a book about sailing, and lined up a fraternity brother to give me some lessons on the Connecticut River. I had heard an adage, "You teach best what you learned last." Surely, I would be a great sailing instructor, since I had so recently learned the skill myself.

However, an acceptance letter then came from New York Telephone, and my plans changed quickly. I had found a real company and felt badly about leaving the camp director quite literally up the river without a paddle. I don't think my father recommended me for a job again.

FEAR IS THE GREATEST MOTIVATOR

When I read my first case at Harvard Business School, I was totally overwhelmed. The case was about a manufacturing company with a huge number of production problems. I had absolutely no idea where to start. If I had been called on in class to make a recommendation, the only thing I would have been able to think of was to close down the entire plant and start over. Somehow, I knew that wasn't the right answer, and I was scared even to attend my first class.

I remembered the words of Napoleon, who said that there were two ways to motivate soldiers—fear and interest, and fear always worked best. I was certainly motivated, and while I welcomed the opportunity to finally study business, it was abject fear that drove me to work as hard as I did. I have never worked harder than I did in my first year at Harvard Business School. (That first case was also the last case of the year—the company did, indeed, have so many problems that it took our class an entire semester to analyze all of them.)

ONCE THE FEAR SUBSIDES, SO DOES THE MOTIVATION

At the end of my first year, my extreme hard work was rewarded. I finished in the top 10 percent of my class. If I had it to do over again, I would have taken it a little easier. I never knew that, though, until the grades came out.

My second year was a breeze. No longer fearful, I took on a salaried job—director of the intramural athletic program. This job entailed scheduling intramural games and hiring students to referee the games (for $10 per game). If one of the teams did not show up for a game, the referee still collected the $10. I soon figured out which teams rarely showed up for their games, and scheduled myself to referee those games. Many times, I could collect two fees for the same hour.

I also gave blood regularly during my two years in Boston, earning $25 per pint. I have O-negative blood, which makes me a universal donor and much sought after by the hospitals. When my eight-week waiting period expired, Massachusetts General Hospital would call me and invite me to come see them again. On a couple of occasions, I went to a second hospital and sold a pint in between my visits to Massachusetts General Hospital.

USE JOB INTERVIEWS TO POLISH YOUR SELLING SKILLS

Even though I had little interest in working for a large company, I signed up for many job interviews anyway. It was a good way to practice my selling skills. Since I really didn't care whether I got a job offer or not, I became a more desirable commodity.

In every sales situation, one party inevitably becomes the buyer, and the other party does the selling. In all circumstances, it is best to be the buyer. The challenge is to assume the role of the buyer even though you are really trying to sell yourself. A job interview is a perfect example. In my case, it was natural to assume the role of the buyer because I really didn't care. However, if you really do want a job, you can still become the buyer by reminding yourself that even though you want a job, you don't necessarily need *this* job. That way, you can assume the buyer's role and increase your chances of being selected. I was offered a full-time job at almost every company I interviewed.

After a while, I got tired of interviewing for jobs I had no intention of accepting. That freed up time to start a business. In the summer between college and graduate school, I had accepted a summer internship with New York Telephone. Needing a place to stay in New York City, I found a service called the Roommate Placement Service. Although I never actually used the service, I thought it was a good idea. (While waiting at a bus stop, a Wesleyan student recognized me and invited me to stay with him for the summer.)

I found that there was no such thing as a roommate placement service in Boston, so I started one. Both apartment renters and people seeking a place to live would pay me a $25 registration fee, and another $25 when I successfully negotiated a match. The business was profitable from the first month. In the one entrepreneurial course that Harvard offered, I had to make a business plan for a prospective new business. I used the Roommate Placement Service of Boston as my topic. I got a very low grade; the professor commented that the business was "impractical." Today, there are four such services in Boston, and in most metropolitan areas throughout the country.

I tried to continue operating Roommate Placement Service of Boston from a distance after graduation. Everything went well for about three months, and then my sole employee disappeared with several weeks' worth of deposits. I closed down the business and gave our accounts to a competitor who had recently come on the scene.

SPARE-TIME ACTIVITIES CAN BE BIG WINNERS

In the spring of 1963, I was a full-time student, social chairman of my section (very part time), had a half-time salaried job, was running a full-time business on the side, and spent a good deal of time in job interviews. This allowed me time for one more activity: chairmanship of the New England Small Business Placement Club. (Was it any wonder that my grades fell so that I finished in the absolute center of my class?)

I now had a budget to pursue my interest in finding a small business to work for in Vermont. I secured a list of every Vermont company with more than 40 employees, and sent each a letter offering the services of several soon-to-graduate Harvard Business School students. I'm sure that I was the only one who really wanted to end up in Vermont. My search was successful, and a new chapter in my life began.

WHAT I LEARNED

- *To paraphrase Mark Twain, Don't let your classes in school interfere with your education.*   Somehow, the real learning always seems to occur outside of class.
- *If you have an idea, and the passion to carry it out, finding money is easy.*   Over 200 million Americans have credit cards, and each one is a *source* of money for you to start your business. All you need to do is ask.
- *Time is the critical factor that ultimately determines how much you can accomplish.*   Most entrepreneurs underestimate by a factor or two how much money they will need to get started. Even worse, however, it usually takes three times as long as they expect to get to profitability.
- *Every selling situation offers you the opportunity to be the buyer.*   Take it! The buyer has all the power, even if he or she doesn't deserve it.
- *All unhappiness in life can be traced to the divergence between our expectations and our experience of what has happened.* Manage your expectations, and you will experience considerable happiness.

Chapter 3

Vermont Ski Lodge: Building a Business to Meet Ladies

How to Get Your Boss to Finance Your Venture

Upon graduation from Harvard, I became assistant to the president and personnel manager for Carris Reels in Rutland, Vermont. Aside from my two summer intern positions and teaching, it was the only job I ever had working for someone else in my entire life.

My salary was $10,000, a princely sum in Vermont in 1963. I was the only employee in the company with a master's degree. Half of my salary was paid by Carris Reels, Inc., and half by Rutland Plywood Company, a sister company owned by Henry Carris and Robert Bigelow. Paying me in this manner was designed to keep my outrageous salary a secret.

Before heading for Vermont, I approached a bank in Boston for a $500 loan to set up housekeeping. The banker agreed to the loan if I could get a letter from my new boss (Henry Carris) stating that I actually had a job. Henry Carris hand-typed this letter himself because he did not want anyone in his company to know how much I would be paid.

THE BALANCE SHEET IN YOUR HEAD IS MORE IMPORTANT THAN THE ONE ON PAPER

I did a quick inventory of my net worth. I had $20 in my pocket, a car, and enough clothes to cover me for a few weeks. My outstanding debt exceeded my tangible assets by at least 10 times. It would have been a good time to declare bankruptcy. My education loans alone equaled 30 percent of my take-home pay. While I may have been bankrupt in a financial sense, in my mind I was at the beginning step on a journey to untold riches.

Fortunately, I had a place to stay—for free. My parents had purchased a summerhouse 10 years earlier at an estate auction. A 10-room farmhouse on 100 acres in East Wallingford, Vermont, about 15 miles south of my work, purchased for the grand sum of $2,000.

The best part of the deal was that the estate offered no money down and payments of $20 a month toward the principal (no interest payments.) In today's world, it's hard to conceive of such bargains. I could see that my lifelong ability for buying valuable things with no money down had come naturally from my parents. Maybe it's genetic.

On the downside, the house lacked a few amenities, such as an indoor bathroom or hot water. The price was right, however, and I figured that it was the perfect place to hang out until snow came or until I could find better digs, whichever came first.

GREAT BUSINESS OPPORTUNITIES CAN BE FOUND AT AUCTIONS

I didn't have to wait long to find a place to live. An old schoolhouse in Florence, Vermont, was being offered for sale by the town on a closed-bid-auction basis. The highest bid received by July 1st would buy 4 acres and a five-room schoolhouse built in 1920.

I only had 37 cents in my checking account (an all-time low if you don't count the multiple times I was overdrawn). Of course, this did not deter me from making a bid of $4,850 on the schoolhouse. To my utter surprise (and panic), I won the bid. I had 30 days to come up with the money, and I still hadn't received my first paycheck.

(Management people only got paid monthly, I learned.) I discovered that I was the only bidder, a fact that caused me more than a little concern. What did everybody else know that I didn't?

I retreated to my unheated, cold-water flat (as I called my parent's summerhouse—it usually evoked lots of sympathy) to plan my strategy. Where would I get the money? I came up with three possible sources: my favorite Harvard professor, and the only two people I knew in Vermont (my boss and a life insurance agent who had found me on my first day in town). Everyone else whom I knew was as broke as me.

My favorite Harvard professor had told us that the two most important things to remember were (1) every business is for sale, and (2) money was no problem. This was a message I could really believe in. My first call was to Harvard (from a pay phone—this was before calling cards), where I got good news and bad news. The good news was that the professor was vacationing in Europe for the summer (surely, he must be feeling extravagant and might loan me some money). The bad news was that he had been fired, possibly for telling gullible students like me that money was never a problem when you wanted to buy a business.

That left me with two names, and one of them, my boss, had taken this inappropriate time to take a family vacation. So, I had to seek out the life insurance agent. I'm sure it's the first time that anyone ever called him.

INVENT A GOOD REASON FOR PEOPLE TO INVEST

I knew that I might have difficulty convincing a prospective investor to put money into a place for me to live. There had to be some commercial idea to whet his or her interest. But what could you do with an abandoned schoolhouse that was miles from anywhere? And *anywhere* wasn't much of anything, either—Rutland, Vermont, with a population of 18,000, was 12 miles away. (I might mention that Rutland has grown over the last 37 years, and now it is a booming metropolis of 18,100 people.)

My idea was to start a bunk-style ski lodge and charge about half of what any other ski lodge charged. No matter that the major ski area, Killington, was almost 30 miles away. Surely, budget-minded skiers would travel this far to save big bucks.

I had two ulterior motives to wanting to start a ski lodge. First, it would be a place for me to live, with luxuries like indoor plumbing and hot water. Second, it would be a great way to meet girls.

I didn't mention my ulterior motives to the life insurance agent, but outlined how I, and any potential investor, could get rich by converting the worthless schoolhouse to a thriving ski lodge. He seemed a little dubious, but he said that he would get back to me. Experience has taught me that "I'll get back to you" is a polite way of saying, "Get lost!"

A week later, my boss finally returned home and I made him the same pitch. To my shock, he said, "Sounds good. I'll put in $1,000, but first I need to talk to my lawyer."

EVERY ONCE IN A WHILE, LAWYERS DON'T SQUELCH THE DEAL

Whenever a deal involves talking to a lawyer, three things inevitably happen. First, it costs you far more than you expected. Second, your share is less than you hoped. Third, the deal never gets done.

There is always the exception, however, to prove that there really are no rules in business. If you really go for it, anything might, and sometimes does, happen.

The lawyer listened carefully to my proposal and said he would like to talk to his partner. Since I thought a deal had no chance of getting done if it had to be passed by a lawyer, I figured the chances of two lawyers approving it were too small to calculate.

Sometimes, though, even lawyers can be swingers. The two lawyers and my boss put in $1,000 each, and together owned 50 percent of the corporation (which they performed the legal work to set up). For my 50 percent, I put in my winning bid, my promise to manage the ski lodge for a year (weekends and nights) with no salary, and my smile.

The deal got even sweeter when my partners agreed to co-sign a $10,000 loan at the bank to pay for converting the schoolhouse to a ski lodge. The pieces were all together, and Chateau Ecole was born.

My head was swimming. Less than a month after arriving in a strange city, nearly destitute and knowing only two people, I was president and half-owner of a corporation, and I had a $10,000 line of credit at the bank—not to mention a roof over my head, indoor plumbing, and a haven for ski bunnies.

NOTHING IS SWEETER THAN TURNING DOWN A PROSPECTIVE INVESTOR

When the life insurance agent heard that my boss and the lawyers had invested in my deal, he wanted to join us as well. Not only did I get everything I went after, but I was turning down prospective investors at the same time. It was surely a heady time in my life as a young entrepreneur.

When I told the Florence town fathers that I planned to start a ski lodge in the schoolhouse, they feared that I might strain the capacity of the town water supply. I planned to have 160 beds, and only 900 people lived in the town, so their fears may have been legitimate. The town agreed to lower the purchase price by $1,300, the cost of drilling my own well.

My dream of having indoor plumbing was postponed by several months because the well driller couldn't start until early in November. However, I moved into the schoolhouse and worked evenings and weekends all summer on renovations.

Frank Kurant, the local plumber, took me under his wing and allowed me to be his helper and student. Together, we created four showers, four sinks, and two toilets in the former cloak closets in each of four classrooms. We also converted the fifth classroom into an apartment for me, and converted the coal furnace to oil.

PEOPLE WHO WORK WITH THEIR HANDS AND LOVE THEIR WORK ARE THE BEST OF ALL PEOPLE

Frank Kurant was the first craftsman I ever met who truly loved his trade. Since then, I have enjoyed the company of other gifted workers—electricians, architects, carpenters, masons, painters, and heavy-equipment operators. For the most part, they are the happiest and most content of all the people I have ever known. They have been lucky, or plucky, enough to have discovered what they love, done their homework so that they become extremely proficient, and pursued their profession with passion. They are the best of all people to hang out with. Somehow, their enthusiasm and passion is contagious and provides inspiration for everyone who comes in contact with them.

RENT IT BY THE NIGHT OR SELL IT OUTRIGHT, WHATEVER MAKES A PROFIT

When I set out to find 80 bunk beds, I found the cheapest price in the area was $250 each, or $20,000 for all I needed. This was double the amount of money that I had budgeted for renovations, and it would require more bank financing (not a problem because of my partners' cosignatures). It seemed like a very large sum of money, though.

After a trip to the library and many phone calls, I discovered a manufacturer in Maryland who could supply beds for only $120 each. There were two problems, however: (1) The minimum order for this price was 150 bunk beds, and (2) it would cost another $20 per bed ($3,000 total) to deliver the beds from Maryland to Vermont.

I have long believed that there are no problems in business, only opportunities to be creative. So I got creative. Our Carris Reel trucks delivered plywood reels all over the country, and usually returned empty. I asked a truck driver how much he would charge to go slightly out of his way and pick up the beds for me on his next trip to Maryland. The answer was $25, and one so-called problem was by the boards.

At a cocktail party that was attended by Rutland's most prestigious families (at least, by their reckoning), I mentioned to several people (actually, anyone who would listen) that I had 70 extra bunk beds, which I would sell for only $200 each, a great saving over the $250 lowest price in town. It seems that many people were actually in the market for bunk beds at the time. During fall foliage season, and again during Christmas and school vacations in ski season, the chamber of commerce advertised on the radio for people who might have an extra bed or two to accommodate the overflow of tourists in the area. Many people were equipping spare bedrooms, garages, or even barns with bunk beds, and earning some extra dollars.

I sold all 70 beds at the cocktail party and earned a profit of $5,600 (more than one-half of my annual salary at the time). This was the first time that I experienced a phenomenon that has repeated itself over and over again: The first product or service with which you start in a new business is often not the most profitable one. Its role is to get you into business. Once you are set up in business and talking with suppliers and customers, you often discover different markets about which you never dreamed with your first product.

Who would have ever guessed that in my first year in the ski lodge business, my biggest profit would come from selling bunk beds (and later, sheets, blankets, and pillows—sold to the same people who bought the bunk beds)?

MAKING IT IS EASY—MARKETING IT IS NOT

With the renovations well under way, I turned to my own true love, marketing. At the library, I copied down the name and address of every college in New York, New Jersey, and New England. I made up a simple brochure offering the lowest-priced accommodations in ski country and sent it to each college, addressed simply to Ski Club.

Probably 90 percent of my letters were never delivered. Most colleges don't even have ski clubs. At least one letter got through, however, and the University of Rochester Ski Club eventually sent a full busload or two of college students about half the weekends for my first year in business.

The only other marketing effort I made was to try to join the Killington Lodging Bureau. Their brochure was distributed by the thousands, and my price would be far cheaper than anyone else's. The only problem was that to become a member, your lodge had to be within 20 miles of Killington, and mine was a full 28 miles away.

Other lodges in Pittsford, 5 miles closer to Killington than was Chateau Ecole, had been turned down.

Since I have always believed that the sale begins when the prospect says no, I was ready for the challenge. I found a topographic map and traced a way through the mountains on mostly dirt roads. I could get to Killington from Chateau Ecole in exactly 19.8 miles. I offered to give the lodging director a ride to prove it, but he believed me after seeing the route on my map.

I was allowed to join the Killington Lodging Bureau, and my success was assured before we got running water. Apparently, it didn't matter that none of the dirt roads on my map were open in the winter, but just in case, I never mentioned that little fact.

IN THE BOONDOCKS, IT IS EASIER TO FIND WORKERS ON CHRISTMAS THAN DURING DEER SEASON

Getting the water turned on ended up being an even greater challenge. The first busload of college kids was due to arrive on December 3rd, and the well drillers didn't start until November 12th. They had drilled 250 feet by November 15th, and I was feeling fairly confident that they would finish on time. My neighbors had hit water at about 300 feet.

On the 16th, however, none of the well drillers came to work. I called the owner in a panic. "Where are they?" I asked.

"It's deer season," he calmly responded, as if I knew that virtually everyone who worked with his hands in the state of Vermont was in the woods during deer season. (It is a lesson that I have learned a dozen times since then, and, somehow, it always comes as a surprise.)

"When will they come back?" I asked hopefully.

"Depends if they get their deer."

"How long is the season?"

"Two weeks."

I calculated that if they didn't get their deer, there would be only two days to complete the well, hook it up, and be ready for my skiers. Not much room for leeway, but possible. Then he hit me with the bomb. "Of course, there's doe season."

I figured that it was time to start the sale when the customer said no, but I quickly learned that some things, like deer hunting in Vermont, are nonnegotiable.

Unfortunately, my well drillers never got their deer that year. Fortunately, they did not have doe permits. They returned to the job, drilled 20 more feet, and I was in business—at least until the hot-water heater burned out on the first day that all 16 showers were turned on at the same time. Such is the life of any new business—it's all ups and downs, just like the toilet seats.

SOMETIMES, HAVING THE LOWEST PRICE WORKS

My business plan was to offer ridiculously low prices and hope college kids would come by the busload. I figured that the only way to make a profit at such low prices was to keep expenses to an absolute minimum. This meant essentially no advertising, and I would be the only employee. Since I had a full-time job weekdays, running a 160-bed ski lodge all by myself provided more opportunities to be creative.

Running Chateau Ecole by myself was actually easier than I feared. Mostly, the skiers were there on weekends, and my biggest time-consuming job was cleaning the bunkrooms and bathrooms after they left Sunday morning. When skiers came during the week, they usually checked in after I got home from work, and they were gone for the day first thing in the morning.

THERE IS DIGNITY IN EVERY KIND OF WORK

I remember reading an interview with a Yale graduate who had come from a wealthy family. He said that his background prevented him from buying a used truck and starting a trash collection business like his friend had (the friend later became quite rich when he sold out to Waste Management, a public company). It never occurred to me that a good education and family might be a liability if someone wanted to start a business of his or her own.

No matter what, I never felt that any work was beneath my dignity. If unpleasant work was required to move the business forward, so be it. I had an MBA from Harvard Business School and cheerfully (usually, at least) cleaned out eight toilets every weekend all winter. I couldn't imagine not doing it.

The income statement for a typical ski weekend was as follows:

120 skiers ($11 each)	$1,320
Meals cost total	360
Utilities	100
Building costs (tax, mortgage, repairs)	100
Miscellaneous	100
Total expenses	660
Profit	$ 660

Each weekend, my ski lodge earned three times as much as I did at my full-time job, where I was paid $200 a week. (Of course, I had to share my ski lodge profits with my partners.) Cleaning toilets didn't seem like much of a price to pay for such riches less than a year out of school.

At the end of the first year in business, I approached my investor-partners and offered to buy them out for $2,500 ($1,000 in cash and the balance, with interest, over the next two years). They accepted my offer, and I soon owned 100 percent of my first business. They each made 150 percent on their investment in one year.

FIND A MENTOR TO TEACH YOU THE ROPES

While it may seem like running Chateau Ecole was my major activity in my first year out of graduate school, it really wasn't. After all, I had a full-time job at Carris Reels. Henry Carris was the most important mentor of my business life. He and I were the only people at the company with a college degree, and I think he used me as a sounding board. We talked for hours about business, and I learned far more about running a small company from him than I ever did at Harvard.

Henry advanced my business career in many other ways—introducing me to the chamber of commerce (where I became president two years later) and nominating me to the board of directors of the Rutland Savings and Loan Association.

Perhaps Henry Carris's greatest gift to me was firing me less than one year after I started. I clearly was not a company person. My biggest problem was getting to work on time. I just couldn't do it. Work started at 8:00 A.M. and I rarely made it before 8:30, even if I left home (20 minutes away) at 7:30—I would stop at the post office and start talking to someone. I consistently stayed at work two hours later than the other employees, but no one ever saw me then. However, they did see me when I came in late, and it became a real issue, especially after my exorbitant salary became public knowledge.

BELIEVE IT OR NOT, THE BEST WOMEN CAN BE FOUND IN THE BOONDOCKS

Before I accepted my job offer at Carris Reels, I had asked Henry what the prospects were for meeting a nice young lady in Rutland. "Oh, that's part of the job," he said. "My wife has already picked out your bride." When I arrived in Rutland, I asked to meet my bride, but was told that she was spending the summer in Europe.

Leslie Pratt returned to Vermont on September 1st, we met, and got engaged a week later. On our second date, we went to an auction and bought a 12-burner industrial stove for the ski lodge. Then, she headed back to St. Lawrence University (a five-hour drive away) to finish her senior year in college. I would have visited her at school, but I was working every night and weekend creating the ski lodge. So we courted by telephone and mail. Sometimes, I think the most significant ongoing endeavor of my entire life has been selling something by mail, only this time I was selling myself.

On a Sunday in January during her Christmas vacation, after the skiers had left, Leslie and I got married at the local church in the presence of my sister, her husband, and the minister. I got Monday off from work, and we drove to New York City for a one-day honeymoon. We hardly knew each other. I still wonder at how impetuous we were. Looking back, it seems ironic that I started a ski lodge as a way to meet women, and found my wife before the first ski bunny came to stay.

In June, Leslie graduated and moved into Chateau Ecole. She seemed a little less than thrilled at moving into her first house with 160 potential, and sometimes actual, housemates. Maybe putting her in charge of those eight toilets was not such a good idea.

On the fateful day she moved in, she even had more concern when we learned that I had just been fired from my first (and ultimately, my only) full-time job. I had absolutely no cash, having just paid back my investors, and it would be almost six long months before the skiers returned. At least we had a roof over our heads until I could find something that created a positive cash flow.

There is a sequel to my getting fired. Two years later, it looked like Henry Carris's son, Bill, would not join the company after college, and Henry was looking for an eventual successor. He offered me my job back at triple the salary I had been making. Apparently, several of the production methods that I had installed had resulted in profits going up 10-fold, and this value wasn't clear at the time I was fired. I declined Henry's generous offer, mostly because I was making even more money in the businesses that I was running on my own. Besides, I could sleep until 9:00 every morning if I wanted.

WHAT I LEARNED

■ *There are willing investors for every sound business.* If you can't convince investors to back your business, you probably couldn't market the business, either.

■ *The first product or service is usually not the most profitable one.* The role of the first idea is to get you away from working for someone else and into business for yourself. Your customers then tell you what they really want (instead of your first product), and you are off and running.

■ *The sale begins when the prospect says no.* It gives you the opportunity to be creative and to turn the prospect into a customer.

■ *Getting engaged a week after you first meet a woman is probably a little hasty.*

Chapter 4

Real Estate Investing: Learning about Leverage

How to Build a Real Estate Empire with No Money Down

$\mathcal{G}$etting fired from your first job after graduate school is a cause for soul searching. I concluded that I must not be a very good employee and should probably work for myself. That way, if I ever got fired again, it would be my own doing and not someone else's.

I decided to become a real estate broker. It is a little ironic that after struggling through four years of college and two years of graduate school, and amassing a pile of debt in the process, I decided on a profession that I could just have easily started right out of high school.

My biggest fear was passing the state real estate exam. I had agreed with Leslie that if I failed the exam, I would swallow my pride and take a real job in New York or Boston. Such a thought totally terrified me. If I couldn't keep a job in a friendly little company in Vermont where I was an important part of the management team, how could I survive in the big city?

The spectre of big-city living (and worse, a salaried job) scared me into studying like I had never studied before. By the time exam day arrived, I felt I knew enough about the subject to teach a course on it.

I passed the exam with one of the highest marks ever recorded, and the following week offered a course on how to pass the exam. Teaching this course kept money flowing in until my first real estate sale closed.

I also began teaching business courses at Castleton State College, the first of many teaching assignments that put food on the table while my entrepreneurial adventures were grinding toward profitability (or dissolution, as was often the case).

THE FIRST MONEY IS OFTEN THE HARDEST

During the summer, I got lots of real estate listings, but made only one sale—and it was anything but easy. A schoolteacher from Connecticut and her unemployed husband wanted to buy a small cabin on half an acre from a farmer in Brandon (asking price $3,000). She had only $300 in cash and asked the farmer to finance the $2,700 balance. He agreed to do it, if I would co-sign the note. If the farmer had any idea of my financial condition, he wouldn't have wasted his time. However, I must have looked prosperous in my VW convertible. Desperate for my $180 commission, I co-signed the note. At last, I had made my first sale.

IF YOU'RE ALMOST TOTALLY BROKE, IT'S TIME TO TAKE A VACATION

By late in September, I had not sold another house, and my total liquid net worth was down to $200. What do you do when you're down to your last $200 and ski season (and possible income) is still three months away? We decided to take our first vacation. I figured that if we waited another two weeks, we might be down to nothing and not be able to afford a vacation at all.

We headed for New Orleans, staying with college friends whenever we could. Our only credit card was a Gulf Oil gas card. Imagine our surprise when we discovered that this card was also good at Holiday Inns. We stayed away an extra week and arrived home with less than $5 to our name.

GOOD THINGS HAPPEN AT AUCTIONS

The very next day, we went to an auction, hoping something might be available in our price range. I left a note on the Chateau Ecole front door diverting any prospective real estate customers to the auction.

To my eternal surprise, a dentist from Connecticut arrived in Vermont, saw my ad in a local paper, drove to the ski lodge, and found me at the auction (no easy feat since he had never seen me in person). Before the weekend was over, he had purchased three investment properties and hired me to manage them. We were in the chips!

Entrepreneurs are not careful people. If they were, they probably wouldn't start half of the businesses they do. And they certainly wouldn't take off on a vacation with the last funds they possessed. But somehow this foolhardiness often works out in the end. (It helps to be lucky.) Leslie often said that it was never easy being married to an entrepreneur, but it wasn't boring.

Real estate was my business and Better Realty my company ("Better Buy Better," "Better Properties for Sale," etc.). I would do almost anything, though, to make a buck if it didn't take much time. The *New York Herald Tribune* (now out of business) sent me a tear sheet with a copy of a small classified ad that I had run. On the same page were details of a contest—select an ad from their paper and tell why you like it in 25 words or less. I sent back by return mail: "This ad captures Vermont's verdant green countryside, shimmering white snow, kaleidoscopic autumn colors. But most of all, it appeals to me because I wrote it."

Those words won an all-expense first-class vacation in California. I cashed the first-class tickets in for tourist class and got $500 extra to spend. Continuing our string of good luck, when we got to the plane, all of the tourist-class seats were full, and we were put in first class anyway.

ALWAYS BE ON THE LOOKOUT FOR IDEAS TO COPY

While in California, I scoured the real estate pages looking for ideas. (I've always believed that emulation is better than creation.) One ad offered a free trip to Hawaii for the couple who bought a particular house. Now there was an idea I could use.

Back home, I had a listing that I was desperate to sell. For three months, I couldn't even get anyone to look at it for the asking price of $10,500. I was also the owner of this property, paying interest and taxes on a vacant house every month.

I called my travel agent, confirmed that a trip to Bermuda could be had for $500, and advertised the house: "Free trip to Bermuda for the couple who buys this house for $11,000." Four people visited the house the first day, and one agreed to buy it. "Could you lower the price if we didn't take the trip to Bermuda?" the buyer asked sheepishly. I agreed to reduce the price by $500, and the deal was completed.

The reason I owned that house was because I had a promotion called Better Realty House of the Month. Under that heading were the words, "I think this property is such a good value that if it doesn't sell at this price in 30 days, I will buy it myself *at this price.*" Every month, I listed a different house, and either sold it or bought it myself. This program got me a lot of listings, each seller hoping I would select their home for the guaranteed sale next month.

The other thing this program got me was a lot of houses. In my first two years in the real estate business, without a cent of my own money to start, I accumulated 23 properties. (Clearly, I was either not a very good salesman, or I couldn't say no to a good deal. It was probably a little of both.)

Real estate is something you can buy with hardly any money of your own. Dozens of books have been written about how to do it. One of them, *How I Turned $1,000 into a Million in Real Estate in My Spare Time,* by William Nickerson, was the one that motivated me.

My plan was to buy absolutely any property I could as long as I didn't have to put any money of my own down (this was easy because I had none), and the rental income from the property could cover all of the mortgage and tax payments. I didn't care what the price was, only the financing. I figured that if I just broke even on a cash flow basis, I would be reducing the mortgage, and the property values would rise over time with inflation. Somewhere down the line, I would surely get rich.

I got financing in many ways, but the two most popular were second mortgages from the sellers and the real estate commission. If it was my listing, I usually got to keep 6 percent (my commission) toward the down payment; if it was another broker's listing, I could usually convince him or her to take the commission as a third mortgage. This way, the other broker was assured of making a sale, and his or her income would come as a steady payment each month, including interest. The real estate business is usually a feast-or-famine affair, and this was a way for brokers to level out their cash flow. Anyway, they almost always agreed to my offer.

On one multiunit apartment house, I had three mortgages lined up (the bank, the seller, and the agent), but I was still $5,000 short of what was needed to close. I tried to think of who might benefit if I owned this property, and my fuel oil dealer came to mind. I offered him the oil business for all of my properties, including the big one that I was about to buy, if he would loan me $5,000 secured by a fourth mortgage. He agreed, and we closed the deal.

IF THE FINANCING IS RIGHT, YOU DON'T HAVE TO INSPECT THE PROPERTY

One of the first properties I bought was while I still had a job (it is more convenient but not always necessary to have a job and income when buying real estate). A broker advertised a 10-room farmhouse and 120 acres for only $365 down. I called her and said I would buy it. She asked if I would like to look at it. I said no thanks, as long as $365 was all I would need.

It took her six months to close the deal, as it was a complicated arrangement with the Farmers Home Administration on the house and five acres, and a second deed for 115 acres with financing by the seller. I bought the property and rented it to a ski club for $1,500 for the winter, gaining back my down payment, and more, in one week.

I was now in the land development business. In the next two years, I divided some of the land into 10-acre lots and sold enough to pay off the mortages in full.

I retained 70 acres for myself and used this land as security for loans to start several businesses in the future. Many years later, I learned that the "town road" serving my land was actually privately owned, and my land had no access, leaving it virtually worthless. Fortunately, this was not public knowledge when I borrowed the money.

YOU CAN'T START A HOG FARM WITH A SINGLE PIG

The other moneymaking adventure that I tried was to buy a piglet. We housed it in a chicken coop in the backyard, but it often got loose and pretended that it was a dog. One day, I was saying good-bye to some real estate prospects in my driveway—two couples from New York. Around the corner of the house came our golden retriever, followed closely by our tenants' German shepherd, followed closely by a huffing and puffing pig. The couples from New York gasped in disbelief. As they drove out of the driveway, I heard one of them say, "Have you ever seen such an ugly dog?"

The pig ended up not being my best investment. First of all, it was always getting into trouble. One Sunday morning, my next-door neighbor (who lived one-quarter of a mile away) knocked on our door and woke us up. He was livid. Our pig had eaten parts of every prize pumpkin that he had been raising for the county fair. He had won ribbons for six consecutive years, until now, he said. Each day, he would inject milk into the pumpkin vines to make them grow larger. And now he had nothing to show. Fortunately, he did not ask for financial consideration, and these were the days before people would sue for such damages.

In spite of what I had heard about pigs, our pig became a finicky eater. Twice a week, I would root through the dumpster at the local supermarket and find good things (mostly vegetables) for it to eat. Then, I would visit a large restaurant where they saved a large garbage can full for me. Most of what I collected remained uneaten, however. He seemed to like only hot dogs and cottage cheese, aside from an occasional milk-fed prize pumpkin.

After four months, our pig weighed only 40 pounds, while his brother and sister from the same litter (owned by my bookkeeper) weighed 170 pounds. I had learned a valuable lesson. You can't raise just one pig. Without competition for food, they aren't piggy at all. I always felt that competition was a healthy thing, and my pig-raising experience was living proof.

SLUM LANDLORDS DESERVE EVERY CENT THEY EARN

For the most part, the properties I bought with no money down were multifamily low-income places in need of repair. The owners' willingness to take a second mortgage on these properties was a good indication of how eager they were to get rid of them. They had discovered, as I later did, how horrible it is to be the owner of low-income housing (it is probably 10 times worse today with all the health and fire regulations). Owning such properties is not a privilege, it is a curse.

On one Rutland street, I owned four adjacent houses, which had 15 total living units. Every single one was occupied by single mothers with children. On the first day of each month, they would receive their welfare checks. I think they were called Aid to Dependent Children checks. I would collect all 15 signed checks, go to the bank to cash them, and return with their change.

While no men were supposed to be living in my 15 apartments, I was convinced that if a census were taken at midnight, at least 15 adult males would be found. If these unwed mothers married their boyfriends, they would lose their benefits. Our welfare system was clearly not working perfectly, although I surely don't know the answer.

My properties were a hotbed of domestic disturbances. The police were often called to assist, and for some strange reason, they always called me to let me know that there was a disturbance in one of my apartments. Even if it was at two o'clock in the morning. I always appreciated their concern.

One day, I got a call from a tenant who said that her bathroom wasn't working. As I drove to her place with my plumbing tools aboard, I was thinking that maybe I wasn't the plumber I thought I was—just the week before, I had replaced all of the old zinc pipes in the building with copper ones.

I also thought that it was strange that she said her bathroom wasn't working. What could that mean? Why hadn't she said, "The toilet is broken," "The sink is clogged," or "The faucet doesn't turn on" (all words I had heard many times before)? When I arrived, I learned why she used the general term *bathroom*. Her now former boyfriend had cut out all of the copper pipes and sold them for scrap.

I could tell you a dozen similar stories, but I think you get the picture. Owning this kind of real estate really sucks. Just because you can buy it with no money down doesn't mean that you should. In fact, in most cases, it means you shouldn't.

SPEED KILLS, EVEN WHEN IT INVOLVES SEIZING A BUSINESS OPPORTUNITY

I have always prided myself on my ability to move fast when I get an idea. Maybe I move fast for fear that I would get cold feet if I thought about it much. This inclination to move fast proved to be my undoing in my real estate career. If I had moved a little more slowly, I would not have acquired 23 buildings and over 80 headaches (apartment units) before I found out what a difficult business it is to be in.

THE ULTIMATE LENDER OF LAST RESORT— YOUR MOTHER

There is one good reason why you should borrow money from your family members: They might loan you the money because they love you, and they won't pay too much attention to your financial condition or the merits of your business propositions.

On the other hand, there are at least a thousand reasons why you shouldn't borrow money from your family: one for each day that the loan is outstanding. Once the loan is made, you can never take a vacation, buy a car, or even go out for dinner. If you do, you will hear something whispered by jealous siblings or aunts or uncles or any other of your extended family members. "Of course, if he didn't have that money his mother foolishly loaned him, he couldn't be spending extravagantly like that." No matter if you have been working 80 hours a week for five years, as long as that loan is outstanding, every single expenditure you make is scrutinized by your entire family.

Sometimes, however, even if you know how awful borrowing money from your family can be, there just doesn't seem to be any other choice. (At my advanced age, I can now resolutely assure you that there are always other choices, and they should always be sought out and used before going to Mom.)

Back in 1965, I wasn't so smart. The deal of the century (or so I thought) had just come along, and I needed $1,500 in cash within 72 hours or I would miss out. I called my mother. Somehow, she had saved up that amount of money, and she was willing to loan it to me interest-free in exchange for 50 percent of any profit that I made on the deal. I took the money, figuring that I could close out the loan and make a tidy profit in no more than 60 days.

There is an old saying about starting a business: Everything in your business plan will end up costing you twice what you expected and take three times as much time as you had expected. (My experience bore this out, and my solution to the problem was to dispense with the planning. That way, I wouldn't be disappointed.)

Sometimes I planned in spite of myself, as in the case of my mother's loan—I planned on paying it back in 60 days. Almost three years later (over 1,000 days later, in fact), I was finally able to repay the loan. But I'm getting ahead of the story.

The property involved was a real fire sale. Situated on 4 acres at the end of a dirt road, this four-bedroom farmhouse had been partially destroyed by a fire. Every room downstairs was blackened, and a few partitions were completely gutted. The frame seemed solid, however, and most of the necessary repairs appeared to be cosmetic (or so they appeared to my trusting eyes).

The owner of the property had collected the fire insurance and offered to sell the blackened structure to the first person who showed up with $1,500 hard cash. That person, thanks to my mother, was me.

EMOTION, NOT REASON, DRIVES PEOPLE TO MAKE PURCHASES

Throughout my adult life, I have read how-to books about as often as most people read the comic strips. My favorite book at this time was called *The Magic Power of Emotional Appeal* by Roy Garn.

The premise of the book was that all people are preoccupied most of the time, and you can only break through this preoccupation and get their attention by appealing to one of four emotional appeals. Each person is predominantly motivated by one of the following emotions: money, romance, ego, and self-preservation. I quickly tried to figure how I could use these emotional appeals to sell real estate and, particularly, my emotionally financed scorched estate.

Emotional Appeal No. 1—Money

Money-obsessed people were easy to sell to, but they weren't much fun—all that they cared about were numbers, numbers, numbers (e.g., costs, returns on investment, resale values, leverages, payback percentages, etc.). I tried to attract this kind of person with a classified ad in the *New York Herald Tribune* and *Boston Herald*—"Fix-Up Special, only $3,950." When someone responded to this ad, I besieged him or her with every number I could think of.

Money-obsessed people were usually the most gullible buyers—their desire to make a killing in real estate would blind them to reality. After all, most of them had been brainwashed by the real estate how-to books, and they were easy pickings if I could arrange financing for them. Unfortunately for me, I couldn't get a bank to make a loan on a burned-out house with no furnace. I had somehow missed the fact that there was no furnace—when I peeked in the cellar, the electricity was turned off, but I had just assumed that there must be a source of heat there. (Yes, I know that to *assume* makes an *ass* out of *u* and *me*.)

Emotional Appeal No. 2—Romance

Romance-minded people are not just interested in romantic boy-girl, boy-boy, or whatever kind of relationships. They are turned on by beautiful things, new things, travel, all kinds of animals, and other warm fuzzies of every kind.

I loved to sell to romantic people. You never had to deal with numbers, and keen observation of beauty counted for more than harsh reality. I once sold a house to romantics who fell in love with a clump of birch trees and a nice view in winter (once the leaves had fallen). They totally ignored the crumbling foundation. After all, how can you compare temporal objects like poured concrete with eternal beauty? In the end, everyone gets exactly what they desire.

I tried to appeal to romantic types with a classified ad in the *New York Times*—"Deer in Your Front Yard." This ad attracted many out-of-state visitors who were thrilled by the beauty of Vermont. Many of them bought country properties from me, but somehow the scorched walls didn't quite seem romantic to them, in spite of the cute little Bambis in the front yard. They soon found that Vermont was crawling with deer. Later, after they moved here and experienced deer devouring their entire flower garden, the romance was gone forever.

Emotional Appeal No. 3—Ego

Ego-driven people are primarily interested in their self-importance and what other people think of them. I tried to appeal to them with an ad in the *Wall Street Journal,* which read, "Your Own Castle at the End of the Road." While I got a good response from the ad, the reality of my burned-out house didn't exactly qualify it for castle status.

The most blatant ego-driven prospect I ever encountered had responded to the castle ad, and was coming to Vermont to be the general manager of the newly built Grant's Department Store. When I met him at the airport, he pointed at my little Volkswagen and said, "I can't get in that little thing. I'm accustomed to a rather large Cadillac." His words implied that his greatest fear was that someone might see him in my little car.

We were 6 miles from town, and the Rutland airport did not have rental cars available yet, so he had no choice but to slither into my tiny car and hope no one would see him. As we drove down the residential streets of Rutland, he wanted to know what kind of people lived there. "I want to be where the doctors and lawyers are," he said.

After a totally frustrating day of showing him everything I knew was for sale in all of Rutland County, I finally said, "Okay, tell me exactly what kind of home would make you happy." His response was precious: "I want something that people will drive by and think, 'There's a $200,000 mansion,' but I want to pay no more than $60,000." A pretty tough assignment, even for a creative real estate broker like me. I gave up and drove him to his hotel.

This man did find his house, but he didn't get it from me, and he got just what he wanted. A ski lodge at Killington had experienced a major fire that virtually destroyed the entire inside and miraculously left the façade untouched. It had been condemned as unlivable. The Grant's manager convinced the town that he would make it livable, and they allowed him to buy it and move in. While he may have felt important, I don't think he entertained at home much for the next couple of years.

Emotional Appeal No. 4—Self-Preservation

Self-preservation people are safety-minded, cautious, and fearful. I also figured they might tend to be older. Most young people, it seemed to me, believed themselves to be immortal. I placed an ad in the *Christian Science Monitor* (average reader age over 50 years old)—"For the Couple Who Will Live to Be 100." This single ad pulled more responses than any classified ad I ever ran. Like all of my other classified ads, it does not say one thing about the house I had for sale. But it said volumes about the people who responded.

When the self-preservation folks arrived to check out my properties, I talked about the clean, fresh air we had in Vermont, the low pollution, and almost no crime—in short, a place where you could plan to live to be 100. (I never mentioned that the cold winters also resulted in one of the highest suicide rates in the nation.)

For some strange reason, none of the self-preservation people were interested in my $3,950 property. I think they believed that I said it was perfect for the couple who would live to be 100 because that was how long it would take to fix it up.

My emotional-appeal advertising campaign had resulted in many real estate sales, but little interest in the subject property. In retrospect, the greatest thing I gained from buying it with my mother's money was to use it as a bait-and-switch device: I got many people to Vermont to check it out, and then I sold them something more desirable (and expensive).

In desperation, I offered to sell the property to a hard-working carpenter with eight children and a terrible credit history. Of course, I had to finance the property entirely myself. He had nothing for a down payment (something familiar to me—it almost endeared him to me). I charged a high interest rate with the understanding that he would quickly fix the place up and make it eligible for a bank loan (with me co-signing if necessary). This understanding was better as a concept than it was reality. A man supporting eight children had little energy or money for house repairs. His wife used her creativity and decorated the house to go well with black walls.

Now, I not only had an angry unpaid mother (although she didn't mention it *every* time we communicated), but the town fathers were extremely upset with me. This one new family increased the total number of kids for the town to educate by 3 percent, with virtually no tax revenue coming in. A selectman called me one evening and told me that the cost of educating these kids would be five times the cost of the house every year for the next 10 years, or worse, if more kids came along. There truly are a lot of things to think about when you are doing business in a small town.

I did like the carpenter, however, even when he couldn't make the first mortgage payment. He agreed to come to work for me on my growing collection of tenant houses, and I deducted the mortgage payments from his weekly paycheck.

Almost four years later, and with much begging on my part, a local bank finally agreed to finance the property (with my signature and a promise to keep the carpenter employed for at least three years). I split the profit with my mother, and was lucky or smart enough to never again borrow from my parents.

ASK QUESTIONS AND PEOPLE WILL THINK THAT YOU KNOW SOMETHING

My real estate endeavors eventually led me into banking. I had discovered a thing called a *blanket mortgage*. This was back when most mortgages were held by the local bank or savings and loan association, and not sold to Fannie Mae. The concept was that if a bank took one mortgage (a blanket one) on several properties all at once, then risk would be reduced. If something bad befell one of the properties in the portfolio, the bank still had equity in all the other properties to secure their position.

I thought that the blanket mortgage was a wonderful idea and was able to convince the president of the Rutland Savings & Loan Association to think the same way. My boss at the time, Henry Carris, was on the board of the Savings & Loan.

At least 15 of my 23 properties were financed with a blanket mortgage at this small bank. Then, I reached the lending limit of the bank, and I was cut off. The directors wanted to keep an eye on me (or so I thought at the time), and I was invited to join their board of directors.

When the man who had been president of this bank for 40 years suddenly died, I was nominated to be its president at the ripe old age of 26. I asked the nominating committee why they had selected me, and they answered that it was because I asked so many questions at the board meetings. They thought I was testing them, when in fact I was trying to figure out how they made loan decisions so I could use the information to get loans for myself from other banks. Clearly, there is no such thing as a stupid question.

When my grandmother read about my appointment in the local paper, she called and said, "Congratulations, it will look so good in your obituary."

ADVERTISING DOESN'T PAY—IT COSTS!

When I was the newly elected president of the Rutland Savings & Loan Association, I tried to think up some ways to get people to think about us without spending money on advertising. Advertising is a long-term investment. In the short run, it is almost always a loser. Most small companies do not have the luxury of long-term thinking. They are in survival mode. This was the case at our bank.

Banks aren't really very exciting topics for publicity articles. The only time a bank usually makes the news is when some officer is caught embezzling or someone tries to rob the place.

In the midst of my thinking about my bank advertising challenge, I made a daily visit to the Rutland Restaurant for some coffee and gossip. (This restaurant is still there, virtually unchanged, 35 years later. Same owner, and still the best place to learn what's going on in Rutland.)

After several cups of coffee, I headed for the men's room. On the wall in front of me, someone had neatly printed "JESUS SAVES." I don't know what caused me to do what I did next, except that I was thinking about how to get my bank some publicity. I took out a pen and wrote under those words "AT RUTLAND SAVINGS & LOAN."

Over the next few days, several of my friends mentioned that they had seen some interesting graffiti about my bank at the Rutland Restaurant. I figured that I was on to something good.

IF YOU HAVE A GOOD IDEA, RUN WITH IT,
ESPECIALLY IF IT DOESN'T COST ANYTHING

Over the next several weeks, I visited every public restroom I could find, writing "JESUS SAVES" in black ink, and "AT RUTLAND SAVINGS & LOAN" in blue ink. I did this in every restaurant and every hotel (okay, there was only one in Rutland). I even tried the bus terminal, but I couldn't find any space on the walls. I decided that most bus patrons probably weren't big bank customers, anyway.

Looking back, I realize that I should have enlisted a female recruit and covered the ladies rooms as well. Everyone knows that women control over half the wealth in our country, but back in 1965, we weren't so smart.

My simple publicity stunt got a few chuckles and even a few new customers. It didn't cost anything, and I got a real kick out of doing it.

RIDE THE HORSE IN THE DIRECTION IT IS GOING— IF THE HORSE DIES, GET OFF

In spite of my low-cost publicity efforts, I realized that our bank was too small to ever be an economic powerhouse. It had originally been set up to be a nonprofit community bank, and for more than a half-century, it had successfully managed to avoid profits every year. We were by far the smallest bank in town, and our competition was offering new services (and lower mortgage rates), which we couldn't match. There was no way we could realistically compete with the other lending institutions.

I realized that the kindest thing that I could do for our bank was to merge with a larger savings and loan association. We soon became the Rutland branch of Burlington Federal, and I was invited to be on their board of advisors. I figured I already had enough banking credentials for my obituary, so I declined the offer. I never would have been a good board member anyway.

WHAT I LEARNED

■ *You can build a real estate empire with little or no money down.* But just because it's possible doesn't mean that you should.

■ *Managing real estate (especially low-income properties) is one of the worst possible businesses imaginable.* The prideful pleasure that you enjoyed by taking a title with little money down will soon be forgotten when you encounter the agonies of managing your properties.

■ *Never borrow from your mother.* Or, at least until you have exhausted every other source of capital you can think of. Money borrowed from family is tainted, and it often involves a psychological price that is far greater than any interest you could pay.

■ *Emulation is as good as creation.* Don't be afraid to copy someone else's good idea. If it works for them, it will probably work for you.

■ *There is no such thing as a stupid question.* Ask enough questions and you might be named president of the bank.

Chapter 5

Equipment Rental Business: "Don't Buy It, Rent It!"

How to Have the Owner/Seller Finance Your Entire Business Purchase

The Taylor Rental Store in Rutland, Vermont, was an experiment being carried on by Dealer Supply Company, a hardware store equipment wholesaler in Springfield, Massachusetts. Cecil Goodheart, Dealer Supply's sales rep in Vermont, had come up with the idea of setting up an equipment rental store to create a captive customer for equipment sales. Rutland was the guinea pig store. Cecil owned it and was expected to buy all of his equipment needs from Dealer Supply, although no royalty payments on sales were required, as is the standard for other equipment rental store franchises.

BUYING FOR NO MONEY DOWN DOESN'T MEAN YOU CAN'T LOSE MONEY ON THE DEAL

I bought this Taylor Rental Store for two reasons: (1) Cecil offered it to me for no money down, and (2) the store had a ton of tools that I could use for my real estate renovations. I didn't really have any idea if it was a good business or not.

At first, all I cared about was whether I could pay one-third of my cash collections to Cecil, as I had agreed, and still have enough left over to pay for my help and other operating expenses. On this score, I was pleasantly surprised (of course, I was not taking out a salary).

After six months of positive cash flow, Dealer Supply offered to give me 100 percent financing if I opened a second store in Barre, Vermont. I liked the unfamiliar feel of a positive cash flow and readily agreed.

Shortly after opening the Barre store, I went to a trade show for equipment rental stores and quickly learned how little I knew about the rental store business. Among other things, I learned that I could buy most of the equipment directly from the manufacturer for about 20 percent less than Dealer Supply charged.

Dealer Supply got angry when they discovered that I had purchased some equipment directly from the manufacturer. They told me I couldn't use the Taylor Rental name if I didn't buy everything from them. (Exclusive buying arrangements were subsequently ruled illegal by the courts, and Dealer Supply set up a royalty payment on sales as their way of making money with Taylor Rental Centers.)

As long as I was not expanding my business significantly (i.e., not buying lots of new equipment), I would be just as well off by keeping my relationship with Dealer Supply. By this time, however, I was hooked by the equipment rental business and had dreams of an empire in my head. I dropped the Taylor Rental Center name and created Green Mountain Rentals, Inc.

GRIEVING WIDOWERS SHOULDN'T GO ON A CRUISE

In a trade magazine, I read about a rental store for sale in North Haven, Connecticut. I hopped in my car and headed south to find an almost bizarre situation. The owner, a nice older man named Leo Kornicker, had lived his entire life in New York City. A few weeks after he retired from a midlevel job with a chemical company, his wife of 45 years died suddenly. In an attempt to get his mind off his significant loss, he took an around-the-world cruise, where he met a lonely 50-year-old never-married woman from Connecticut. They fell in love and were married on board the ship by the captain.

Before they reached port, she also convinced him to take a portion of his retirement savings and buy a business for her nephew who was "a good kid" but had "some difficulty keeping a job." He purchased North Haven Rentals for $80,000, a price equal to the prior year's rental sales.

The nephew now had a good-paying job—a manager, no less! His first executive decision was to close the store for the lunch hour so he could go home and enjoy a beer with his wife. His second decision was to get rid of the U-Haul trailers because it was too hard to hook them up when it got cold.

Not surprising, the business started to deteriorate. First-year sales fell to $60,000. When I arrived in June, Leo Kornicker was trying to run the store himself because the nephew was taking a few weeks off to rest (he was burned out from the stress of running the business).

Leo had never owned a car, nor had a license, nor touched a gas engine. Much of the equipment was not in working condition, and sales looked like they would be about $40,000 for the current year.

At the end of the business day, I drove Leo home and we sat in the living room with his wife. In my head, I thought $40,000 would be a fair price for his business, since that would be about what they would do this year (most stores sold for a price equal to the last year's sales). By fixing the equipment and hiring a good manager, I figured I could easily get sales back up to $60,000.

We discussed the rental business, and I told them that I was the owner of two other very successful rental stores. We agreed that his equipment was in poor shape, and that the business needed a large chunk of cash to finance the purchase of new equipment, repair the existing equipment, and to do some serious marketing. Expecting some negotiations on the price, I offered $30,000 for the business. Leo and his wife retreated to another room to consider my offer.

Sometimes the Real Sale Starts
When the Customer Says Yes

Their desperate state became apparent when they returned and accepted my offer without even making a counteroffer. While they were in the other room, I had time to plan the rest of my negotiations. If I played my cards right, I could get this store, *and another one* somewhere else, all with no money down. At least, that was the goal that I had set for myself as I sat in their living room that day.

"I would like to pay $10,000 in cash, and you hold a note for $20,000," I said, as if I were finishing the sentence I had earlier started with "I'll pay you $30,000 for the business." They retreated to the other room once more to consider my new terms, and soon they returned with their acceptance. "We have confidence in you— we think you can make it a success," they said. They seemed relieved, thinking the deal was done.

In my mind, the sale was just beginning. The important part of the negotiations had not been discussed yet. I continued my earlier sentence, "I would like you to hold this $20,000 note, and not have a first security interest in the equipment I am buying. Your security will be the full net worth of my successful rental company, as well as my personal guarantee. We have agreed that your store needs a lot of new equipment, and the bank will not lend me money if someone else has a first lien on everything in the store."

Perception Is More Important Than Reality Most of the Time

The Kornickers seemed to feel comfortable with my words *full net worth of my successful rental company* and *personal guarantee,* and they agreed to these final terms. In reality, neither my company nor I had a positive net worth at the time. Perception is always more important than reality in these matters. It's only when things go badly that reality sticks its ugly head into the picture.

I drove back to Vermont with dreams of rental stores 3 and 4 dancing in my head. My empire was expanding quickly. Now, I needed to find a banker to finance the North Haven store.

I had already learned the importance of cultivating bankers in my real estate activities. Part of developing this important relationship is to educate the banker about your business. I got to work and wrote a 20-page report on the equipment rental industry. With trade industry statistics and charts, I demonstrated the following five facts about the industry:

1. Rental stores typically earned gross rental income each year that was equal to the cost of their equipment.
2. Rental stores could afford one-third of their income for debt repayment (I had proved this in the Rutland store).
3. The going price for rental stores was the previous year's gross sales.
4. In California, rental stores had $10 in annual sales for every person in the market area.
5. In New England, rental stores had only one-tenth of these results per person, suggesting that the industry on the East Coast was in its infancy and destined to boom.

With these facts attractively presented in my report, I headed back to Connecticut to find a banker. I visited the chamber of commerce first. "Where can I find a forward-looking aggressive banker?" I asked.

"We can't recommend one bank," they said. "All the banks are members of the Chamber."

The Most Valuable Information Lies between the Lines

From my experience, this is *always* the answer that chamber of commerce staff members give. The trick is to engage them in a conversation, and they will soon tell you with body language and tone of voice what their words are not telling you. I learned that in North Haven, the president of the chamber was a commercial banker. Since I was also a chamber president, we would have something in common. He was clearly my guy. I asked for an introduction.

After we had commiserated over the common hassles of being a chamber president (endless meetings and internal politicking), I showed him my report and asked for a $50,000 loan to be secured by $80,000 in equipment value. I explained that I was buying a store worth $60,000 (the last year's sales) and would buy $20,000 worth of new equipment. This would make $80,000 worth of value on which he would have a first security interest. It didn't seem relevant that I was only paying $30,000 for the $60,000 worth of equipment.

Doing Your Homework Always Pays Off

He granted me a $50,000 loan, telling me that no one had ever made such a well-presented and thorough loan application to him in all his years of banking. I had done my homework and won.

I used $10,000 of the bank loan to make the down payment to Leo Kornicker, $20,000 to buy new equipment, and I had $20,000 left over to use for starting a new store. I deposited this money in a savings account in Glens Falls, New York, while I hired a manager and got set up in Connecticut.

Two months later, I met with a banker in Glens Falls, told him that I had $20,000 in a savings account in his bank, and needed a $40,000 loan to start a rental store in his city. I recycled my equipment rental industry report and got the loan.

In each of the next two years, I bought an existing store, using a local bank loan for the down payment and the seller for the rest of the financing. The store in West Hartford, Connecticut, was double the size of any of my other stores, and specialized in party equipment. With our equipment, someone could have a wedding reception for 2,000 people. We had at least that many chairs, place settings of fine china, silverware settings, linen napkins, champagne (and four kinds of other) glasses, and hundreds of round tables, linen tablecloths, silver serving dishes, and so on. My plan was to make this equipment available for special-occasion rentals at my other stores as well.

My sixth store was the only rental store in Manchester, New Hampshire, a fast-growing city two hours east of Rutland.

I soon learned that it was a lot more fun buying these stores than it was running them (much like my real estate investments). At first, I had the only rental store in the area in every location, except for West Hartford. But then, competition started erupting everywhere. The rental store business was an easy-entry business. Banks would look at statistics, much like those that I had put down in my report, and happily loan 80 or 90 percent of the start-up costs for a new store. Since the equipment was being bought at wholesale and might be sold almost at cost in the worst of situations (a bankruptcy auction), banks were quite willing to set up almost anyone in the rental store business.

Several national equipment store franchises entered the picture. Dealer Supply set up a separate Taylor Rental Center company, had an IPO, and sold dozens of franchises (including one in Rutland). In a single year, A-Z Rental, a California company, set up one new franchise every 72 hours.

Beware of Stupid Competition

Much of these new entrepreneurs became what I call *stupid competition*. They did not place any value on their own time. If they could get anything—anything at all—for the rental of a piece of equipment, they would take it, as long as it covered the cost of depreciation. Our published price lists soon became wish lists. Our major customers (building contractors) soon learned that they could get on the telephone and call around to all the rental stores in town to negotiate lower and lower prices.

With prices eroding all over the place, and much of our expected business being shared by new competitors, it was becoming increasingly difficult to meet the loan payments on my six stores. I had learned how to generate real cash by buying a new store and negotiating favorable financing, but now I was questioning the long-term viability of the business itself. If I stopped buying new stores, where would I get the cash to cover my earlier purchases?

The past was catching up with me, and the negative cash flow was getting uncomfortable. Before I gave up, however, I decided to try out some creative marketing ideas to see if I could increase revenue. After all, my business degree was in marketing, not operations.

My efforts to think up marketing ideas led to writing a book and coming up with an idea for a new company, but that is a story for the next chapter.

Two years after assembling the six-store miniconglomerate of equipment rental stores, I decided to sell. It was becoming difficult to compete with all of the emerging competition, and there was not a match between my personal skills and interests and what it took to succeed in this business. (Mostly, it would have been best if I had been a good mechanic who could keep all the machines in running condition.)

It's Easier to Buy Something Than It Is to Sell It

When I was a young teenager, my grandmother, Louise Sanford, an entrepreneur in her own right, gave me sage words of advice: It's always easier to buy something than it is to sell it. Over the years, I experienced the truth in her words many times over—with cars, houses, and even businesses. (Some people would argue that this principle also applies to spouses, but I don't think I want to go there.)

It had actually been quite easy for me to buy six rental stores scattered across New England. Selling them became quite a different matter, especially since none of them were making a profit. How could I sell a money-losing business with new competition coming on the scene every month? The only thing that I had going for me was that our headquarters was located in Vermont. Maybe somebody would undertake the challenge in exchange for the opportunity to live in a place with a higher quality of life. I placed an advertisement in the *Newark* (New Jersey) *Star Ledger,* hoping that there might be someone in that area who was eager to get away from the crime and traffic jams.

About 10 people responded to my ad, and I invited them all to visit me on the same day in my new company's office in Natick, Massachusetts. Only two perspective buyers came, but I put them in separate rooms and got a little auction going between them. I ran back and forth between the rooms and encouraged them to increase their offers or risk losing out to the other guy. The "winner" agreed to pay me $50,000 in cash and assume all my loans for the four northern stores.

Not only did this fellow want to move to Vermont, but he was also seeking an employment opportunity for his wife and son. The entire family achieved their goal of moving to Vermont, but experienced a long struggle with the business.

Two years after buying the stores, the man from Newark came to Massachusetts and asked me to buy them back, saying he had been a real pigeon to have bought them. He wound up selling the stores one at a time over three years, all at a loss.

I merged the two Connecticut stores and sold them in a separate transaction. All of the banks and people who sold stores to me eventually got paid in full, including interest, although some had to wait longer than they expected to finally get their last check.

In retrospect, my rental stores provided me with a wonderful internship. I learned valuable lessons about running a small business with multiple locations. In the end, I realized that there was no fit between me and the rental store business. My experience there helped move me toward another business, however, which was considerably more appropriate to my personal skills and interests.

WHAT I LEARNED

- *Do your homework before you ask a banker for money.* An important part of getting money from banks is to educate your banker. He or she needs to know enough about your business to feel comfortable about loaning you money. If your banker doesn't understand the business, you don't have a chance of getting the cash.

- *Just because you can get 100 percent financing, or buy something with no money down, doesn't mean you* should *do it.* The business itself has to make sense, both now and in the foreseeable future.

- *Beware of easy-entry businesses.* If it's so easy to get into this business, people will. The Great American Dream is alive and thriving. New adherents are being born every day. Some people reach retirement age and look around for businesses to start. Easy-entry businesses will attract stupid competition, and very few will succeed. (The biggest reason that so many restaurants fail is that they're so easy to get into. All the equipment you need to start up is available for pennies on the dollar from earlier restaurant owners who have gone belly-up.)

■ *Make certain that there is a match between the entrepreneur's skills and interests and what it takes to be successful in a particular business.* If the business needs a good mechanic and you are a good marketer, don't get into that business. It is destined to fail.

■ *It's always easier to buy something than it is to sell it.* Keep this in mind when you are thinking about taking on a new acquisition. Do you *really* want it, both now and forever?

Chapter 6

Retail Toy Store:
A Christmas to Remember

How to Get a Bank to Open
Its Vaults for You

It all started innocently one early July evening while John Simon and I were sipping martinis. John was the personnel manager at the Rutland GE plant. Over the winter, we had experimented with making drier and drier martinis, until one day we dispensed with the vermouth altogether. I'd like to think that those dry martinis were largely responsible for what followed.

The idea, first proposed by John, was to rent the largest store we could get our hands on (starting in November), fill it up with toys that we got on consignment, close the store down the day after Christmas, and return all the unsold toys to their owners. "I'll drink to that," I said, raising my glass. It sounded to me like a perfect business with virtually no downside. Our only risk would be the rent. We figured our wives could be unpaid clerks, even though they were both at home with our young children. ("Bring the kids to the store," we told them, "they'll have hundreds of toys to play with.")

FIGURE OUT WHAT THE HOMEWORK ASSIGNMENT IS BEFORE YOU DO IT

Before going ahead with any new business, especially one that is hatched up while drinking gin, you must do your homework. I knew that. In this case, I figured that doing my homework would be a simple matter. How complicated could a simple retail toy store be? All I would have to do would be to visit a few toy stores in the area and get an idea of what the competition would be like. While I couldn't find any toy stores in Rutland in 1968, there were three large department stores—Sears, Ames, and Grants (now defunct, Grants resembled today's Kmart).

In mid-July, I visited our major would-be competitors and was amazed to discover that it was hard to even find the toy department. They had almost no selection of toys. John was right—this town really needed a good toy store. We could be the only game in town!

Half of the job of doing your homework consists of knowing what to study. In my case, checking out the competition was a good idea. Checking it out in July instead of December, however, was a critical mistake. My oldest son was barely a year old, so I had never experienced visiting the toy section of large department stores at Christmas.

My wife and her family were fiscally conservative and risk-adverse. They liked the security of cash, didn't like debt very much, and waited to buy cars (or even summer homes) until they had cash to pay. In their eyes, about the best thing that I had done in my first five years of marriage was to have salted away $500 in a savings account. And now, I was planning to squander it all on a new business!

We found an empty building that exceeded all of our expectations. Three floors on the corner of Merchants Row and West Street (known as "the busiest corner in the State of Vermont"). The former tenant, JCPenney, had recently moved out and left many shelves and display fixtures behind. The only problem was that the building rented for $3,000 a month, and John and I had only $1,000 between us.

In a small town like Rutland, you know just about everyone, or even better, you know something *about* almost everyone. We knew that the owner of the building liked his liquor, sometimes to excess. We set up a meeting with him at his house and introduced him to our version of the dry martini.

At first, he was adamant about getting $3,000 a month, particularly for a short-term rental. We pointed out that it was too late to get a new major tenant before the Christmas season. Surely, the building would look a lot more attractive with a thriving toy store in it than if it were vacant. If we were really successful, we might rent it out at full price on a long-term rental. And finally, we would keep the place heated and prevent the pipes from freezing during some of the coldest winter months. In the end, the martinis, his fear of additional utility costs, and his urgent need for cash resulted in our renting the building for October, November, and December for the grand total of $1,000.

When we set out to secure our inventory, we learned that perhaps we hadn't done quite enough market research. It seems someone else had already come up with the idea of getting toys on consignment for the Christmas selling season. Toy wholesalers would not even grant 30-day terms. In fact, they wouldn't deliver toys on a cash-on-delivery (COD) basis—their only terms were cash in advance. We had just blown our entire stash for the rent. Sometimes, doing your homework involves more than just checking out the competition.

DON'T BORROW MONEY FROM BANKS . . .

John and I retired to my house and plotted our strategy. We needed some money, fast. My considerable borrowing experience had taught me one thing about banks: You don't borrow money from banks. This may seem like a pretty bizarre statement. After all, as Willie Sutton said when asked why he robbed banks, "That is where the money is." Banks, however, are institutions, and they have rules—extremely conservative rules—about how money should be loaned out.

. . . BORROW MONEY FROM BANKERS

Bankers are individuals with all sorts of feelings and prejudices. They often make decisions that are based on emotions rather than rational analysis. If they like you or your business idea, they might be willing to bend the bank's rules a little to accommodate you. The trick, therefore, is to borrow from bankers, not banks. One bank officer might reject a loan application outright, whereas another lending officer might be enthusiastic about it. In our case, John and I had to decide who, among the 10 or so commercial lending officers in our area, might be interested in financing a toy store.

We listed the names of each banker and wrote down what we knew about them. One man, Arlan Mahoney, stood out. Arlan had eight children. We used to joke that Arlan's wife was part Irish and part Xerox. Who better than Arlan Mahoney to lend us money to start a toy store?

The next morning, we sat in front of Arlan's desk and told him about our idea. He confessed that he and his wife had talked about starting a toy store themselves. "Except at Christmas, you can't even find a toy in this town," he said, "Every time we go out to buy a birthday present for one of the kids, we can't find anything." John and I glanced at one another, tacitly agreeing not to mention our intention to close the store the day after Christmas.

I have long believed that many bankers are really frustrated entrepreneurs in disguise. By backing entrepreneurs like myself, they can vicariously be in business for themselves. Arlan didn't dare take the chance of opening a store on his own (who could blame him with eight dependents?), but he could be a silent partner in our store.

There was a potential problem, however. One of the silly rules at Arlan's bank was that we should have some sort of collateral for a loan. I remember my answer to Arlan's request for collateral. "You know me better than that, Arlan, I have a lot more ideas than I do collateral, and you said yourself that this is a good idea." In the end, he agreed to give us a $7,000 unsecured personal loan *if our wives would co-sign the note.*

Now, I was in a real panic mode. Given my wife's aversion to debt, I knew it wasn't going to be easy. Fortunately, I knew a little about the toy business, and I thought I had some arguments to justify the loan. Dick Fish, the sales rep from New England's largest toy wholesaler, had told us about a brand new toy this year called Marvel the Mustang. It was a large plastic hobbyhorse on wheels. As the rider bounced up and down, the horse would move forward. Nothing like this toy had ever been offered before. "Trust me, you can't go wrong with this toy," he said prophetically.

Marvel the Mustang would be supported by millions of dollars of national advertising, and every kid would want one for Christmas. In early market tests, the demand had been so great that Dick feared that the manufacturer had not made nearly enough to satisfy the Christmas demand.

NEVER TRUST A SALESPERSON WHO SAYS, "TRUST ME"

The suggested retail price for Marvel the Mustang was $18.00, and our cost was $9.90. I figured that we would undercut this retail price by plenty and sell our entire inventory in a few days at our discounted price of $16.88. We were planning to allocate $4,000 of our $7,000 loan to buy 400 Marvels, and as soon as we sold them ("a near certainty given our discounted price," I told my wife), we would have enough to repay the loan in full. Our profit on this toy alone would be $2,800, a small fortune, even though I had to split it with John.

After much discussion with our wives and promises of washing thousands of dishes, our wives co-signed the note. We were finally and officially in the toy business!

What Dick did not tell us was that the suggested retail price for a popular toy at Christmas was a joke. Essentially, not a single retail store would consider trying to collect the suggested retail price. The job of a salesperson is to sell, not necessarily to tell all of the truth. Mr. Fish had done his job well.

Not only was Marvel the Mustang the soon-to-be hottest toy in history and what we expected to be our financial salvation, its large size would serve us in another way. It was packed in a 3-by-4-foot box and took up lots of room. We stacked them all the way across our ample plate-glass windows. The store was so large and our resources so low that we needed some bulk to make the place look lived in. Still, even with 400 Marvel boxes, the store seemed barren.

We sought out Arlan and asked him to come visit our store, now named Toys 'N Games but not yet open for business. I will never forget Arlan's statement as we walked through the front door. "Our store looks a little empty doesn't it?" *Our* store, he said. He was, indeed, a real partner!

"How much more money do you need?" he asked. Although we had planned to plead for $5,000 more, his "our store" remark gave me great confidence, and I blurted out "$10,000" before John could say anything.

SAVE YOURSELF SOME ANGUISH AND DON'T BOTHER READING THE SMALL PRINT

"Let's go back to the bank and take a look at the note you signed," he said. "Maybe we can advance you that much without getting your wives' signatures again."

Sure enough, the note that our wives had co-signed included some fine print that said that their signature guarantees applied to the $7,000 original loan "or to any additional sums advanced to the primary borrowers [John and myself] related to the same business enterprise."

So John and I got an additional $10,000, and we didn't even have to tell our wives. It didn't seem fair, even at the time. However, most documents that you sign at the bank really aren't fair—they are written by the bank's attorneys with only their interest in mind.

My advice is to forget about reading the small print, but totally know in your heart that you will most certainly pay any loan back—with interest and attorney fees. It's a certainty like death and taxes (only bankruptcy may save you). So don't sign the document unless you fully expect to pay everything back as promised.

GOING-OUT-OF-BUSINESS SALES AND AUCTIONS ARE GOOD INDICATIONS OF BUSINESS RISK

Have you ever thought about starting a restaurant? It seems like thousands of people have thought about it and actually done it. And based on the number of restaurant equipment auctions, thousands of people have failed. I always keep my eyes posted on going-out-of-business auctions to identify businesses to stay away from.

I had never seen a going-out-of-business auction for a toy store. I did find a company in Boston, though, whose only business was buying the inventory of toy stores that had gone bankrupt or closed down after Christmas the year before. Apparently, there were many such stores, a fact that left us a little uneasy about our upcoming new business. Finding this store in Boston *before* we started Toys 'N Games would have been an important part of doing our homework.

John and I rented a U-Haul truck, got fifty $100 bills from the bank, and headed for Boston. We made some truly great purchases at the closeout wholesale toy store. The prices were so low that we multiplied our cost by five to set our retail price. Even with that markup, we could sell last year's Hot Wheels model cars for 88 cents, while the retail price was 99 cents. We also bought a 12-foot Christmas stocking full of wrapped presents to give away to some lucky person who visited our store.

Our grand opening took place on the Wednesday before Thanksgiving. Given our limited budget, we spent money on only two promotions. The first was the rental of a full-length bear outfit. Because I had the MBA, we thought it was appropriate that I should be the bear outside the store. For three days, I waved to passersby and lured dozens of shoppers to Toys 'N Games.

DON'T FEATURE PRICE IN YOUR ADVERTISEMENT IF YOU HAVE THE HIGHEST PRICE IN TOWN

The second promotional effort was the only advertisement we ever placed. It was a 3-by-4-inch newspaper ad in the *Rutland Herald.* There was a small picture of Marvel the Mustang at our superdiscounted price of $16.88, and an invitation to come in and register for the 12-foot-high Christmas stocking.

I eagerly ran to get that morning's paper. I couldn't wait to see how great the impact of our ad might be. I was shocked at what I found. In the same issue of the *Rutland Herald,* Grants Department

Store ran a two-page centerfold advertisement with a 16-by-12-inch picture of Marvel the Mustang and their price—$9.97. Welcome to the toy business, John and Terry.

My immediate reaction was utter panic—not that we wouldn't be able to sell a single Marvel the Mustang, but that my wife would see Grants' ad. Fortunately, the center page was easy to remove and quickly destroy.

THERE IS NO PROFIT IN A LOSS LEADER— THAT'S WHY ITS FIRST NAME IS LOSS

John and I met for lunch to discuss our now-serious situation. In an effort to ease John's fears (and my own as well), I recalled a couple of concepts from Marketing 101. The first was *loss leader,* a strategy to get shoppers into your store in hopes that they will buy lots of other things in addition to the item that you are practically giving away. Hopefully, offering Marvel for only $9.97 was a tactic that Grants would only keep in effect for a few days.

The second term was *bait and switch.* This tactic involved luring people into your store with a great offer, but having little or no inventory (or a broken sample), and then convincing the customer that another (higher-priced) product was even better. My greatest hope was that Grants was conducting a bait-and-switch campaign.

We left lunch and headed over to Grants, leaving our sandwiches unfinished. In fact, our stomachs felt sort of nauseously sick every day from Thanksgiving until Christmas that year.

When we walked through Grants' front door, I got a double shock. First, fully half of this large department store had somehow been transformed into a football field–sized toy store. I remembered back to my July visit when I couldn't even find the toy department.

Second, in the middle of this gigantic collection of toys, there was a mountain of Marvel the Mustangs reaching to the top of their 14-foot ceiling. You would need a ladder to reach the top. My bait-and-switch hope was rudely dashed to bits.

"Not to worry," I reassured John, "they'll only keep this price for a few days." My stomach rumbled ominously.

For the next two weeks, I raced to the mailbox to get the newspaper and check out the Grants ad. On the days when Marvel was advertised at $9.97, I cringed. It was becoming a little more difficult to tear out the ad because it usually wasn't a full page any longer. The price, however, was still $9.97.

On the days when there was no ad, I ran down to Grants to see if they had raised the price. They never did. It was on one of these visits that I approached the manager to see if I could learn anything about his selling strategy. I asked him why the piles of toys were so high that people couldn't reach the top. He explained that it was Grants' policy to present an image of great bulk. "We have no back room," he said, "everything we have for sale is right out there for everyone to see."

I asked him what happens when someone puts a toy on layaway. "If you have no back room, where do you put the item someone has laid away?" I asked.

He replied, "We leave it right out there on the floor. But we have computer reports that ensure we don't sell more layaways than we have in stock."

Two weeks before Christmas, and our situation was becoming desperate. Even though many of our smaller toys were selling, we still had 400 unsold Marvels. We had almost $3,000 in cash, but still owed $17,000 to the bank. At our current rate of sales, we wouldn't be able to pay off half of the loan.

GO FOR IT! WHEN YOUR STRATEGY ISN'T WORKING, CHANGE SOMETHING

John and I brainstormed far into the night and couldn't seem to come up with a single good idea until very late when our dry martinis had really taken effect.

I don't know where it came from, but it just popped out of my mouth. "Let's corner the market," I said. "We thought Marvel was a great buy at $9.90 from our wholesaler. Now we can buy it for only 7 cents more from our major competitor, and pretty soon, we'll have the only Marvels in town. Then we can get our $16.88, and maybe even more.

I had heard of people trying to corner the market for potatoes—and silver, and even wheat. It seemed to me that every story I had ever read about cornering the market had ended in disaster. But in every case, you couldn't help but admire the daring entrepreneurs who attempted to build their own monopoly, even if they crashed.

Here was my chance to be a swashbuckling financial baron who cornered the market for Marvel the Mustang in Rutland, Vermont, in 1968. Wow!

It all sounded so logical that night. The next day, I was too hung-over to do anything else but carry out the clandestine plan plotted the previous evening. I drove a U-Haul truck to Grants with two employees from my rental store and a toy store clerk. I handed out $20 bills to everyone and told them to head for the Marvel the Mustang pile.

Fortunately, each box had a plastic handle on the top, but the boxes were so large that we could only carry two at a time. Each of us would go to a different checkout line to avoid suspicion. Once we made our purchases, we would deposit the boxes in the U-Haul and return for another load.

Over the next week, Grants' pile slowly lowered, and our pile increased enormously. It was the longest week of my entire life. My biggest concern was the nagging thought that I had a $17,000 unsecured loan outstanding that my wife did not know about, coupled with the knowledge that it was becoming more and more evident that we would be totally unable to pay it back.

Another concern was Arlan Mahoney, who understandably was looking for some money. His bank was diagonally across the street from our store, and he could see customers walking out of our store with bags of toys in their arms. Yet, we had not repaid one penny of our loan.

For the two weeks preceding Christmas, I felt like a hunted man. I mentally accused Arlan of stalking me. I never picked up a telephone, no matter how long it rang. If I were in the toy store, I stayed near the back, behind one of the large toy soldiers that was tacked to a column.

Our checkout lady had one important job in addition to ringing up the sales—to keep a lookout for Arlan Mahoney. If he started coming across the street, she would turn the store sound system way up high, a sign for me to duck out the back door and make a hasty retreat. For two full weeks, I successfully avoided personal contact with a man who worked about 200 feet away from me and was trying very hard to reach me. (In 1968, mercifully, no one owned an answering machine.)

Eight days before Christmas, we still had not sold one Marvel the Mustang. We now owned almost 800 of them. Grants only had about 20 left, and we had bought every one of Ames Department Store's supply (another competitor offering Marvel for $9.97).

BEWARE THE SALESPERSON BRINGING GOOD TIDINGS (FOR HER- OR HIMSELF)

Dick Fish, the wholesaler rep, came into our store, rubbing his hands in glee. "How are things going?" he asked.

"Not bad," I answered, trying to disguise my absolute panic.

"How's Marvel the Mustang selling?" he asked.

"Not well," I answered.

"I can't believe it," he responded. "They're selling like crazy down at Grants." Somehow this statement wasn't much of a surprise to me.

Then he hit us with the bombshell. "I've just received the largest order of my entire life. Grants Department Store has just ordered a boxcar of Marvel the Mustangs. We'll get it to them in three days."

"A boxcar?" I asked incredulously. "Like in a train boxcar?" How big is that?"

"Real big," Fish said, grinning from gill to gill.

LUCK IS MORE IMPORTANT THAN SKILL WHEN SOLVING MOST BUSINESS PROBLEMS

That night was the longest night in the longest week of my life. Our only alternative was to sweat it out and hope the boxcar didn't make it before Christmas. Patience is not a virtue enjoyed by most entrepreneurs. I was no exception.

In 1968, Christmas fell on a Monday, and Vermont had Blue Laws, which prohibited retail sales on Sunday. We had decided to stay open anyway, pay the $200 fine, and try to sell off any inventory we had left. Being the only toy store open on Christmas Eve might just save our skins, we hoped. It's amazing how creative your imagination gets when you are in a situation like ours. Now, I understood the proverb "A drowning man clutches at straws."

On the Wednesday before Christmas, with less than four legal shopping days before Christmas, we sold our first Marvel the Mustang! Hurray! Sensing that something important had happened, I hustled the two blocks down to Grants and entered the store. To my everlasting delight, the pile was gone.

Even more significant, I found two young mothers in heated discussion with the store manager. The women had put Marvel the Mustang on layaway and wanted it now. They weren't buying the manager's promise that a boxcar was on the way. These ladies were angry—desperate may have been more accurate. They were soon at Toys 'N Games, bless their hearts.

When disappointed layaway customers or last-minute shoppers came to our store, the dialogue went something like this.

"$16.88 for a Marvel the Mustang? Why so much? They only charge $9.97 at Grants."

"I didn't think Grants had any left."

"They don't."

"Well, if we didn't have any left, we would charge $9.97, too."

Invariably, they would grumble and buy Marvel the Mustang at our price; often walking out with a box that had "Grants Department Store" stamped on the end.

By Thursday, three days before Christmas Eve, the trickle of Marvel buyers had turned into a torrent. Apparently, hundreds of families had put it on layaway at Grants, not because they were short of money, but because they did not want to try to hide a toy this large for weeks before Christmas. Many people who never normally made layaway purchases had made an exception this year with Marvel the Mustang.

IF YOU SCREW UP NEARLY EVERY BUSINESS DECISION YOU MAKE, PRAY FOR A MIRACLE

Someone up there surely was watching out for us. Grants' computer model missed the layaway phenomenon, and the boxcar did not arrive until the day after Christmas. By Friday, we had taken in enough money to pay Arlan his $17,000 in full. Any money we took in on Saturday would be pure profit. We would not have to stay open on Sunday.

On the following Wednesday, we donated our remaining inventory, worth about $400, to an orphanage. And we closed the store.

I have two fond memories of Toys 'N Games to this day. The first was splitting several thousand dollars of undeserved profits with John and then filling a large Christmas stocking with $20 bills for my wife. She deserved it more than I did. For someone who had bravely (and usually silently) endured the vagaries of my up-and-down entrepreneurial life, it was the first real cash she had ever realized for herself.

The second fond memory was giving away the 12-foot stocking full of presents. The first person whose name we selected was a well-to-do single woman with no children. We quickly put her name back in the bowl. We didn't know the second selection, but the address was in the best part of town, and we put that one back, too. The third choice was a real winner—a single mother from the poorer section of town with a 10-year old boy and an 8-year old girl. I still remember their happy faces as all three carried the stocking from the store.

PETER LYNCH IS RIGHT—USE YOUR OWN EXPERIENCE TO MAKE A KILLING IN THE STOCK MARKET

In January, after our December closing, I was visited by a salesperson from the Mattel toy company. They had a new program called "Toys on Consignment." You (the toy store owner) paid Mattel $2,000 up front and received a selection of toys for that year. You didn't even know what toys you were going to get. The toys would come in July, and you had to agree to display them until Christmas. If they weren't sold by then, you got your money back.

He explained Mattel's reasoning behind the new program. The Christmas selling season was so short that manufacturers often got caught off guard and couldn't make enough of the hot toy to satisfy the seasonal demand. (My experience sure corroborated this.) By getting all the new toys on store shelves in July, manufacturers could get an early reading on which toys they should make lots of for the Christmas season.

I told the salesperson that my toy store days were over, but I loved this "Toys on Consignment" idea. I would use my share of the profits to buy shares of Mattel stock. In the next couple of years, the stock soared, and I sold it for a 300 percent gain, more than tripling my ill-gotten toy store gains. Two years after that, in 1973, the oil crunch caused plastic prices to skyrocket, and Mattel stock fell to almost nothing (eventually being delisted, I believe.) Once again, it was better to be lucky than smart.

In retrospect, Toys 'N Games was an extremely rare business event—both a financial success and a rich learning experience. I learned how important it is to do your homework. The retail toy business was different than anything we had encountered in our short business lives, and we should have either worked for or interviewed several toy store owners (in far-away states) before jumping in.

I also learned how important it is to go for it. Taking the big chance of cornering the market was our salvation. It was an ostensibly foolhardy decision (I would never do it again), but it saved my business life at the time.

WHAT I LEARNED

■ *Sometimes you can do just about everything wrong and still come out a winner.* It is far better to be lucky than it is to be smart. The only way to be lucky is to give it a try—you can't win the game of business unless you get in the game. Go for it!

■ *The most important part of doing your homework is understanding the assignment.* Market research is essential, but be sure to collect relevant information. Don't check out what your retail competition is doing in July when most of their sales come at Christmas time.

■ *Don't borrow money from banks.* Instead, borrow money from bankers. It is important to establish personal relationships with commercial lending officers at several banks—before you need money. Teach them about your business so they will feel comfortable lending money to you when you eventually need it.

■ *In some industries, suggested retail prices are meaningless.* For example, popular toys are often sold as loss leaders during the Christmas selling season.

Chapter 7

Self-Publishing: My First Book

How to Sell Something before It Even Exists

Since I had so many businesses in the late 1960s (ski lodge, toy store, equipment rental stores, and real estate agency), I thought it would be a good idea to join the Rutland Region Chamber of Commerce. In my first year as a member, the annual membership drive offered a first prize of a set of luggage for the person who signed up the most new Chamber members. I wanted both the luggage and the distinction of being the top seller, so I hit the pavement in earnest. Of course, I won (otherwise, I wouldn't be telling this story).

The next year, the membership chairman named me as team captain. In this capacity, I directed the efforts of six people, each of whom contacted about six members to renew their membership, and about three non-Chamber members as well. As team captain, I was not eligible for the individual prize that was awarded for superior performance.

PROMOTE YOUR BEST SALESPERSON, AND SALES DECREASE

My entire team sold fewer new memberships than I had personally sold the prior year. This story is typical of what happens in many businesses—the top salesperson is promoted to sales manager, and sales go down. The skills of a salesperson usually don't transition easily into success as a sales manager. It's a similar phenomenon with good entrepreneurs failing as managers.

IF SALESPEOPLE CAN'T MANAGE, MAYBE THEY CAN WRITE A BOOK ABOUT SELLING

In early 1969, I owned six equipment rental stores scattered throughout four states—Vermont, New York, New Hampshire, and Connecticut. I spent a great deal of time driving to these stores and making unannounced visits. My goal was to keep close tabs on employee honesty. The equipment rental business is conducted mostly in cash, and there is no inventory to trace. In many respects, it is more dangerous than owning a bar.

I had one inviolate rule for my managers: Every piece of equipment owned by the store either had to be physically in the store or listed on a numbered rental contract. A single violation of this rule meant instant termination of the store manager.

TRUST YOUR INTUITION

I had to fire only one manager, and I communicated precisely how it happened to my other managers. I had made a surprise visit one Friday to my Glens Falls store and did a quick inventory review. Everything was in order, but I had a funny feeling about my Glens Falls manager. (Intuition is not an attribute possessed only by women; it is usually more powerful and dependable than conscious reasoning.)

Saturday was the busiest day in the rental business. I correctly figured the manager would never expect me to return for another visit the very next day, especially because I had told him I was spending the weekend camping with my family.

When I returned Saturday afternoon, three large pieces of equipment were gone from the store and no contract had been made out. Clearly, the manager was running his own rental business on the side, using my equipment as his inventory. I told him to leave the store immediately and later learned that all the cash from the register had left at the same time.

I never got to go camping. Instead, I had to commute to Glens Falls and manage the store until I hired a replacement manager.

USE DRIVING TIME FOR CREATIVE THINKING (FIRST, TURN OFF THE CAR RADIO)

All this driving between stores gave me a great opportunity to think creatively without telephone interruptions (this was before cell phones, of course). Mostly, I thought about how I could increase business at my stores.

One day, I decided that there must be a book about how to advertise and market an equipment rental store and that I should find it. I examined *Books in Print* thoroughly and found many publications about how to market small retail stores, but nothing about how to increase the business of an equipment rental store.

My first thought was that if I were seeking this kind of book, other equipment rental store owners must want one also. So, why not write it myself? The idea of *Advertising and Promotion Ideas for the General Rental Store* by Terry F. Allen was born.

THE BEST OF ALL BUSINESS SCENARIOS—SELL THE PRODUCT BEFORE IT EXISTS!

First, I had to test the market. Maybe I was unique in wanting such a book. I purchased a list of 1,000 equipment rental dealers (a list compiled from the Yellow Pages). Then, I wrote up the table of contents for my proposed book and sent a letter and order form to the

1,000 prospects, offering them a prepublication discount if they sent money within 30 days. I chuckled a little about this word *prepublication,* since not one word outside of the table of contents had yet been written.

The market test was primarily designed to learn if storeowners would actually buy the book. I also wanted to know how much they would pay. One-third of the order forms asked for $7.50, one-third asked for $9.95, and one-third asked for $12.95.

The response to my mailing was amazing! Over 100 people sent in money and included over $1,000 in cash. In 1969, a first-class stamp was 6 cents, and $1,000 was more than I had earned in one month any time in my life at my highest-paying job.

So, I knew I had a winner! There were 17,000 equipment rental dealers in the United States, so I could expect at least $17,000 when I sent the same ad to the entire list. (The $9.95 price point ended up being the most profitable price to use in the full rollout.)

My local printer said that he could print 2,000 copies of a 115-page perfect-bound book (like a telephone book), 8½-by-11-inch pages for $2,000. I figured that my mailing costs would be $2,000, shipping $1,000, and I would make a handsome profit of $12,000 for writing the book.

BOLD PROMISES CREATE SALES

I believe my high response rate was due largely to the title of Chapter 6 in the table of contents that I sent to the 1,000 rental store owners. It is my favorite chapter title, and I have never seen it used by anyone else. Chapter 6 was entitled "Ten Ideas Each Worth Ten Times the Price of This Book." Isn't that a beautiful title? What a challenge for the author, and an intriguing mystery for the prospect. I could see the prospect saying to himself, "If even one of these ideas is good, the book will be worth it."

When I first created the table of contents, I did not have a single idea that I thought was worthy of being included in this chapter. But I had a great deal of confidence in my imagination. Ironically, several years later, one of the ideas eventually thought up for this chapter ended up becoming my most profitable venture ever (and also my biggest failure when it went bankrupt). But more on that later.

I figured I should hurry up and write the book, as I wasn't sure how long people would wait for a book that they ordered prepublication. I drove to the Harvard Business School library and took out every book they had on advertising and promotion ideas for small businesses. Next, I drove to Southport, Connecticut, home of the *Rental Equipment Register* (the industry's major trade publication), and borrowed every issue they had published for the last 10 years.

Then, my family and I headed for a small town near North Haven and rented an oceanside cottage for the month of May (cheap off-season rates), using my $1,000 windfall from the test to pay the rent and support us for the month. I selected this spot because I had just purchased a rental store in North Haven, and I could spend some time training my new manager.

I completed the book in less than a month. In fact, everything about the book was a success. All 2,000 books were sold with a single mailing. Every book! I do not have a single copy left.

Knowing what I do now about direct marketing, I would have made many more mailings to this same list, earning the same, or perhaps even more, with each mailing. At the time, however, I was totally satisfied with the profits from that single mailing.

DOING IT YOURSELF IS CONSIDERABLY MORE PROFITABLE THAN DOING IT FOR SOMEONE ELSE

I calculated that I had earned more money from this single self-published book than my father had made in royalties from four books that he had written about baseball coaching techniques. His books were 400-page hardcover editions, really wonderful and significant books published by Prentice-Hall. My book (115 pages hand-typed by me) was of lower quality in every respect, yet ended up being more profitable. This clearly demonstrates the difference between being in business for yourself and working for someone else.

ENTREPRENEURS DO NOT LIKE TO TAKE RISKS

A short digression—about risk. You might say that my book example was not an apples-to-apples comparison. In my choice to self-publish, I incurred a risk that I would have avoided if a legitimate publisher had put out the book. But how big was the risk? Only the cost of mailing out the 1,000 test offers—about the cost of an evening on the town. Once I had the results from the test, virtually all of the risk had disappeared.

People who work for someone else often believe that entrepreneurs are great risk takers. Entrepreneurs believe just the opposite. Since entrepreneurs believe that they can personally influence the outcome, in their minds, the risk is minimal. In my book-publishing venture, given the results of my test mailing, I was realistically taking no risk whatsoever.

Studies have shown that entrepreneurs are not likely to visit gambling casinos. They prefer to avoid risks where they have no influence over the outcome. That is gambling, not intelligent risk taking. In the mind of the entrepreneur, it is a critical distinction that is usually lost in the minds of outsiders looking at the life of an entrepreneur.

REINVEST PROFITS QUICKLY
FOR ADDITIONAL RETURNS

I earned more than $10,000 in a single month with my little book, enough for a down payment on two profitable apartment houses. Each month (in my mind) I counted the cash profits from these buildings as royalties on my book, even though no more copies of the book were available for sale.

LEARNING EXPERIENCES ARE MOST VALUABLE
WHEN YOU REMEMBER THEM

A sequel to my first book experience: I promptly forgot everything that I had just learned. Buoyed by my great success, I hired a recent college graduate (editor of his college newspaper) to write the same book for two other industries—hardware stores and florists. There were thousands more of these kinds of stores than there were rental stores. Surely, these books would be a great success, even if the mailing achieved a much lower response rate.

Only this time, I did not test the market. But how could I go wrong? All my student editor had to do was go through my book and substitute *hardware store* or *florist* every time he saw *equipment rental store.* We used the exact same table of contents for our advertisement, and the exact same wording for the marketing literature.

We sent out 10,000 hardware store advertisements and 5,000 florist advertisements, and we sold virtually nothing! It seems that a similar book had recently been offered in both industries (written by known industry experts), and these books were priced at $5.00 compared with my $9.95.

I lost half the money I made on my first book project and learned a valuable lesson. Every market is different, and each one must be tested before you invest your money.

WHAT I LEARNED

- *The best new business ideas come about when you encounter a problem that doesn't have a known solution.* I needed a book that didn't exist, so I wrote it myself. All I needed for success was for enough other equipment rental dealers to have the same need.

- *Trust your intuition.* The absolute best business decisions that I have made throughout my life were those that "felt right." Many times, there didn't seem to be a rational excuse for making the decision, but I knew in my gut that it was the right thing to do.

- *Do market research with an order form.* Don't ask people if they like your idea, but if they'll buy it.

- *Don't be limited by the belief that something must exist before you can take orders for it.* You don't even need a prototype or a photograph. All you need is a hand-sketched drawing or verbal description of what it will be. You might even be lucky enough to get enough capital from advance orders to pay for creating the eventual real product.

■ *Every market and market segment is different.* If you encounter success in one market, don't assume that another market will be similar—the new market must first be tested (with an order form), too.

■ *You can make multiple mailings (same advertising piece, same list), and expect similar response rates.* Sometimes, the fifth mailing of the same piece to the same list yields greater response than the first mailing. (I really didn't learn this until much later, but wished I had.)

Chapter 8

Coupon Distribution Service: "Welcome Wagon by Mail"

How to Raise Money from Angel Investors

How to Have Your Own IPO without an Underwriter

How to Finance Your Business by Selling Franchises

While writing my book on marketing ideas for equipment rental stores, I had to brainstorm "Ten Ideas Each Worth Ten Times the Price of This Book," as I had promised in my sales literature. One of these 10 ideas was to contact new homeowners shortly after they purchased their new home. That is the time when they might need rental equipment—to sand their floors, remove someone else's idea of clever wallpaper, or perform any of the other home improvement projects that only a new homeowner has the energy to carry out. Once the family has lived in the house for a while, the peeling paint becomes part of the landscape and they don't even notice it.

How could I contact new homeowners? The only established program I could find was Welcome Wagon. For $1.50 per contact, the local Welcome Wagon representative would make a personal call on every new family that she could find and deliver a gift or coupon from you, the merchant.

There were several shortcomings to the Welcome Wagon program for me, however:

- Over half of the families contacted were apartment dwellers who surely would not be sanding their floors.
- The welcoming visit usually occurred 3 to 6 months after the family moved in, which was way too late for my purposes.
- The cost of $1.50 per contact seemed like a lot of money (it now costs $3.50 per contact, I believe).

EVERY PROBLEM IS AN OPPORTUNITY IN DISGUISE

I decided to do the job myself. I went to the city clerk's office and wrote down the name and address on every real estate deed recorded for the week. It was unfortunate for me that I lived in Vermont because in every state except ours, Connecticut, and Rhode Island, real estate transactions are recorded at the county level instead of at the city or town level. In 47 other states, I could have found all the new homeowners for the entire county with a visit to a single location. In Vermont, at least at first, I had to drive around to every town in the county to gather these names.

I mailed a gift certificate worth $10 toward the rental of any piece of equipment in my store. In addition, I printed a list of over 250 different items available for rental and offered a $25 free rental if the new homeowner could find the item that was listed twice. Earning the extra rental value involved a close reading of the entire list and often caused prospects to rent items that they may never have thought about before.

The program was a great success. Almost half of the people to whom I sent coupons came in and rented something. When things were slow, we telephoned each new homeowner and personally invited them to visit us. This effort clearly raised our response rate. The average rental was almost double the coupon amount, so we made a profit on every customer who visited our store. I had estimated that the lifetime value of a rental customer was about $300, and it was costing me less than $1 to get a new homeowner into our store.

IF IT WORKS FOR YOU, IT MIGHT WORK FOR OTHERS

My next thought was to offer other merchants the chance to participate in this successful marketing program. If it worked for me, why wouldn't it work for others? As long as the other merchants didn't compete with me, what could I lose by including their coupons in my mailing?

The first nine merchants I visited agreed to participate at 10 cents per mailing. I decided that something was wrong. If the program was that easy to sell, I probably wasn't charging enough. In fact, the only hesitation I noticed on the merchants' part was the price—how could I offer this service for only 10 cents when the Welcome Wagon charged 15 times as much? In addition, I was telling them that my program was even better than Welcome Wagon's because we got to the new families faster, and we contacted only higher-income homeowners who had made a large financial investment in the community. These prospects could be expected to become good, long-term customers, much better than apartment dwellers.

I raised the price to 20 cents per mailing, and to my great surprise, the next 10 merchants I contacted agreed to come on board at the new price. Now, I was getting $2.70 for every package of coupons I was mailing out, and the postage had only increased to 12 cents per mailing.

Still, 10 out of 10 sales suggested that I was charging too little. I started quoting 30 cents per mailing, and finally somebody said no.

I was relieved. I eventually settled on 25 cents per mailing as being the ideal price, and sold another 10 merchants at that price.

DON'T TEST NEW BUSINESS IDEAS ON YOUR FRIENDS

I told my friends about my marketing program, which was not only bringing me lots of equipment rental customers but actually making a nice profit as well. They were universally unimpressed (as most people are by most new ideas). They said that I was a supersalesman selling to people whom I knew, and the program could probably not be duplicated by someone else in some other city.

Of course, to me, that was like waving a red flag at a raging bull. I had to prove that the idea was exportable and not dependent on my selling skills. I chose Glens Falls, New York, as the test city. I had a rental store there, and it was in a state that recorded deeds at the county level. I discovered that the local credit bureau published a weekly list of recorded deeds, mortgages, and liens for only $50 a year. About 400 deeds a year were recorded, so my cost of new homeowner names was only about 12 cents each.

I figured that I had better give my program a name. After much brainstorming, I was delighted with the name I invented: *HO*me-owners *W*elcome *D*a*Y* (or HOWDY) coupons. I drew up a silly little logo that displayed the name in the shape of smiling lips. Really hokey!

I hired a meat salesman to sell HOWDY coupons in Glens Falls. On Fridays, he did not make any sales calls for the meat business because his customers (mostly restaurants) had already placed their orders for Saturday delivery. I agreed to pay him 25 percent of all cash that we collected from all the sales he made.

In about six weeks, he had signed up 36 merchants at the rate of 25 cents per new homeowner mailing. Except for restaurants, he only accepted one merchant for every business category (e.g., hardware store, insurance agent, etc.).

I did the math:

Revenue per mailing (25¢ × 36 merchants)	$9.00
Sales commission (25%)	$2.25
Cost of new homeowner name	.12
Cost of printing (1¢ per coupon × 36)	.36
Assembly and mailing labor	.50
Postage and envelope	.20
Total cost per mailing	$3.43
Profit per mailing	$5.57

IT DOESN'T HURT TO HAVE BIG DREAMS

Since there were 60 million homeowners in the United States, and every year about 20 percent of these homeowners moved, there were 12 million new homeowners each year. I figured that if I only covered 10 percent of the market, I could make a profit of $6 million a year from HOWDY coupons. It all seemed so easy then. I was convinced I would soon be a multimillionaire. All that I had to do was replicate a sure thing that had been easy to sell in two cities. The only thing I had to fear was someone else coming up with the idea and getting the program set up before I got there.

My usually morbidly pessimistic accountant encouraged me to go all out and expand the program dramatically and fast. "Your cost of goods sold is only 7 percent," he (incorrectly) calculated. "This is like selling water. Are you looking for investors?" I couldn't believe such enthusiasm coming from him.

The numbers did look promising, however, and there seemed to be a need to move fast to take advantage of this perhaps fleeting opportunity. I decided to raise investment capital from other people to ramp up this new business in far less time than I could do it with my own resources.

At first, I tried every banker in town. They all looked at the cash flow in my rental store business (which was sadly not positive) and concluded that I could not handle any more debt. That meant that I would have to sell some equity to get the money in a hurry. Banks don't buy equity.

FIND YOURSELF AN ANGEL

I had heard about angel investors, but I didn't know any. Angel investors were people with capital to invest in start-up companies. They were sort of private venture capital companies. Often, they have earned their money with their own successful business, and could offer management advice as well.

I decided that there must be some angel investors in Boston, a mere three-hour drive away. First, I polished up my business plan, which was simply a statement of what had happened in Rutland and Glens Falls, with plans to roll out to 15 other states in three years. I got in my car and vowed I wouldn't return to Vermont until I had raised at least $50,000. I did not have any appointments or even any names of possible angel investors when I left.

On the drive to Boston, I thought about who might be interested in HOWDY coupons if it grew into a big company. Who would be suppliers to this company? Two kinds of businesses came to mind: (1) printing companies (for the coupons and mailing packages) and (2) computer service bureaus. Each month, we would have to send a list of new homeowners to each merchant along with an invoice that charged according to the number of mailings we sent out. This was before the days of personal computers, and service bureaus were used by many businesses to perform these kinds of functions.

USE THE POSSIBILITY OF NEW BUSINESS
TO OPEN DOORS

I stopped at a telephone booth on Route 128 outside Boston and looked under "Computer Service Bureaus" in the Yellow Pages. The closest listing happened to be about three miles away from the phone booth—on the Babson College campus in Wellesley. I telephoned the company, told them I was a potential $100,000-a-year customer, and wanted to visit with the president. He said to come right over.

We talked for almost two hours, and my enthusiasm for HOWDY coupons became contagious. He loved the idea. "Why settle for 10 percent of the new homeowners each year?" he said, "Why not hit 20 percent of them and make over $10 million a year?" I whole-heartedly agreed with him, and then went on to explain that I needed a little seed capital to roll the idea out to a national or even a regional basis.

"I don't know if any of these guys would be interested," he said, "but they all invested money in my company and are on my board of directors. If you get started, it will be good for us, so they might give you a serious look." He scribbled down four names and telephone numbers, in pencil, and passed me the rumpled piece of scrap paper.

To me, that piece of paper felt like pure gold. I had the names of four angels, and I knew the heavens were looking out for me.

I raced back to my lucky phone booth and made four calls, reaching the angel himself on three of them. The first man was leaving the next morning for a three-week vacation in Greece, but he invited me to visit him, when he returned in a month, at his Louisburg Square home (perhaps the most prestigious address in all of Boston).

The second angel invited me to meet with him at his office the following morning. The third angel, Luther Breck, to my great delight and astonishment, said to come right over, and his office was literally only 300 yards from my phone booth.

Everything was going much faster than I ever expected. I thought it would take me a week or so just to find an angel investor, and now I was on my way to meet one in person a few hours after I had arrived in Boston. I wasn't even sure what I should offer in the way of equity to an investor. I really didn't have much to offer. No real company, that is—no employees, no assets, not even a telephone number.

I entered Mr. Breck's office in hopes of getting part of the $50,000 I needed to get started, armed only with a business plan and my enthusiasm. At the last minute, I decided to offer 50 percent of the company for a $50,000 investment. That would be more money than I ever had in my life at one time, and I thought that I could easily parlay it and HOWDY coupons into millions of dollars of profits every year. So what if the investors got half those millions? I would also get half, which was a darn sight more than anything I had experienced to date.

Luther Breck had inherited Brecks of Boston, a mail-order firm that specialized in selling tulip bulbs from Holland. He had recently sold his company for $5 million and was keeping himself busy with angel investing. He told me about his first three angel investments, one of which had already gone belly-up, and the other two were well on their way to the same end. I began to doubt his business wisdom or his willingness to back another fledgling start-up.

WHEN THE CUSTOMER SAYS YES, SHUT UP AND START WRITING

Finally, after two hours of wonderful tales, he asked me why I was there. In five minutes I blurted out the entire story. "I can see the direct mail opportunities in this business," he said, "You can sell a ton of stuff to those new homeowners, and sell their names to a whole bunch of companies as well."

"Here's the deal," he said, "I'll loan you $25,000 for two years, interest at 10 percent payable quarterly. At the end of the two years, I have the option of converting my loan to stock, and I will own 10 percent of your company." He extended his hand toward me, gave me a big smile, and asked, "Do we have a deal?"

I couldn't believe it. Here he was, offering me a proposition that valued my idea for a company at two and a half times what I was willing to accept—and he hadn't even read my precious business plan.

I remembered a cardinal rule of selling: When the customer says yes, stop talking and start writing. I suppressed my thought about mentioning the business plan and shook his hand.

Like many angel investors, Luther Breck was interested in HOWDY coupons because it was in an industry he knew, and he could be a mentor for me and an advisor to the company, as well as being a financial partner. At his age and stage in life, he did not want to be involved in the day-to-day operational details of running a business. On the other hand, he liked the idea of people coming to him for advice and direction, much like what he provided when he ran his own company. From my experience, very few angel investors are primarily motivated by making money when they invest in other companies (after all, they already have money). More important to them is the opportunity to be a mentor and to participate vicariously in the growth of the entrepreneur's business.

The first lesson in getting money from an angel investor is to find one who made his or her fortune in a business that is related to yours. He or she will not only provide expert advice at no cost, but will be more likely to invest than someone who is unfamiliar with your industry.

BE AWARE OF IMPROPER BOSTONIANS

The next morning, I met angel investor number 2 in his downtown office. He was late for the appointment, complaining that his chauffeur had trouble with the Rolls-Royce. We exchanged introductions. Fortunately, I had been warned by his secretary that while his name was spelled Pierce, it was pronounced 'Purse.' "Old Boston name," she explained.

Our conversation immediately took a downturn when he opened a small worn book on his desk and asked how I spelled my name. "What's that?" I asked.

"A list of prominent Boston families," he answered. I assured him my name was not to be found there. I resisted the temptation to add that I'd bet there were many "Pierces" in the book.

I felt that this guy was more interested in intimidating me than he was in hearing about HOWDY coupons, but I launched into my story. To my ultimate surprise, Mr. Pierce did not totally reject my deal. He said that he would not invest directly, but that he might loan me some of his stock, against which I could borrow. Somehow, he figured that would lessen his risk, but of course, it wouldn't. If I couldn't pay back the loan, he would lose his stock. But I was encouraged that the rest of my nest egg was close enough to taste.

Then, he dropped a bombshell that I knew meant I was doomed: He wanted to run the proposition by his accountant first. Accountants and lawyers are in business to say no. That is their job, and they usually do a very good job of it. They will never get in trouble by saying no, and if once they say yes and the client loses money, they may be out of a job.

Accountants and lawyers perform a valuable service documenting the deal, but if they are given the responsibility to decide whether or not to do the deal, they will almost always kill it. They have nothing to gain by agreeing to the deal (the client makes all of the profit), and they have a whole lot to lose if the deal goes bad.

I learned two things about angel investors from Mr. Pierce. First, they need entrepreneurs as much as entrepreneurs need angel investors. In fact, he was paying someone to find investment opportunities for him. Knowing that angel investors really need you helps make it easier to seek them out and pitch your deal.

Second, I learned that unless an angel investor made the money himself, he isn't a very good prospect for investing in you. Mr. Pierce had inherited his money, and the idea of really taking a risk was uncomfortable for him. While he might look, walk, and talk like an angel investor, he really wasn't a very good prospect. Letting his accountant make the final decision gave him away. No successful entrepreneur I ever met would delegate decision-making powers to an accountant.

SOMETIMES, ANGEL INVESTORS ARE LIKE LEMMINGS

In the afternoon, I met with angel investor number 4, a delightful, easygoing, and intelligent self-made man named John Reynolds. After less than an hour, he agreed to put in $25,000 "on the same terms as my friend, Luther Breck." He never looked at my business plan either. I couldn't believe my good fortune. Not only was I getting all the money that I needed, but it was coming from a nice guy who could help me with business advice as well.

I returned to Vermont with dollar signs dancing in my eyes. I was extremely proud of myself, having raised $50,000 to start a business from complete strangers in less than 48 hours.

All it took was an idea, a business plan, and some enthusiasm. You might think that I really didn't need the business plan, because neither investor actually read it before committing his money. However, going through the process of creating the plan forced me to think about and investigate all of the important issues (e.g., competition, how to collect names, how to deliver the service, costs, etc.). Having done that investigation gave me the confidence (and knowledge) to sell the idea with enthusiasm and conviction. I knew that there were no questions an angel might ask that I didn't have an answer for.

Mr. Reynolds taught me something important about angel investors: They have friends. In fact, every angel whom I have met seems to be part of an informal network of other angel investors, and if you talk to enough angels, one of them is likely to take a shine to you and get you the cash you need to get started.

SOMETIMES, IT HELPS TO HAVE A REPUTATION AS A WHEELER-DEALER

Now that I had secured $50,000 of start-up capital, I needed a place to set up shop. Before I could find something to rent, a woman mysteriously appeared at my door with a proposal. She had come to me because someone told her I could make real estate deals quickly. She and her husband were in the middle of a divorce and needed to sell a four-apartment commercial property really quickly. The selling price was $50,000.

There was an interesting twist to her offer. A federal agency wanted to tear the building down and build a retirement home on the land. While the agency was willing to pay $60,000, it couldn't buy the property for another six months when funding came in. The divorcing couple had already been waiting for a year and did not want to postpone their divorce any longer.

It seemed like a perfect deal for me. The two first-floor apartments were vacant and would provide free office space while we got the business started. The upstairs apartments would pay the mortgage and taxes. In six months, we would have a better idea of how large an office we needed, and whether it should be in Rutland or in Boston to be near the service bureau I felt a moral obligation to employ.

I was attracted to a "sure" $10,000 gain for waiting six months. A few years earlier, this sum had been my entire salary for a year of full-time labor.

The federal agency couldn't really sign a purchase and sale agreement, but they wrote a letter indicating their intention to buy the property for $60,000 "if and when they got funding and permission from the town to build." With this letter in hand, I went to my angel investors to get their agreement to make a real estate deal with some of their money. They seemed happy to think that I was keeping the $10,000 windfall profit inside HOWDY coupons rather than in my own pocket. The truth of the matter was that I could never have done the deal myself because I lacked money for a down payment.

YOU DON'T HAVE A BUSINESS
UNTIL YOU FIGURE OUT HOW TO SELL IT

Having secured office space in record time, I shifted my focus to hiring salespeople. I needed people all over the country to set up the program in their local area, and then move on to something else. This wasn't a full-time job, but a part-time project that would end as soon as they had contacted all the likely prospects in their town.

My idea was to hire college students. I thought it would be a great summer job. I could go to one spot (their college) and hire salespeople for all over the country without traveling to distant cities. It seemed like the perfect solution for my selling challenge. I headed for Boston once again—the home of more than 60 colleges.

My first stop was Babson College, the site of my good luck a few weeks earlier. I got more than I bargained for when I interviewed my first prospect. He introduced me to his marketing professor, Colonel Ed McGee, whose specialty was a course called Creative Marketing Problem Solving. Ed loved the idea and thought it would be a perfect subject for a semester project for his students.

The next week, I spoke to two of Ed McGee's classes. I showed them the results of my success in Rutland and Glens Falls and samples of the coupon packages. I posed two problems to the students: (1) how to make this idea into a national company, and (2) to come up with a better name for the service than HOWDY coupons?

This idea of finding a better name was Ed McGee's—he thought HOWDY coupons would suggest hamburgers to merchants in Boston. Furthermore, the problem-solving process he was teaching was ideally suited to finding a name for a service, product, or company. Students were organized in teams of four who had to creatively brainstorm at least 200 possible names, and then put on their critical hats and select the best one.

Fifteen student groups were set up, and each group created both a written and an oral presentation of their ideas at the end of the semester. I offered a $100 prize for the best report and another $100 to whichever group came up with a name that we adopted.

What an inexpensive and fabulous situation this was—the students had lots of fun, and I got a ton of great ideas (and a new name) for almost nothing. In addition, four of the students (including Ed McGee's son) ultimately became full-time salaried employees. Many others became sales reps, and several even offered to invest money in the business. It was a win all around, and I was giddy with delight.

Returning home after my initial presentation to the classes, I got a phone call from Steve Steinberg, a business law instructor at Babson. He had been alerted by a student who sat in the first class that I addressed. Steve sat in the back row during the second class. He told me that he had some extra time during the week (his classes all fell on two days) and would like to try selling HOWDY coupons in the Boston area.

We agreed to meet halfway between Boston and Rutland to get him the sales materials he needed (sample coupon packages and sales contracts—business cards would follow). I realized that Steve was someone out of the ordinary when he got out of his new arrest-me red Corvette. My seven-year-old Volkswagen looked pretty dismal in comparison. I thought it was most ironic that he was planning to go to work for me instead of the other way around.

Steve proved to be one spectacular salesman, the best we ever had, in fact. Within a month, he had signed up more than 40 merchants in the Boston area, and some were huge. He had agreements for us to contact new homeowners in at least 20 cities for the *Boston Globe,* Star Super Markets, Hood Milk, and Merrill Lynch. Wow! I was more convinced than ever that we had a major success on our hands. I also concluded that we should probably set up our main office in Boston to be close to our largest customers.

When the student reports were submitted, we had a new name for our company. The winning group had winnowed over 200 possible names to a mere 9 names, which included Community Ambassadors, Welcome Neighbor, Welcome Belle, and Homeowners Welcoming Service. Almost as an afterthought, they added Merchants Welcome Service to the list so they would have an even 10 choices.

MARKET TESTS DON'T HAVE TO BE EXPENSIVE TO BE EFFECTIVE

This group did the one thing that none of the other groups had done: They market-tested the list. Doug Leeds, project leader, walked down the main street in Wellesley and showed the list to 20 merchants. "If these ten names were in the Yellow Pages under New Family Welcome Programs, which name would you call first?" he asked. An astonishing 15 merchants selected Merchants Welcome Service.

It seems that many of these merchants had been participating in Welcome Wagon for many years, and felt neglected because most new families thought the Welcome Wagon lady was being charitable when she called on them. They didn't realize that Welcome Wagon was a commercial venture (owned at the time by the Gillette company, in fact), and the merchants were paying dearly for her services. Merchants Welcome Service would properly credit the merchants as the sponsors of the program.

I never in a million years would have thought up this name for our company, yet it was the perfect name from the perspective of the most important party—our customers, the merchants. All the other proposed names focused on the homeowners who weren't paying us a cent.

The process of finding a name for Merchants Welcome Service will always remind me of the importance of doing market research by talking to, and listening to, the people who pay your salary—your customers.

Doug Leeds not only won both $100 prizes, he came on board as our marketing director when he graduated. Doug was one of the most creative people I've met, and he later moved on to own the largest point-of-purchase advertising agency in the world.

School was now out, and we had recruited over 30 college students to set up a Merchants Welcome Service program in their hometowns, wherever that might be. Our instructions to them were quite simple:

1. Make certain that a list of new homeowners is available in your town (in most areas, a credit bureau or the county published a weekly list of deed recordings).

2. Sign up as many merchants as you can. We suggest you charge 25 cents per contact, but what you charge is up to you. If a merchant wants exclusive coverage in the program for his or her category, charge double the regular rate.

3. The best source of prospects is the Welcome Wagon program. Find a new family who has recently been contacted by Welcome Wagon, get the list of participating merchants, and contact them. These merchants are already sold on the idea of contacting new families, and we do it faster at about one-sixth the cost.

4. Do not argue with the merchants about what kind of a gift or discount to offer—the important thing is to get him or her signed up for the program.

We offered our sales reps a choice of commission schedules— either they would get 25 percent of every dollar the merchant ever paid, a lifetime annuity in some cases for a single sale, or we would pay a one-time commission of 15 percent of what we expected the merchant would pay during the first year, based on the population of homes in the city.

Every single sales rep selected the 15 percent alternative. It seems that they had a need for instant cash (and no other job to fall back on like our Glens Falls meat salesman).

CASH FLOW IS ALWAYS KING

Every new sale cost us real cash at the beginning. We had to print a year's supply of coupons and pay the sales reps in advance before we collected anything from the merchant. We figured our program in a new city would become a positive cash flow after four months, and then profits of about 90 percent on every dollar collected would start. (In retrospect, I would have insisted that the salesperson collect a deposit from the merchant. The deposit should have been at least as large as the salesperson's commission. This policy would have made for a more difficult sale, but it would have made a considerable difference in cash flow for us.)

We foolishly spent a big chunk of our start-up capital on a used printing press. At the time, it seemed like a brilliant decision. We could print brochures, customer coupons, and sales rep business cards in less time and for far cheaper than an outside printing firm could.

KEEP EXPENSES VARIABLE RATHER THAN FIXED WHENEVER POSSIBLE

Start-up firms cannot afford the luxury of fixed costs. Buying a press (as well as the operator to run it) is a fixed cost. Farming out the printing to a printing company is the appropriate way to operate until you have a positive cash flow from operations.

We were now in a situation in which we had used one-third of our start-up capital to buy some real estate; another third for a printing press, platemaker, and office equipment; and every new customer whom we added on was costing us more up-front dollars. I was counting the days until the real estate would sell when I read in the *Rutland Herald* that the proposed federal retirement home was seven stories high, and the longest ladder in the fire department only reached to five stories. It was unlikely that the city would give permission to build such a large structure. My stomach quite suddenly had developed some chronic gurgling sounds.

A few weeks earlier, I had been giddy with excitement over our impending great success; now I was totally depressed because I was almost completely out of money. My mood was not helped when some vandals broke into our office and scattered over 200 piles of coupons (each pile had 1,000 merchant coupons) into one big pile in the middle of the room and then dumped a gallon can of red paint on the pile. It took us two weeks to separate out the coupons without red paint and return them to their rightful piles.

I remembered that several Babson students had offered to invest money in our company. Although he had not committed to invest, one of Doug Leeds' best friends was Edsel Ford, who had just inherited some $20 million on his 21st birthday. Maybe we could get him and the others to come on board if we made a public offering of stock.

The normal way to have a public offering is to find an underwriter who will buy your stock (and then sell it to lots of smaller investors.) Such an offering involves registering with the Securities and Exchange Commission (SEC), spending tens of thousands of dollars on legal and accounting expenses, and waiting nine months or so before you get any money. This alternative was not available to us for the simple fact that no underwriter in his right mind would even look at us, and we had no money for legal or any other kind of expenses.

There was an exemption from full registration, however. Regulation A allowed for offerings under $500,000. (A similar exemption, Regulation D, now allows stock sales up to $1.5 million). Under Regulation A, you could sell stock without an underwriter, and you could register the offering more quickly and less costly with a regional office of the SEC.

For us, this meant Boston. The person in charge was a warm and charming lawyer (whose son was Charles Colson, later to gain notoriety at Watergate). The elder Mr. Colson had earned his law degree at night while traveling throughout New England in a sales position. He appreciated my bootstrap efforts to raise money and helped me through the administrative red tape in record time—about 90 days.

BEWARE OF DISAPPEARING INVESTORS

When we finally secured permission to sell stock, the potential investors had carried out a disappearing act (or had just invested their money in something else). Only about 15 people bought stock, in amounts from $200 to $10,000. In total, we raised just over $50,000, mostly from my friends who believed in me more than the business deal. For the three months that we spent raising the money, just about all of our time was focused on selling stock rather than running the business. By the time we finally got the money, it was virtually all gone, either from the selling costs (travel and registration expenses) or from adding on new customers, each one of which took money out of our nearly empty pockets.

DON'T SEND A BOY TO DO A MAN'S JOB

Depending on students to sell our service was, ultimately, a disaster. One of two scenarios resulted. First, the student encountered difficulty in selling the service. After a dozen or so rejections, he or she would quit selling and find a job as a lifeguard for the rest of the summer. To make matters worse, a student would make three or four sales before quitting, receive payment from us, but leave us with too few merchants to profitably collect the names and mail out the coupons. We were left with incomplete and unprofitable programs set up in 17 states from Maine to Louisiana. In addition, we had paid out thousands of dollars in sales commissions and printing costs.

In the second scenario, the students encountered great success and soon had earned enough cash to keep them in beer for the rest of the summer. These students then quit working altogether. One month into the summer, none of the 30 student sales reps were working any longer for Merchants Welcome Service. Although this was temporarily good for our cash flow, it did not auger well for the long-term health of the company.

SELLING IS ALWAYS THE LARGEST CHALLENGE

Like most businesses, selling the service became our largest obstacle to success. By the end of our first summer, we had moved to a second-floor office (rent $200 per month) in Natick, Massachusetts, to be nearer to our major customer base (thanks to Steve Steinberg's efforts). Our full-time staffers all made sales calls and added on a couple hundred merchants in greater Boston. I spent a day myself selling in Lexington, and made seven sales in one day, a record. I didn't really like this kind of selling, though, and almost always found an excuse to do something else.

We were learning other discouraging things about our service. The merchants who originally signed on in Glens Falls were not renewing their service at the end of the year. The biggest reason was that they had offered such small incentives that it wasn't worthwhile for the homeowner to redeem the coupon. We had failed to convince the merchant that the long-term value of a new customer was worth an extremely generous gift to get him or her into the store for the first time. Second, the salesperson had so oversold the service that the merchant's expectations could never meet the inevitable reality of our program. I have learned over the years that straight-commission salespeople will do anything to make a sale, including overstating, lying, or even forging the merchant's signature. None of these activities helps to create a long-term client for the company that must deliver the service.

Other problems centered around the merchant. Most of them did not monitor the results from their advertising efforts, so they never knew what was working for them. I went to one of our furniture merchants looking for a testimonial, since I knew one of our home-owners had recently bought over $2,000 worth of furniture from him. He told me that as far as he knew, the program wasn't working for him, and he was planning to cancel. (The single sale I knew about would have paid for several years of our service.)

Merchants are notoriously fickle, and they often switch to a different advertising gimmick every year (usually turned on by some hard-selling, enthusiastic straight-commission salesperson). Even if our program worked well for them, many merchants preferred to take a chance that some other promotional program might do even better.

On the other hand, if merchants were sold properly in the first place (had reasonable expectations and offered a generous incentive) or participated actively (followed up our mailing with a phone call welcoming the new homeowner and extending a personal invitation to come to the store), they might stay with Merchants Welcome Service as long as they were in business.

FRANCHISES ARE NOT FOR FAST FOODS ALONE

Clearly, I needed a new way to sell the program. I couldn't afford to employ salaried salespeople (a fixed cost), and I had had my fill of straight-commission sales types. I decided to franchise the program. For an investment of $3,500, a person could purchase exclusive rights to sell Merchants Welcome Service in an area that averaged a population of 500,000. We would provide the franchise with sales materials, sample coupons from other areas, contracts, business cards, a comprehensive training manual, and three days of personal training at our headquarters in Natick.

The franchisee would do all the selling, and we would gather the new homeowner names, print the coupons, do the mailings, send the list of new homeowners to the merchant each month, and bill the merchants. We wouldn't mail out any packages until at least 12 merchants had signed on. Fifty percent of all money collected would go to the franchisee, and we would keep 50 percent for our fulfillment services.

Fortunately, there was a relatively easy and inexpensive way to sell franchises in distant cities. Each weekend, an "Own Your Own Business" exposition was held in a different city by a trade show company. For $500, I could rent a booth alongside 20 or so other companies that were offering such opportunities as vending machine routes (e.g., selling candy, maps, compressed air, etc.), a localized TV guide publication, and a dozen franchises from mufflers to sub shops to car washes. Virtually all of these opportunities were gold mines for the sellers and guaranteed total losses for the unfortunate buyers.

I soon got a call from a man in California. "I represent the National Business Opportunity Referral Service," he explained. "We're sort of like the Better Business Bureau for franchise opportunities. Every single exhibitor at the show you are attending uses our service."

"How does it work?" I asked.

"When you have a prospect who is on the fence and can't make up his mind, you ask him if he would like to talk to someone familiar with this opportunity—a service much like the Better Business Bureau. You give him our toll-free 800-number, and he calls us for a reference."

"What do you tell him?"

"Anything you tell me to say."

"Do you want to know anything about me or my company?"

"Of course not. Just pay me $25 for every phone call I handle. Very few suckers ever call us and end up not buying your deal."

I never used this fraudulent service, even though it put me at a competitive disadvantage to the other exhibitors who did use it. I realized that I was competing with sleazy hustlers who were peddling the American dream to mostly gullible neophytes.

While my franchise was one of the few legitimate business propositions for sale, it required a great deal of hard work and selling skills. My competitors sold good-sounding but impossible-to-make-money deals, which required little more effort than going around collecting money from vending machines. The gullible show attendees bought at least 20 of these worthless business deals for every legitimate deal that was sold.

Every Merchants Welcome Service franchise that I sold for $3,500 would net me $2,000. I spent an average of $500 for traveling to the city and the hotel, $500 for the booth, and $500 for materials and training. In 24 weeks (working only weekends), I sold franchises in 20 cities, netting us $40,000. This cash literally kept us alive while we were building the company.

I had learned that selling Merchants Welcome Service was a really difficult thing for most people. On the other hand, for natural salespeople, like myself, I suppose that it came very easy. I was determined to sell franchises only to people who had already enjoyed the selling experience in some other area. At the back of my booth, I placed a sign that read:

IF YOU HAVE SELLING EXPERIENCE, I CAN SHOW YOU AN EASY WAY TO MAKE $50,000 A YEAR IN YOUR SPARE TIME. IF YOU DON'T HAVE SELLING EXPERIENCE, PLEASE DON'T STOP HERE.

I soon learned the magic of the negative sell. No one wanted my franchise more than someone who was told he couldn't have it. People with absolutely no selling experience were demanding that I sell them the franchise. The harder I argued that they would fail, the more they wanted it.

In the end, I sold the franchise to someone with sales experience whenever I could, but I really needed the money, and rather than go home empty-handed, I always caved in to someone waving a $3,500 check at me, regardless of my feelings about his or her likely success. I rationalized my actions by remembering that most of the other opportunities at the show cost $10,000 or more, and these well-meaning but naïve folks were a whole lot better off losing only $3,500.

In the end, 18 of the 20 franchises failed. The two who succeeded got together and formed a partnership. Eight profitable (for them) years later, I bought back their franchise for $170,000, but now I'm getting way ahead of myself.

We never really made a profit with Merchants Welcome Service, except for selling the franchises. However, the lessons that I learned in this never-to-be-successful business served me a hundred times over in my future business endeavors. There is no education so valuable as what you learn while failing at something you believe you can do. Merchants Welcome Service was one wonderful learning experience for me, more valuable than my six years of formal higher education.

WHAT I LEARNED

■ *Successful new companies are created around markets, not products.* New companies are either product-driven or market-driven. In product-driven companies, an entrepreneur or investor comes up with an idea for a neat new product, which he is certain will be bought by millions of people. Market-driven companies are started when someone wants something and can't find it in the market. The entrepreneur starts a company to satisfy that need. For me, I was usually the person who couldn't find what he wanted in the market (like an inexpensive welcoming program directed at new homeowners). It doesn't have to be that way, however—your customers, friends, relatives, as well as books, newspapers, and magazines can all be sources for new business ideas. Every time you hear about a problem that someone is having, there is a good chance that you have discovered a good new business opportunity. Market-driven new companies are almost always successful, and product-driven companies almost always fail. Don't fall for that neat new product idea, but be ever vigilant for difficult problems that you can solve for someone.

■ *It's virtually impossible to build a viable, long-term business using straight-commission salespeople.* Straight-commission salespeople are likely to do most anything to make a sale, including promising things you might not be able to deliver. When a better sales opportunity comes along (or what they perceive as a better opportunity), straight-commission salespeople are gone in a flash.

■ *Finding good salespeople is one of the most difficult of all business challenges.* The best salespeople have a combination of ego drive (it's important to them to score with a sale), empathy (they listen to and appreciate customers' needs), and positive self-concept (they do not treat rejection as a personal failure).

■ *Be a seller of franchises, not a buyer.* The major advantage of most franchises is unique information about how to run a particular type of business. Rather than paying a huge franchise fee (and perhaps royalty fees forever), you can gain this same information from books or other people in the same business. Just go to a distant state, and a franchisee or other person in that business will probably tell you everything that he or she knows (or that you need to know) about succeeding in that business. Of course, every rule has an exception or two. However, for every McDonald's, there are 1,000 franchises that are not worth the paper they are drawn up on.

■ *No opportunity is so fleeting that you must move at break-neck speeds to get it.*   The speed of the Internet may have changed this advice, but for most companies, it is still true. We made many expensive mistakes at Merchants Welcome Service. If we hadn't been in such a hurry to cover the entire country before someone else did, we could have made the same mistakes on a whole lot less money.

Chapter 9

The Information Industry: Selling a Product and Having It to Sell Again

How to Get Your Customers to Completely Finance Your Business

Six months after starting Merchants Welcome Service, we were out of cash. We closed down all of our operations in seven states because there were not enough merchants signed up to cover the cost of compiling the new homeowner names and mailing out the coupon packages. We now operated only in Massachusetts.

We expected to have some capital in a few months when the real estate in Vermont finally closed, but that was an elusive date that kept getting pushed further out. (It would be almost another full year before we got our investment back.)

DESPERATE TIMES CALL FOR DESPERATE MEASURES

What could we sell to make some quick cash? I wondered if there would be a market for the list of real estate sales we had in our computer. What if we sorted all the sales by street address in each city, and published an easily referenced monthly directory? No one

inside our company thought it would be valuable until we had compiled at least two years of data. At the time, we had six months'
worth of sales in only 2 out of 14 counties in Massachusetts.

A 100-year-old company, Banker & Tradesmen (B&T), domi-
nated the real estate information business in Massachusetts. Their
weekly publication listed every real estate sale and mortgage in the
entire state for only $75 a year. Most of their revenue came from
advertising. In many counties, we used their weekly list as our
source of new homeowners.

B&T was not computerized. They manually typed each real estate
transaction and pasted up a list for their publication. (This was
important to us, because it meant that they could not easily sort their
data and compete with our proposed product.)

An important drawback to my idea of selling a compiled list of
transactions was that we would, in some respects, be competing with
B&T. This meant that we could no longer use B&T as a source of
data. We would have to incur the extra expense of hiring someone to
go to each county registry of deeds each week. Although this would
considerably increase our fixed costs, I felt that if we did the data collecting ourselves, we might be able to find a market for companies
who wanted the information faster than it was available in B&T.

In spite of my team's pessimism, I thought we had to try selling
our own computerized list of data. If we didn't do something, we
would soon be out of business.

DO YOUR MARKET RESEARCH
WITH AN ORDER FORM (AGAIN)

We got a list of every real estate brokerage firm, real estate
appraiser, and bank in Massachusetts and sent out 5,000 mailing
packages. For $50 a year, we offered a monthly list of all real estate
sales in one county with a cumulative list every six months. (Middlesex, the largest county, cost $100.) "With this list," I wrote, "you
can drive down any street in the state and know the selling price of
any house on the street that sold during the last year. To find the
same information in a weekly publication, you would have to read
through 52 separate issues."

INFORMATION RULES! SELL IT, AND YOU STILL HAVE IT TO SELL AGAIN

To everyone's utter surprise, we got 500 orders with $50 checks enclosed—$25,000 in real cash. This was enough to finance our new business—*Real Estate Transfer Directory*. Not only did this single mailing get us the start-up capital that we needed, but it opened our eyes to the wonderful world of selling information. From this point forward, my primary business focus became selling data. It is the only product I know of that you sell and still have to sell to someone else. Your success depends on how many times (and different ways) you can sell the same information.

The good news was that we had $25,000. The bad news was that we had an obligation to deliver a year's worth of data in 14 counties. At the time, we were operating in only five counties and had only a few months' data for those counties.

Quickly, we visited every county courthouse and were delighted to discover that the large counties offered a daily or weekly listing of deeds and mortgages for a nominal fee ($60 to $100 per month). In the smaller counties, we usually hired the same person who was collecting data for B&T (often getting a copy of what the collector sent to B&T).

We made a second mailing and signed up another 500 subscribers. Before the year ended, we had 1,300 paying customers for *Real Estate Transfer Directory* and were taking in far more from our list of real estate sales than we were from Merchants Welcome Service.

LEVERAGE THE VALUE OF DATA BY FINDING NEW MARKETS

Next, we offered a weekly list of sales, which was guaranteed to get to our customers before B&T. We sold this list primarily to insurance agents and fuel oil companies. The first fuel oil dealer who arrived at a new homeowner's door usually got their home heating and service business for as long as they owned the house. Most every fuel oil company had a salesperson whose primary target was new homeowners. Competition for new business was intense, and we ultimately signed up over 30 fuel oil dealers in the state.

For an additional fee, we provided our weekly-list customers with a telephone number for each new homeowner. Calls to directory assistance were free at that time. We added two full-time people to make the calls. The weekly-list service ultimately became a daily list, and we promised to get the new homeowners' names in our customers' hands within 48 hours of the deed being filed. By that time, the fuel oil companies were paying our entire data collection costs in Massachusetts.

DON'T EXPECT A COMPUTER TO BE YOUR FRIEND

Our computer service bureau could not turn around our data fast enough to meet the standards we had promised our customers. We were forced to rent our own computer. It was a real dog by today's standards. First, it cost $3,000 a month to rent, and it had about $\frac{1}{100}$th of the power of today's PCs (which cost less than $1,000 to purchase). Second, the data were keypunched onto a 96-column card. We were collecting too much information to fit on a single card, so each record required two cards. The first 15 columns of each card had to be used as an identifying code to keep the two data cards together.

Every time we created a compiled list of sales, we had to sort several thousand dual-card records. Sometimes, it took two weeks to do the job, with three shifts of people working 24 hours a day. Today's computers could do the same job in less than a minute.

I spent many nights until the wee hours of the morning feeding the card sorter while I tried to do accounting or other work. One early morning I dropped a box holding several thousand punched cards, and had to start the sorting process all over again.

WHEN YOU'RE ON AN ELEPHANT HUNT, DON'T SHOOT THE RABBITS

Being one of the few small companies to have a computer at the time eventually proved to be a curse. Most of all, it encouraged me to get into a whole host of businesses we shouldn't even have considered.

Steve Harris, founder and owner of the Writewell Company, gave me this valuable advice: "While you're on an elephant hunt, don't shoot the rabbits." Of course, Steve was nearly 80, a direct marketing genius (and one of the warmest, sincerest, and most wonderful men who ever lived), and I was a 33-year-old know-it-all. I ignored his wise counsel.

Our biggest rabbit was a marketing program for auto dealers. Instead of having each car salesperson make out a 3-by-5-inch card for each sales prospect, we would enter this information into the computer. (Dealers liked this program because when the salesperson left, which he or she usually did sooner or later, the dealer would own the customer profile.)

Each month we would search the database and give each sales rep reasons for contacting people on his or her prospect list (birthday, car purchase anniversary, and the big one—last loan payment). We also wrote a monthly newsletter, printing several different variations with each salesperson's picture on the edition for his or her prospects.

The only reason for us to be in this business was one large auto dealer customer, our computer, and our printing press. We had nothing else, certainly not all the important skills that were needed to succeed in this business. Eventually, we failed, of course.

DIVERSIFICATION DOES NOT USUALLY RESULT IN REDUCED RISK

Our computer also provided the excuse to get into other businesses, such as printing computer so-called personal letters to new home-owners or any other prospect list. We even agreed to keypunch the entire alumni list for a local college and print their alumni directory. All of these were attempts at diversifying (a wonderful-sounding word that makes it seem like you are reducing risk). They all failed miserably, not only in an economic sense, but even more so because they distracted us from the elephant hunt (i.e., expanding our base of customers who wanted our real estate transfer information).

My employees complained that I was coming into work every Monday morning with a new business to start, and they hadn't even started processing the orders from the business I started the week before. Clearly, I was the one who was being distracted by the rabbits and neglecting the elephant. Successful companies can handle an entrepreneur for so long, and then they have to get rid of him.

GET A JUMP START WITH A GOOD BUSINESS NAME

Now that we were offering so many different services, our company name did not make much sense. Our fastest-growing service was the weekly and daily lists, and these were neither Merchants Welcome Service nor *Real Estate Transfer Directory*. In addition, the auto dealer program had grown to five significant customers, and represented about a quarter of our sales.

Lyman Wood, creator of the Garden Way cart and a dozen or so successful mail-order businesses, said that the way to find a name for your company is to take your best friend out in a boat on a large lake, and don't come back until you have thought up a name. Hunger eventually forces you to make a decision. As weird as the name may sound at the time, two months later it will sound perfect.

I would like to offer four small pieces of advice on naming your company:

1. Have it suggest the most important service that you are providing.
2. Make it pronounceable.
3. Don't make it so specific that it will hinder future diversification.
4. Don't use initials.

To illustrate this last point, I have selected some companies who use initials in their name from the Fortune 500 list. Listed to the right of each company is a second company that is the next largest company on the Fortune 500 list. For how many of these companies can you name their most important product line? Remember, each company on the left is *larger* than the company on the right.

USX	Lockheed
AMR	Coca-Cola

IBP	Philips Petroleum
CSX	El Paso Energy
TJX	Nike
FPL Group	Campbell's
VF	Automatic Data Processing
GPU	Southwest Airlines
PPL	Eastman Chemical
FMC	Clorox
USG	Barnes & Noble
AES	Times Mirror

If you are like most people, you could not identify the major product of the "initial" companies, but had no trouble with the companies with a full name. The message is simple: Don't use initials in your company name unless you want the public not to remember anything about you or what you have to offer.

The company name we came up with—Auto-Data Systems—was not much better than using initials because it was intentionally confusing. We hoped that our auto customers would think that we were predominantly involved in the car business, and everyone else would know we had a computer. A few years later, *every* business had a computer, and we were easy to forget.

Speaking of confusing names, shortly after we first offered our first real estate data product, I read in the *Boston Globe* that there was to be the semiannual meeting of the Metropolitan Mortgage Bureau. To me, this sounded like a quasi-public organization, perhaps like the Better Business Bureau. Since our list included every mortgage recorded in the state, I thought I would attend this meeting and see if I could sell some of our services.

DON'T JOIN YOUR COMPETITOR FOR LUNCH UNLESS YOU HAVE BEEN INVITED

I arrived late for the lunch meeting, which was scheduled in a conference room at a downtown hotel. For once, my proclivity for lateness paid off. Had I been on time, I never would have been invited in. A waiter saw someone in a business suit standing outside the door and directed me to the only vacant seat in the horseshoe-shaped banquet room. I noticed that I was the only one without a nametag. The waiter placed a filet mignon dinner in front of me. "Who are you with?" the older gentleman at my right asked. I started to mumble an answer, but was drowned out by the president of the organization who stood up to speak.

"For fifty years," he reported, "we have been publishing a list of every real estate sale in the Commonwealth of Massachusetts. We have printed each sale on a three-by-five-inch card so that our members could sort the sales by street address in each city. This has been a valuable service for our constituents and has paid for our elegant banquet each year. But now there is a dark cloud on the horizon. It's called *Real Estate Transfer Directory*. They offer a computerized list of sales for only $50 per county per year. At that price, we will soon be out of business. Does anyone have any ideas about how we can combat this threat to our existence?"

I could feel my face turning red, and I immediately realized that I could never be the spy that I had fantasized about as a child. I was torn between wanting to get out of there as quickly as I could and wanting to stay to learn what they were planning to do about us. I stayed. They decided that we would soon be out of business because we were charging so little. All they had to do was wait it out, they concluded. I asked my neighbor where the men's room was and headed home. I vowed that next time I would call to find out what the organization actually was.

THERE ARE TIMES IN AN ENTREPRENEUR'S LIFE WHEN HE OR SHE SHOULD NOT GET OUT OF BED FOR AN ENTIRE YEAR

We expanded our services to Connecticut, collecting a nice capital infusion by selling *Real Estate Transfer Directory* in advance. Although the data would be considerably more expensive to collect in Connecticut (deeds were recorded at each local town, rather than at the county), I figured that oil companies alone would almost pay for the entire data collection cost. We hired 10 part-time collectors to cover about 20 towns each, agreeing to pay their travel costs as well as a nice salary.

A second promising development was a wonderful office building in Framingham, Massachusetts, large enough to handle our expansion for many years. The best part of the deal were the magic words *no money down,* but how we got to that point was a story in itself. A real estate broker approached me with the offer. Someone in his family died, and he had been asked to handle the sale for the estate. He thought a $90,000 price would be a great buy for me and also fair to the estate.

DON'T ALWAYS TRUST THE BANK PRESIDENT

I signed a purchase and sale agreement and went to a bank in Framingham asking for a mortgage loan. I asked to speak to the president, as I was hoping to sell him our real estate data and sign him up for Merchants Welcome Service at the same time. The president seemed receptive to all my proposals, especially the real estate. He was familiar with the building, but had not realized that it was for sale. He would give me an answer in a week.

Four days later, I got a call from the real estate broker. While the executor was gathering trustee signatures for our sale, someone had come along and made an oral offer on the building of $100,000. He thought this was a little strange because he was the sole representative of the estate, and had not told anyone but me about the property. He told me not to worry. The property would still be mine, but I might have to go up to $100,000 for it, still a fair price.

I happened to visit the next-door neighbor, an auto parts dealer, to tell him about my pending purchase and to learn if he might be interested in renting a few parking places from me. "Funny thing you should be talking about that building," he said, "Just this morning, I had a weird visit by the president of a Framingham bank. He said the bank wanted to buy the building to use for their computer operations, but the property was in an estate being handled by the trust department of the Shawmut Bank of Boston, an affiliated bank. He asked me if I would be interested in buying the building. He would finance the purchase 100 percent, and would agree to buy the building from me six months later and give me a $25,000 profit on the deal."

Now I knew where the $100,000 bid had come from. I immediately went to the president of the bank and told him what I knew. I agreed not to say a word to anyone if he would give me a $100,000 loan on the building. He agreed, and I owned a nice piece of real estate, on which I soon got a $30,000 second mortgage to help finance some growth for Auto-Data Systems.

Next, we offered our services in Westchester County, New York, again collecting money in advance from real estate brokers and appraisers. Then we encountered a real snag. The competitive supplier of real estate data, *The Westchester Law Review,* was given access to the deeds a full month before they were available to the general public (and we were considered to be the general public). Oil companies or welcome program subscribers would not tolerate ancient information. I tried everything I could think of, including hiring a lawyer to write the county a letter threatening legal action, and offering to pay rent (in cash if the county registrar of deeds wanted) for a desk behind the counter so we could get access to the deeds. Nothing worked. Once, after my sixth visit to the registrar of deeds pleading my case, he offered to have one of the registry employees (his nephew, in fact) copy down the deed information for us during his lunch hour if we would guarantee him at least $20 per hour. I readily agreed, but the nephew was hopelessly unreliable and rarely even showed up for work.

Our expansion to New Jersey appeared to be on the fast track when I visited the Records Publishing Company, a small family business that had published a list of real estate deeds in New Jersey's four largest counties for over 50 years. Each weekly list was manually typed on a mimeograph master and run off in the basement every weekend (mimeograph is a now obsolete form of copying that only senior citizens will remember).

The real estate publication was a sideline to the family's other business interest, had no full-time employees, and no sales efforts of any sort were carried out. They had kept the business going only because it had been earning a cash profit of $35,000 a year with little or no effort.

I explained to the owner (the son of the company's founder) that we were planning to publish a computerized listing of the same data and charge only $75 per year compared with his price of $88. I addition, our customers would get an annual compilation of the data for reference purposes absolutely free. "I expected that someone with a computer would come along and steal this business from us some day," he said. (Without computerizing the data, he couldn't offer a sorted list of records.)

I told him that I didn't want to steal his business, but buy him out instead. He agreed to sell it to me for no money down and 60 monthly payments of $1,000 with no interest. The present value of this price was less than one year's profit, but he understood that something was better than nothing. We hand-wrote a purchase and sale agreement, with the closing in 30 days.

As part of the sale, I agreed to keypunch all of the sales data for the first six months of the year, using his weekly reports as a source, and to sell an annual directory of all the sales. We would split the profits from this special directory.

I returned to Massachusetts and hired seven full-time people to enter the New Jersey data into our computer, spending several thousand dollars that we didn't have. On the night before I was to return to New Jersey for the closing, I got a phone call at 10:30. I was half asleep, but I still remember the call as if it came yesterday.

"Hi, I'm Steve M. calling from the offices of Records Publishing Company in New Jersey. I work for Real Estate Data, Inc. (Nasdaq symbol, REDI), and we have just signed an agreement to buy this company from the owners. Our lawyers have examined your purchase and sale agreement, and they assure me that it won't stand up in court. In addition, we have the right to all the past information they published, and we will sue you if you try to sell any of it."

Steve went on to say that this was his first job out of Harvard Business School, and his new boss had put him in complete charge of the negotiations. He spoke with a swagger, clearly proud of the great deal he had just negotiated.

"How much did you pay, if I might ask?" I asked.

"That's the best part," he replied. "You know, they were making $35,000 a year with no marketing whatsoever, and we figured we could at least double this profit. We agreed to pay them $35,000 a year for 38 years," he crowed.

"So you will pay them over a million dollars for what they had agreed to sell to me for $60,000?" I said. There was a long silence on the other end of the phone. A weak voice finally sounded, "Will you have some compassion for me, and not tell my boss?" he fairly begged.

DON'T PICK A FIGHT WITH AN 800-POUND GORILLA

I was angry and vowed to go into competition with them in New Jersey, anyway. I went to my lawyer and asked whether we could publish the back information we had been given. He referred me to a copyright lawyer specialist, who, for $1,000, assured me that I could not be stopped legally.

I sent out advertisements for the weekly service (with an annual compilation) in New Jersey for $60 per year. A large number, perhaps half, of Records Publishing Company's subscribers sent checks. Then REDI got a restraining court order against us, protesting our publication of the data that we had been given by Records Publishing Company.

My copyright lawyer specialist referred me to a similar lawyer in New Jersey who reassured me that we were entitled to publish the data that had been freely given to us for just this purpose. The only problems were that he needed a $5,000 retainer (which I didn't have) and that the court process would take from six to nine months (by which time the data would be too stale to sell).

When I decided to take on REDI in New Jersey, it was for purely vindictive reasons. I was angry that they had squelched the great deal I had negotiated. When I charged only $60 a year for our service (instead of the $75 I had originally planned), I was more interested in hurting them by taking away their business than I was in making a profit for us. This time, I was not bullying an old man with only a small interest in his business (as I had with Records Publishing Company), but a well-financed public company that was intent on owning the real estate data market throughout the country. REDI essentially lowered the price to zero, giving away the weekly sales data free to any customer who also subscribed to their real estate map service. (Most real estate brokers were already getting the map service.)

Our newly acquired subscribers started sending in cancellation notices, asking for a refund of their unfulfilled subscription. We didn't have any money to send them.

As bad as things were going in Westchester County and New Jersey, they got even worse everywhere else.

In 1973, OPEC decided to dramatically increase oil prices, and the supply of oil dwindled to a drip. The fuel oil companies who were underwriting our entire data compilation costs could not take on any new customers. They dissolved their marketing departments and cancelled their daily list service with us. We lost a monthly cash flow of over $10,000 in a single week, and all our expenses stayed the same.

We took drastic action to reduce overhead. We laid off over half our staff. We closed down marginal or money-losing businesses—the auto dealer program, the computer services (e.g., the alumni directory compilation), Westchester County, and all of New Jersey.

CRIME ONLY WORKS IN THE SHORT RUN

In Connecticut, we had a real problem. We could not afford to pay our data collectors, yet we had collected money in advance for an annual list of all real estate names. We had no money to refund to these customers. Desperate again, I decided to take the calculated risk of being sued for stealing the information from the *Commercial Record,* a weekly publication in Connecticut that was owned by our Massachusetts competitor, B&T. Our plan was to use their information to satisfy the subscriptions that we had already sold for the balance of the year and then to cease publication.

We were amazed at how fast they caught us. It seems that in anticipation of our pulling such a caper, the *Commercial Record* inserted fictitious real estate sales in each weekly publication. When these fictitious records showed up in our monthly list, we were toast. A letter from their lawyer presented their evidence and told us to cease and desist or they would sue us for everything we had. We tried to decide whether their suit would be more or less expensive than paying the claims of the subscribers who didn't get what they paid for. Not a fun experience to go through for an entrepreneur who thought everything was going great just a few weeks earlier.

And it never did become fun. In mid-March 1974, I decided that our only alternative was to file for a Chapter 11 bankruptcy proceeding. The Internal Revenue Service had put a lien on our building because we had not been able to pay withholding taxes. The bank was planning to shut us down because we had not reached positive cash flow as we had projected.

MAKE SURE THAT YOUR EMPLOYEES AREN'T AFRAID TO GIVE YOU BAD NEWS

For me, the final blow came when I discovered that our accounts receivable were only half what I believed they were. Our sales manager, Miriam K., had hired three telephone salespeople to sell weekly lists in all the geographical areas we covered, as well as several counties in upstate New York. Unbeknownst to me, these salespeople were offering free-trial subscriptions to our lists. Their pitch was, "Try these lists for 60 days. If you don't want to continue, just write 'cancel' on the invoice and you will owe nothing. We will even pay the postage on the envelope you send back." Very few of the companies they called refused this free-trial offer.

When the cancelled invoices started coming in, our bookkeeper (per Miriam's orders) piled them in the corner of his office and did not make note of the cancellation in our accounting system. Miriam had told him that I was in a state of extreme stress and could not handle any bad news.

We were showing a paper profit every month, thanks in large part to these bogus booked sales. Based on these figures, I got an additional $30,000 loan from Bank of Boston, secured by receivables that did not exist.

The day I discovered the pile of unrecorded cancellations in the bookkeeper's office was the day I decided that bankruptcy was our only choice.

Chapter 11 is not technically a bankruptcy, but an arrangement with your creditors. You (the company) are allowed to continue doing business and are not allowed to pay any of your unsecured bills (except taxes) while you make an offer of settlement to your creditors. If over half of the unsecured creditors (in both number and by amount of money owed) agree to your offer of settlement, then all the creditors are forced to accept the same terms.

The mechanics of a Chapter 11 bankruptcy are quite simple and painless if your creditors cooperate. (The emotional aspects, at least for me, were an entirely different matter.)

I borrowed $15,000, with a second mortgage on my house, to pay the legal bills for the proceeding (payable in advance, of course). I wrote an emotional letter to all our creditors, telling them how hard we had worked, how I had not collected a salary for five months, and how close we believed we were to profitability, if only we could get back on our feet.

We offered all unsecured creditors shares of stock in our company for their claim—one share for every $5 they were owed. I donated my personal shares to satisfy the unsecured creditors so that none of the existing shareholders would suffer a dilution of their interest in the company.

Over 95 percent of our creditors agreed to take stock in the company as payment in full for their claims (the other 5 percent were required by the court to accept the same terms). We were free to try again.

ALL CREDITORS ARE NOT EQUAL

The bank, being a secured creditor, could negotiate different terms. They agreed to limit their claims to the accounts receivables that we could collect. They also insisted that I no longer run the company. Understandably, they did not believe that I did not know about the bogus receivables. In any case, if I was so stupid as not to know that much about my own company, I should not be entrusted with running it.

Ironically, at least to me, the bank decided that Miriam should run the company. I think it helped that she agreed to work for five months with no salary. I agreed to give her 10,000 of my personal shares as compensation.

CHAPTER 11 IS OFTEN NOT THE END, BUT A NEW BEGINNING

Everything that I had ever feared about life after a Chapter 11 bankruptcy proved to be wrong. Until we got into another cash crisis, things improved amazingly. Not only did creditors stop hounding us for old bills due them, they eagerly sought to sell their services to a company with a clean balance sheet. Every single creditor, except for American Express, extended credit to us.

Several people suddenly appeared at our door asking to buy the company. Now that we had no debt, we became an attractive acquisition candidate. Since I had decided to enroll in the doctoral program at the University of Virginia and was losing confidence in the way Miriam was running the business, I decided to sell. The purchase price was $150,000, payable over six years, with annual principal payments of $25,000 plus interest. The first two years' payments would pay off our federal and state tax liabilities, since these are not forgiven in a bankruptcy proceeding. After two years, our stockholders could be reimbursed for most of their investments.

Unfortunately, the real estate market turned sour, and the company I sold out to went bankrupt themselves. I had a choice of dropping out of the doctoral program and returning to try running the company again or accepting their settlement offer of $20,000, which would go to pay our remaining bills and legal expenses. I accepted their offer reluctantly, and Auto-Data Systems was dead.

Everyone had lost money pursuing my grand dream. I lost more than anyone, financially and psychologically. That was no consolation to me when I reviewed the list of investors and suppliers who had lost so much. The original investors, Mr. Breck and Mr. Reynolds, actually didn't fare too badly. They received interest on their money for two years and were able to take their losses as an ordinary loss rather than a capital loss. Since the top income tax rate at the time was 70 percent, Uncle Sam covered most of their losses for them.

Some of the early purchasers of our stock never should have made their investment, because they couldn't afford to lose it. I felt sorry for them and bought their shares back from them at cost (as soon as I could). One woman, a cleaning lady in a Babson College dorm, had made the minimum $200 investment. Less than a month after I sent her $200 for her shares, she had a heart attack and died (I hope my check did not send her into shock). Her death was a reminder for me—all of my efforts to make Auto-Data Systems a success, or to do the right thing by buying back soon-to-be-worthless shares, ultimately were meaningless concerns in the greater scheme of life and death.

At least I had learned something about running a business, as well as about my own skills and shortcomings. Entrepreneurs are far different from managers, and I was a decent entrepreneur but a horrible manager. Now, I was planning to give up my entrepreneurial dreams and seek the safety of teaching as a career, saddened by the loss of the dream, but satisfied that I would soon be able to support my family again.

WHAT I LEARNED

- *Collecting deposits from your customers is absolutely the best source of start-up capital.* There is no interest to pay on this money, and you don't have to give away any stock. You return the capital by providing a service or delivering a product that presumably has a large margin of profit.
- *When on an elephant hunt, don't chase after the rabbits.* It is vitally important to understand exactly your company's dominant mission, and focus all your energies on that specific business. There will always be exciting new business opportunities that will tempt you. The trick is to only pursue those that directly relate to your company mission.

- *Chapter 11 is often an unfortunate but viable business tactic.*
  Chapter 11 is really not bankruptcy, but an arrangement with
  your unsecured creditors. You gain time to turn your business
  around, and reward those creditors by becoming a valuable
  customer for many years to come. More than anything, your
  business becomes more attractive to a prospective buyer once
  it has successfully emerged from a Chapter 11 arrangement.

- *An entrepreneur works 24 hours a day.* The only good part of
  this is that the entrepreneur has the freedom to choose which
  hours he or she works.

- *When you fail in business, don't take it personally.* Even
  though I learned this lesson many times, I was never able to actually do it. For me, failure is an intimately personal event. No
  matter how many times I have told myself that there is no such
  thing as failure (only learning experiences), it still hurts to the
  core of my being when I lose a lot of money.

Chapter 10

Electronic Video Games

How to Start a Business with $2,000 and Make a $15,000 Profit in the First Week

Early 1974 was a low point in my life. My five-year dream of building a successful business had been shattered. The company was down to eight employees (from 60 a year earlier), and I wasn't one of them.

Fortunately, I had a job teaching entrepreneurship and marketing at Babson College. At the least, there was food on the table for my family. My heart wasn't really into teaching, though. How could I instruct young people how to start and run a successful business when I was such a failure myself?

I continued to work on weekends selling Merchants Welcome Service franchises at the Own Your Own Business expositions. I was working on straight commission, earning $1,000 for each sale. My company made a cash gain of $1,000 on each sale as well, and hopefully gained a productive new salesperson, too. Although I still technically owned more than half the company, not being in charge or even on the payroll caused me to totally distance myself from the business. Part of me wanted it to fail the rest of the way and close the doors forever.

Selling the Merchants Welcome Service franchises at Own Your Own Business shows had become boring. Sometimes, the very first person who visited my booth bought the territory, and I didn't have anything else to do for the rest of the show. Because I was determined to sell the franchise only to people with sales experience, only about 1 out of 20 people who walked by my booth was a legitimate prospect. I started to wonder if there might be something else that I could offer to the other 19 people who passed by.

EMULATION IS BETTER THAN CREATION

Most of the action at the shows seemed to center around the two companies selling electronic video game deals. A few months earlier, the first Pong games had appeared on the market. Pong was a simple game where a blob of light in the shape of a little ball could be deflected by moving a paddle up and down with a knob. Two players would oppose each other, trying to deflect the ball past their opponents.

The first commercial Pong games were placed in vertical boxes that were 6 feet high, and the players would pay 25 cents to stand up and play a game. The Pong games were placed in bowling alleys, airports, restaurant waiting areas, and game rooms—wherever people might congregate for a few minutes.

The second generation of these Pong games was causing all of the excitement at the show. Instead of being placed in a vertical box, the video screen was face up in the top of a small round table. Players could sit down, enjoy a drink, and play to their heart's content. In some California bars, every single cocktail table was a Pong game.

An investor could get into this business for a mere $2,500 for one game, although most purchased five games at the discounted price of $2,000 each. The purchase price included having the machines placed in local restaurants, bars, and other such locations for you. Your only job would be to go around to each location each week and split the proceeds with the owner of the location. The *Wall Street Journal* had reported that these games were taking in $300 every week, so it wouldn't be long before you had your investment back and were raking in quarters by the thousands.

The salesperson would invariably close the deal by saying in a hushed tone to the prospective investor/entrepreneur, "You know, this is a pure cash business" (wink, wink).

Where could I find some of these games and get into this business, I wondered? My prayers were answered when I saw a classified ad in the *Wall Street Journal.* A company in California had a table-model video game for only $790. The ad said that this game was far superior to the Pong games because it was controlled by a joystick rather than a knob. A player could move his or her paddle all over the screen and even hit the ball twice on his or her side of the net. Even better, there were three game choices instead of only one, including solitaire for someone sitting alone.

I couldn't believe my good luck. I had found a new business to start. The next show was scheduled for Orlando in one week. I wired money to California with instructions to ship a game immediately to the Orlando hotel.

This ended up being quite an eventful weekend. First, I had my wife and three sons with me for a trip to Disney World. This was typical for me. I had a long history of spending money on a vacation just before it looked inevitable that I would soon be broke.

Second, I was trying to sell a Merchants Welcome Service franchise and a video game distributorship in a 10-by-10-foot booth at the same time. I had never seen the video game and didn't know how to turn it on or operate it. Unfortunately, the game arrived three hours after the show had started, and the crowd that quickly collected saw how stupid I was. "I think you have to put the quarter in to get it going," one smart observer commented. Of course he was right. I was soon in business.

I decided to sell the game for $1,890 for one, or $1,690 each if five were purchased. I figured these prices were far less that what the competition charged, and would make me a nice profit over my $790 cost.

A rough-looking man soon appeared at my booth and announced that he was the *locator* for that area. For $50 a shot, he would find a location for my buyers and deliver the games as well. Over the next many weeks, I discovered that every show had a locator who served many of the companies that were selling at the show.

ALWAYS HAVE AN ORDER FORM IN YOUR POCKET

I did not have any sales literature or brochures of kind—only the single sample game. I had put in some simple purchase and sales agreements just in case I was lucky enough to sell one.

I experienced unbelievably great success, and it had nothing to do with me. The two competitive booths that were selling Pong games were filled with fast-talking hard-selling hustlers who convinced dozens of people that the video game business was a gold mine. Then, people came to my booth and saw that my game was three times more interesting and selling for 30 percent less. I didn't have to say anything, only write up orders. Before the weekend was over, I had deposits on 27 units, and would make a profit of more than $15,000.

AN ORAL CONTRACT IS WORTH THE PAPER ON WHICH IT'S PRINTED

Halfway through the show, when I realized I had a gold mine on my hands, I telephoned the company in California. Luckily, the owner was there on a Saturday. I told him I was selling lots of his games, and wondered if he would give me exclusive rights to sell the games through Own Your Own Business shows. (There were two such shows operating in different cities each week). In exchange for this exclusive arrangement, I would promise him sales of at least 50 units a month.

"I can't shake your hand right now because you're so far away," he said enthusiastically, "but we've got a deal, and I'm shaking your hand on it over the telephone." I hung up thinking I was on my way to sudden riches.

The next day, a doctor from Orlando who had bought 10 games came back to my booth and asked for the name of the manufacturer in California in case he needed service. Since I had had such a nice conversation with the owner the day before, I gave him the number.

That night, the doctor called me and told me he had just spoken to the owner in California (he was there on Sunday as well), and the owner had said to the doctor, "Don't buy any more games from him—I'll sell them to you for half the price you paid." So much for handshakes over the telephone. Fortunately, for me, the doctor had paid for his games in full and in cash, so I didn't lose the sale.

ALL'S FAIR IN LOVE, WAR, AND
WHEN SOMEONE DOUBLE-CROSSES YOU

I don't take too kindly to people who double-cross me. Who does? I vowed to myself that the one game I had bought from the guy in California would be the only one. But where would I find 26 other games that looked and played like that game, and deliver them to Orlando in the 30 days I had promised? "Probably someone on Route 128 in Boston can make a copy of it," I said to myself.

I flew the sample game back with me to Boston, put it in the back end of my station wagon and started driving up and down Route 128. I stopped at every company that had an electronic ring to its name, showed them the game, and asked, "Can you build some of these?"

One helpful technician said that his company couldn't do it, but there was a guy named Ernie Dennison in Holliston who could probably do the job. Ernie had a small circuit board–manufacturing company and was looking for more work. I headed for Holliston.

Ernie was a delight and enthusiastically jumped at the chance to make copies of the game. Fortunately, for us, the circuit boards were all made with standard well-marked chips and components, and Ernie could order everything off the shelf from an electronic distributor.

CASH PROFITS EASE FEELINGS OF FAILURE

To my great surprise, Ernie promised to manufacture 30 games in 30 days, for only $700 per unit (compared with the $790 charged by the California manufacturer). My profit for the first weekend suddenly increased by $2,430, and I was feeling less like the total business failure that I felt a few weeks earlier when I lost my job at my own company.

For the next two weeks, Ernie and I played tug-of-war with our sample game. He wanted it in pieces so he could fabricate parts, and I wanted an assembled working model so I could take more orders. I managed to get it both weekends and sold another 30 units.

DON'T EVER EXPECT SUDDEN SUCCESS TO CONTINUE

Then disaster struck. My video game competitors in the Own Your Own Business show circuit clearly could not sell their product when I was there with my superior game and lower price. Therefore, they went to the owner of the show and offered him $3,000 per show, instead of the normal $1,000 fee for two booths, and paid for 10 shows in advance. Their only requirement was that I couldn't sell video games in the show.

When the show owner called to convey the news, he said, "It's only business. Don't take it personally." You can still sell Merchants Welcome Service." I was devastated. Just when I thought I finally had something I could get rich with, I was put out of business. Once again, I felt like a total failure who could never figure out how to be successful.

I retreated to my favorite restaurant and hatched a plan. I knew it would be dangerous, perhaps life-threatening (which it ultimately was). I would be slapping the faces of my video game competitors.

Before I started to carry out my plan, I set up a corporation and called it something that reflected my state of mind at the time— IDGAS (which stood for "I Don't Give A S _ _ _"). To make it seem a little more respectable, I lengthened the name to IDGAS Enterprises.

My idea was to go to the hotel where the show was being held and sell my games even though I didn't have a booth at the show. The next show was held in Arlington, Virginia. I hired Jim Miller to help me. Jim stayed in our hotel room with a sample game and lots of order forms.

I hung out in the parking lot, waiting for show visitors to return to their cars. They were easy to identify because they were laden down with sales literature describing a dozen business opportunities. "Did you check out the video games?" I would ask them. "How would you like to see a much better game for $800 less? Our game is so great that they won't let us in the show. You would never buy one of their games if you saw ours." I handed them a picture of our game and invited them to visit Jim in Room 312. Many people took me up on my offer, and we sold 15 games the first weekend.

The next week we tried the same ploy in Charlotte, North Carolina, but the police had been alerted and told me to leave the parking lot. In addition, I got a call in our hotel room from the show owner who said that he liked me and wanted me to know that one of my competitors had a gun and was looking for me in the parking lot. "I saved your life by calling the police," he added.

AFTER GOING DOWN ONCE, A DROWNING PERSON GETS MORE CREATIVE

More creative thinking was clearly required. For the next several weeks, we tried a new strategy. Jim and I would check into the hotel late at night. We would smuggle a game into our room while no one was around, usually using a service elevator. We checked out alternative ways to get around the hotel without being seen. (To this day, I know more about back staircases, service elevators, and fire escapes for more hotels than most people learn in a lifetime.) During the week preceding the show, we would place an ad in the local newspaper for video game distributorships, along with "Call Jim Miller" at the hotel's telephone number. I would call a temp agency and ask for two people to work half-days for the weekend. They couldn't understand why I wanted different people to work each shift, but when I offered $20 per hour for handing out sales literature, they always found me fresh faces. (I'm sure that they paid the workers less than half of what I was paying the agency.)

When our temp workers arrived, we would tell them the entire story. Usually, they felt sorry for us because we were excluded from the show. We told them their job would actually be easier than handing out sales literature. They would get to visit the show.

We gave each temp $3 to buy a ticket for admission. They would visit all of the booths as if they were an opportunity seeker. Their only responsibility was to watch for people who spent at least half an hour listening to the pitch at one of the video machine booths. When they identified such a person, they would watch him or her until they left the show. Then, they would approach that person and say, "I see you were interested in the video game deal. I was, too, and I read about an alternative deal being offered upstairs," showing the person the classified ad in the local paper. "Would you like to go up and check it out with me?" Many people accepted the offer, and we continued to outsell our competitors every week.

The IDGAS business continued uneventfully for a couple of months, but there were some other difficulties. Once, our name almost got us into trouble. We had rented a single room for $50 a month from my old company in Framingham as a base of operations. When we were not out crashing business opportunity shows, we advertised in the Boston papers and sold games from this tiny office.

DON'T GIVE YOUR BUSINESS AN OBSCENE NAME UNLESS YOU ARE WILLING TO LIVE WITH IT

I was sitting across from one of our game tables with an elderly dowager from Plymouth, Massachusetts. She was considering the purchase of two games to give her a little extra retirement income. "Before I buy this game," she said, looking at me directly in my eyes, "you've got to tell me what IDGAS stands for." I think she feared the truth and was worried that this might not be the kind of company she would be comfortable dealing with. I stammered out an answer: "We wanted to be able to diversify into many businesses without being tied to one. In fact, we thought many people might think we were in the gas business, which is sort of a respectable business."

The lady stared at me without saying a word. I could tell she didn't believe one word I had said. To my utter disbelief, she bought the two games anyway.

That night, I did some brainstorming and came up with an answer—IDGAS now stood for Independent Distributor of Games and Supplies. I even had stationery printed up, making it official.

WHEN THE HORSE DIES, GET OFF

I knew that the ending would come as soon as someone came up with a better game—a game that we couldn't copy, that is. We had no capability to actually create one of these machines. When the new game actually appeared, Ernie Dennison bought a Pac-Man game in hopes of having a new product to copy and make. The manufacturers, however, were now more sophisticated, and they disguised the circuitry so that it was impossible to duplicate.

I visited Ernie with the news that the business was over for me. "It's been a wonderful, exciting trip," I said, "We've been riding the horse in the direction it was going, but the horse has died and it's time to get off."

Ernie either didn't understand my analogy or believe that the horse was dead. He was planning, in fact, to build a new plant and extend his assembly line to become more efficient. Already, he had secured a large mortgage from the Small Business Administration to build his new assembly line and building. "But I won't be selling any more games," I told him.

"That doesn't make any difference," he answered, "I have my manufacturing cost down to $350 per unit now, and if I can't sell the games, I'll put them in locations throughout Boston and collect enough quarters in a couple of months to pay for them completely."

He asked my permission to hire Jim Miller as his salesman, and offered him a base salary, adding more to his fixed costs. In six months, Ernie declared bankruptcy.

In retrospect, the IDGAS business vividly demonstrated the difference between the fixed-cost mentality of a manufacturer (Ernie) and the variable-cost mentality of a marketer (myself). The fixed-cost strategy yields lower unit costs if you have a long-enough manufacturing cycle to eventually cover your fixed-cost investment. With these video games, however, we were involved in an extremely short product life cycle. The only appropriate strategy in this industry was to keep every cost variable. I rented a small office on a month-to-month tenancy. My sole salesperson worked on a straight-commission basis. Never once did I have more than $1,000 tied up in fixed costs. The sample game I used to sell others was my sole risk. Eventually, I gave this game to my children, who got bored with playing it within a week and left it in the basement to rust.

WHAT I LEARNED

■ *Plan for the end when you start.* Every business must end someday. If that someday is many years away, you might be able to afford the luxury of fixed costs. Otherwise, keep all of your costs variable, and keep dodging the bullets. In some businesses, the bullets are real.

■ *There are creative solutions to most any business problem.* There are many times during most businesses when it seems like the easiest solution would be to quit. Resist the temptation, and look for a creative solution, as bizarre as it might be.

■ *The psychological state of the entrepreneur determines what level of risk he or she is willing to take.* Looking back, it was foolish to risk my life to make a few thousand dollars. At the time, however, I was filled with intense excitement. I was obsessed with beating out the bad guys. Taking the chances that I took distracted me from the overwhelming feeling of failure that I was having over the breakup of the company I had worked so hard for five years to build.

■ *Be a seller of franchises, not a buyer.* Unless it's McDonald's, you can probably gain all of the knowledge that you need to run a successful business without paying a franchise fee. By all means, never buy anything at an Own Your Own Business exposition. If you follow this single bit of advice, you will save over 100 times the cost of this book.

Chapter 11

The Sex Education Publishing Business

How to Get Your Book Banned and Sell a Million Copies without Advertising

I have always believed that good things happen when you are doing something you love. It was no surprise, therefore, when I acquired a wonderful business while I was playing tennis. It proved to be a love game in more ways than one.

"I've heard you know a little about marketing," my opponent said as we were putting away our racquets. "I'm in the process of buying a business, and I wondered if you might give me some marketing advice."

He clearly assumed that since I was earning a Ph.D. in marketing, I must know something about the subject. Little did he know that the statistical correlation analysis I was then working on had virtually nothing to do with anything in the real world. I didn't want to disappoint him, though, so I confessed that I did know a little about marketing. He offered to pay for lunch, which was the largest consulting fee I had enjoyed for quite a spell.

My tennis opponent was a cartoonist. For several years, he had been doing freelance work for Sex-Ed Press, a small publishing company that was owned by a large midwestern college.

Their major product line was a series of comic books that were aimed at young teenagers. Most of the comics were about sex education (e.g., contraceptive alternatives, venereal disease avoidance, how to say no to sexual advances, etc.), and other comic books addressed drug use, overeating, and anorexia. The company had learned that kids, particularly low-income ones, would not read books about sex education, but they loved comic books that treated the subject in a light-hearted and nonjudgmental manner. The company also offered a series of tape-recorded lectures. One tape, *How Much Is Too Much?* (about masturbation), had sold several thousand copies.

The heart and soul of Sex-Ed Press was Dr. Sam J., a renowned speaker and author in the field of sexology. He had authored most of the books in the series and contributed the profits of the publishing company to his department at the college. Sex-Ed Press had always operated at a profit, although no overhead was charged to the publishing operation.

Dr. J. had agreed to sell Sex-Ed Press to the cartoonist for what seemed to me to be an extremely low price. At lunch, I asked why. "Because he doesn't get any royalties as long as the press is owned by the University," the cartoonist told me. Even though this seemed like a logical explanation, I wondered why Dr. J. decided to sell the business to a cartoonist who knew nothing about marketing instead of someone who could promise considerably increased sales.

We discussed what marketing efforts the company had conducted to date, and they were minimal at best. Dr. J. was a frequent (and charismatic) speaker, and brought his comic book inventory to each of his lectures. Rarely did he sell less than $2,000 worth of books and tapes at the more than 50 lectures he gave each year.

ALL PUBLICITY IS GOOD, EVEN IF IT'S BAD

Once, Dr. J. rented a booth at an educational World's Fair, and a fundamentalist Christian group boycotted his booth. The resulting publicity (it made the front page of several large metropolitan newspapers) caused an avalanche of orders for one particularly obscene (according to the group) comic book, called *Seven Fascinating Facts about Sex*. Orders were received from as far away as Australia. When a revised edition of the comic was published a year later, it was dedicated to the Christian group. Over 1 million copies were eventually sold.

Other than the lecture series and the World's Fair booth, almost no marketing efforts had been made. It was a typical business enterprise run by academics rather than entrepreneurs.

At lunch, I suggested direct-marketing the comic book series to Planned Parenthood groups and other social service agencies who had bought books through Dr. J.'s lecture series. (Sex-Ed Press had never compiled a mailing list of prospects or customers.)

At the end of our lunch, as the cartoonist was paying the bill, he said, "I have learned more about marketing today than in my entire life. I also now know I need someone like you to help run this business. Would you like to be my partner?"

The deal that he outlined was hard to resist. He already had one partner, an obstetrician who had agreed to put up the entire purchase price ($15,000) for a one-half interest. The cartoonist offered to me half of his share (25 percent) if I would direct the marketing efforts on a part-time basis for one year at no salary.

I did some hasty calculations. There were about 200,000 comic books in inventory. Each book had cost about 7.5 cents to print. I never realized comic books were so cheap to make. The average selling price was 75 cents, or 10 times cost. The total retail value of all the inventory was $150,000, or 10 times the purchase price. Assuming Dr. J. continued making lectures, the entire purchase price could be recovered in about 10 weeks.

THERE IS A WORLD OF DIFFERENCE BETWEEN ABD AND DBA

It seemed like too good a deal to turn down, but I did. I didn't think it was fair to the cartoonist, because I didn't expect to stay in Charlottesville much longer. I had completed everything except my dissertation. I could presumably put the initials ABD (All but

Dissertation) after my name. Surely, in a few short months, I could finish that little project and rearrange the letters to DBA (Doctor of Business Administration).

An aside: One of my early friends and a fellow teacher of entrepreneurship, Jeffry Timmons, said that if you lined up all the people in the world on a continuum between doers at one end and planners at the other end, most of the entrepreneurs would be at the doers' end of the spectrum and most academicians would be located at the planners' end. This model suggests that doers (entrepreneurs) might not be good planners. Such was my case. The dissertation that I expected to finish in a few short months wasn't completed for another four years.

About the only reason a person gets a doctorate in business administration is to be able to teach. I taught (marketing and entrepreneurship) at the college or graduate-school level for most of my adult life. Since I never had my DBA degree, I was always paid less than a terminally degreed person. (Isn't that a wonderful term? It sounds like another fatal disease, such as *chronic entrepreneur*.)

Finally, in 1983, eight years after I started my doctoral program at the University of Virginia, I earned my DBA. I celebrated this accomplishment by never teaching full-time again. Now, that's what I call planning.

Back to Sex-Ed Press. After turning down the cartoonist's generous offer, he asked me if I would be his consultant. He was meeting with Dr. J. in Washington in a week to go over the details of the purchase. I agreed to tag along if he would buy me a good lunch.

We found a private conference room at a frequent flyer lounge at National Airport. A purchase and sale agreement was placed on the table. It provided for Sex-Ed Press to sell its assets consisting of about 200,000 comics and other books to a corporation to be formed by the cartoonist. Total purchase price: $15,000 cash. Future editions of these books, or any other books and tapes authored by Dr. J., would provide for a 10 percent royalty being paid to Dr. J. He also agreed to serve as the editor of this new corporation in exchange for free travel to Charlottesville at least four times a year.

I thought this last provision was a little strange, but recommended that the cartoonist sign the agreement. "I sure would love to buy this company on these terms," I said.

As we enjoyed the good lunch that I was promised, a quick glance under the table solved (for me) much of the confusion and mystery I felt about this entire business transaction. The cartoonist and Dr. J. were holding hands. Some pictures truly do say 1,000 words.

LOVE AND BUSINESS DON'T MIX

Two weeks later, I received an alarmed call from the cartoonist. It seems like the gynecologist-investor hadn't liked something about the contract, had done some checking around, and jealousy dictated that he not invest his money.

"You said you would like to buy this business yourself on these terms," the cartoonist said to me. "Do you have $15,000?"

Of course, I didn't have $15,000. The lack of money, however, had never stopped me before, so why should it now?

I retired to my room and created a simple business plan over the weekend. On Monday, I presented it to the banker who lived next door to me. While my business plan was clean, my financial situation was a disaster. Most important, I was in the midst of a divorce.

ALWAYS ASK FOR MORE THAN YOU NEED

The banker was impressed with my plan to pay him back in full within six months. I intended to postpone all my wonderful marketing plans and to keep overhead to absolutely zero until Dr. J.'s lectures provided enough cash to repay the bank loan. I got a loan for $20,000, enough to buy the business, move it to Charlottesville, and invest a little in stock options (an event that eventually changed the rest of my life).

I sweetened the deal for the cartoonist by paying him $1,000 and moving into a vacant room he had in his house. I needed a place to stay, the rent was reasonable, and the room was large enough to hold 200,000 comic books, or so I thought.

I offered Dr. J. a $1,000 monthly stipend for being the editor (in addition to the four trips to Charlottesville a year). Everyone was happy, and in May, we all agreed to a September 1st closing date.

CHANGE ALWAYS BEGETS CHANGE

My 40th year, 1979, was the craziest year of my life. Perhaps it was male menopause. Change begets change. Divorce is a major change. Everything else changed, as well. In the fall of 1979, I was living in Charlottesville ostensibly finishing my dissertation and running Sex-Ed Press in my spare time. I had a full-time teaching job at Babson College in Boston and a half-time consulting job in Fort Lauderdale, Florida.

UNHAPPY MEN BUY NEW CARS

As men in a midlife crisis are wont to do, I purchased a new car for myself. After all, I had given away all my earthly possessions, and I was working so very hard. I surely deserved it. And it wasn't just any car. It was a bright maroon, obscenely huge Ford LTD, perhaps the largest car that Ford ever made, and surely the largest car I ever owned. (Except for the Rolls-Royce I got three months later, but there I go again, getting ahead of myself.)

In late August, one of my Babson students and I headed for the Midwest in my obscenely beautiful car. Our plan was to rent a large U-Haul truck, pick up the 200,000 comic books, and head for Charlottesville. He would drive the truck while I cruised along in my new fancy luxury vehicle.

When we got to the university town and picked up the truck, my student helper got into the cab and promptly hailed me. "Hey, I can't drive this thing—it's got a standard shift." Of course it did, as well as did all of the other trucks for rent in that city.

I will never forget that trip of over 1,000 miles, driving a 20-foot long truck with no air conditioning and a broken radio, while my student helper cruised along behind me in my brand new car. I could see his smiling face in the rear-view mirror. He grinned from ear to ear. I squirmed and sweated in 95° heat and cursed the day I ever met him. (As impossible as it may seem, he caused me even more damage later, but that's another story.)

Arriving in Charlottesville in a miserable but expansive mood, I resolutely went about doing just the opposite of what I proposed in my business plan. Mostly, I created lots of new overhead. I rented a second, larger room in the cartoonist's house. Although comic books are skinny little things, 200,000 of them make a pretty large pile— something that I hadn't figured on. Next, I hired a Ph.D. (in sexology, I think) from Dr. J.'s staff. Although I thought I knew how to market, I knew nothing about the business, and I needed her skills as my publisher.

Next, I bought a personal computer. Digital Equipment had just come out with it, and it only cost $17,000. I leased it for $500 a month for three years. It had about one-tenth of the capacity of today's computers (which cost less than $1,000) and moved at a slow pace that would frustrate any computer-literate person today. For the next two years, Digital lowered their personal computer prices on a regular basis, and I kept comparing my remaining lease payments with the cost of a new computer. Only in the last 10 months of the lease did the total of my remaining payments become less than the cost of a new and much improved machine. This experience was largely responsible for my later disdain for fixed costs of any nature.

In spite of my increased overhead load, the business was an immediate success. I got a free list of government agencies and made enough money with a single mailing to pay off the bank loan. Subsequent mailings put a little money in my pocket.

By November, I realized how little I knew about the subject matter of Sex-Ed Press. The first two books recommended by my editor, Dr. J., advocated gay rights and were directed at young children. Not only was I unsure as to whether these would be my first choice of the first books to publish, but they were designed to be hardbound four-color glossy print editions—a really expensive investment, unlike comic books.

Dr. J. recommended that I give the author a $5,000 advance. I thought that this was a bit unusual because advances are usually given to support the author while he or she writes the book. In this case, both the books had already been written and illustrated. At this point, I learned that Dr. J. and the author were lovers. How objective could he be in recommending that I publish these books, I wondered?

A wonderful new thing (I thought at the time) had entered my life, and I decided it was time to sell. My publisher, the Ph.D. in sexology, agreed to buy the business—now with 150,000 books and a mailing list—for $40,000. She got a $10,000 loan from the same banker I used and paid me the balance over two years. Her monthly checks almost covered my child support payments, so I was free to start something new.

She moved the entire business back to her university hometown and continues to run a successful business to this day.

WHAT I LEARNED

- *The best deals come when you're doing what you love.*   For me, some of the best business opportunities I ever found were on a tennis court.

- *The lack of money is a poor reason not to buy a business.*   If it is a good business proposition, you can always find a source of money to buy the business.

- *It is more important to know how to sell the product than it is to understand the product.*   If you don't understand the product, though, it will probably be difficult to sell it. It would be better to sell the company and find something that you can both understand and sell.

- *There is no such thing as bad publicity.*   The only time to worry is when you are getting no publicity at all.

- *Love makes the world go round.*   Business is business, but love is eternal.

Chapter 12

Stock Options Trading on the Chicago Board Options Exchange

How to Get Someone to Give You $1 Million to Invest and a Rolls-Royce as Well

The time and energy demands of running your own business is widely believed to be stressful on a marriage or other personal relationship. While I believe this to be true, studies suggest that divorce rates are no higher for entrepreneurs than they are for the general population.

Regardless, I think it is ironic that in the only year of my adult life when I wasn't running my own business, my marriage broke up. I believe that the failure of Auto-Data Systems was a contributing factor in our marriage's demise. At least, for me, something extremely important to me had died, and I grieved for more than a year.

Because I did not want my children to suffer economically in addition to enduring the psychological strains of a divorce, I agreed to pay child and spousal support equal to 20 percent more than my entire take-home pay as a full-time teacher at the University of Richmond. My offer made it necessary for me to do something other than full-time teaching to support myself. I was also a full-time doctoral student, so I didn't have a lot of spare time to devote to the activity that would put bread on my own table.

I had been studying the stock options industry off and on since 1973, when the Chicago Board Options Exchange (CBOE) was created. I was fascinated by the relationships between prices of call options at different strike prices and expiration months. I entered a large number of these prices into a computer at the University of Virginia and came up with a rough computer model that predicted what these option prices should be at any given point in time.

In 1977, when I first started playing with my computer model, the option prices on the CBOE were often quite inefficient. (This means that they often deviated by a large margin from the theoretical values generated by my computer model.) Often, there were opportunities to buy calls that were cheap, according to my model, and to sell another series of calls that were expensive in the same stock, creating a position where you didn't care whether the price of the stock went up or down. You would make a profit as soon as the actual option prices became equal to the theoretical values (which they always would at some time, perhaps on the expiration date of the options).

IF YOU TRULY HAVE A MILLION-DOLLAR IDEA, USE IT YOURSELF RATHER THAN WRITING A BOOK

A couple of years later, two economists from the University of Chicago created the Black-Scholes model, a more sophisticated model to predict stock option values. (Actually, their model had only two rather unimportant variables that I didn't have in the model that I created: (1) the interest rate and (2) the dividends.) If Doctors Black and Scholes had found a financial backer and put their model to work in the market instead of publishing it for all to see, they undoubtedly would have become billionaires. The end result of their model was that the options market became far more efficient. Many investors use the model to this day to uncover option-buying or -selling opportunities.

In 1977 and 1978, while the prices were often still inefficient, I decided to try out my model. I started with an unsecured $5,000 loan from my friendly banker. I will not try to confuse you (as I probably have already) with stock option terminology, but will try to explain, in general, the strategy I employed. I purchased at-the-money call options in IBM, which expired in six months, and simultaneously sold the same number of at-the-money call options, which expired in three months. This is commonly known as a *time spread*. Then, I waited three months for the calls that I sold to expire. (I guess that's why they call it a time spread.) When they did, IBM had gone up by $8 per share, and I had to buy back these calls. My $5,000 investment had turned into $10,000 in the first three months, so I placed another identical bet and waited three more months.

In the next three months, the price of IBM fell by $6 and my $10,000 turned into $20,000. In other words, in one three-month period, the stock price had gone up and I doubled my money, and in the next three-month period, the stock price had declined and I still doubled my money. I felt certain I had discovered the golden egg that only exists in fairy tales.

I quickly invested the entire $20,000 in the same manner. This time, the three-month options would be expiring on the third Friday of July 1978—right in the middle of my summer vacation.

DON'T PACK YOUR BAGS UNTIL YOU KNOW WHETHER YOU ARE TRAVELING NORTH OR SOUTH

I had intended to spend the summer with a friend who had a cottage on an island off the coast of Georgia. My plan was to get a jump start on the dissertation I needed to write to complete my doctoral program.

Before heading south, however, I got a call that was forever to change my life. It was from a lawyer in San Francisco named Marshall Thurber. He was planning to operate a school for hopeful entrepreneurs at a mansion he had purchased in a remote part of my favorite state, Vermont. He offered me $2,000 plus travel expenses to teach at his school for four days. Although this seemed like a lot of money for a few days' work, I declined his offer for fear that it would disrupt my dissertation process. (I later learned that Marshall had made two inquiries about where he could find a qualified teacher for his school: (1) Harvard Business School and (2) a New York City–based consultant who, in turn, had called a friend of mine. Both references had recommended only one person, and that was me.)

Two hours later, Marshall called back, raised the offer to $4,000 for four days, plus "you can play tennis every afternoon." I was impressed that he had done his homework and had learned about my interest in tennis. I accepted his second offer and headed north to Vermont when my classes ended. After all, it would only be for four days.

Never Believe That the Job Will Only Last Four Days

The school in Vermont was called The Humanistic Business School at Burklyn, and was unlike any educational anything I had ever seen. Most of the students (and all of the faculty, except me) were veterans of the new-age "human potential" movement in California. They were all graduates of *est* (a new-age multiweekend seminar that taught responsibility in what some of my academic colleagues might call fairly bizarre ways).

Marshall Thurber was described in the media as the "Guru of New-Age Capitalism," and Burklyn was his grand experiment to enable others to duplicate the success he had achieved at Hawthorne/Stone, a San Francisco real estate firm. Marshall was the most charismatic person I have ever known.

I arrived at the school two weeks after it opened. The students had already created their own set of 10 ground rules in the Hawthorne/Stone tradition, which were the following:

1. Make only agreements that you are willing and able to keep.
2. Whenever possible, communicate any potential broken agreement before it is broken: Clear up broken agreements at the first appropriate time.

3. Speak only with good intent.
4. If a problem arises, communicate at the first appropriate time to the person who can do something about it.
5. Tell the truth responsibly, and support others in telling the truth.
6. Get off what clearly is not working.
7. Be willing to share and support so that everyone succeeds (every act is a contribution to the whole, and every act should be a win-win situation).
8. Take responsibility for creating and supporting an abundant environment.
9. Constantly examine and monitor the working environment, making sure that the organization and the players are all in alignment.
10. Acknowledge others for what they have done.

These ground rules, if they were followed, seemed to me to be able to eliminate some of the nastiest things that existed in most business environments. I fell in love with the whole idea of running a business in these terms and soon became more a student than a teacher at Burklyn.

After my four-day stint as a paid teacher, I offered to remain for the remaining four weeks of the school in return for room and board for me and my three sons. Marshall and the students were delighted to have me continue on these terms.

I taught the students a little about accounting and the basics of running your own business, using my personal experience for examples. For many years, I had taught college students the basics of accounting by using a child's lemonade business as a case study. The lemonade business required very few accounting transactions, and it could easily be used to demonstrate a profit and loss statement, a balance sheet, and the relationship between them. Marshall added some right-brained aspects to the lemonade example (little pieces of bright green paper instead of numbers, for example) and made it into a playful game. He called it The Accounting Game, and the students took to it like none of my college students ever had.

A couple of years later, Nancy Maresh, one of the students at Burklyn, asked me if she could try to make The Accounting Game into a commercial venture. I wished her luck and told her that she needn't worry about paying me royalties. Five years later, I read on the front page of the *Wall Street Journal* that The Accounting Game was being used to teach accounting to over 30,000 adults every year throughout the country. Several students called me to ask why my name was not in the article. Apparently, she was no longer following Burklyn's ground rule number 10: Acknowledge others for what they have done. (The current edition of the game now gives credit to both Marshall and me.)

STUDENTS MAKE THE BEST TEACHERS

In exchange for my teaching a little accounting and entrepreneurship, the students taught me a whole new way of looking at the world. I learned about things that were never in my vocabulary. I experienced rolfing (and met Ida Rolf, its founder); I was *rebirthed* by Sondra Ray, author of the new-age best-seller, *Rebirthing;* I learned yoga and how to meditate, said daily affirmations, learned about holistic medicine, chanted ooooms (forgive my spelling), spent time with Buckminster Fuller, learned how to hug, attended (and loved) *est,* and met Jerry Rubin (a member of the Chicago Seven, who had become a new-age stockbroker). Everything was new and wonderful to me in the summer of 1978.

In July, when the IBM call options expired, the $20,000 I had invested 90 days earlier had turned into $40,000. I shared my good news and my computer model with Marshall. He got quite excited about the potential and promised that he could get me $1 million to play with instead of the so-called paltry amounts that I was currently investing.

I felt that managing a large sum of money like that would require full-time attention, and I was determined to finish my dissertation and get my degree. I declined his offer.

Returning to school in September, I was dismayed to learn that my dissertation advisor and mentor had suffered a heart attack and was taking a year's leave of absence. My new dissertation advisor did not like me. For one thing, a local company, Babcock & Wilcox, had sent a letter to the Darden School at the University of Virginia at Charlottesville (UVA) asking for proposals to teach Management by Objectives to their top management executives. I submitted a proposal and won the contract, beating out my new dissertation advisor. (I did not know he was competing for the same contract.)

I submitted eight possible dissertation topics to my new advisor, but he blackballed every one of them, saying I knew more about all those topics than he did. If I wanted to do a dissertation with him, he said, I would have to do it on a topic that was, essentially, a follow-up (and would give academic publicity to) his own dissertation written some 20 years earlier.

IF YOU REALLY WANT ATTENTION, STAGE A SIT-IN

I started to work on the proposal for my advisor's topic, submitting a 12-section draft. He told me not to do any more work until he had read what I had written so far. We scheduled a meeting to discuss the proposal every week for five straight weeks, and he cancelled every meeting, saying he had been too busy to read anything I had written. Finally, I sat on the floor in the hall in front of his office, and told him I would sit there all day, every day, until he read my proposal. He promised to do it by the next day.

The next day arrived, and my advisor acknowledged that he had skimmed over my proposal during breakfast. His only feedback to me was to "tighten up" three of the sections and get back to him in no sooner than one month.

I left the meeting in total despair. Clearly, he was determined to prevent me from finishing the dissertation, and he could afford to outwait me. I returned to the damp basement apartment I was living in (the only place in Charlottesville I could afford). There, I found another letter from Marshall, begging me to drop out of the doctoral program and go to work for him on the floor of the CBOE. "Write me and tell me what it would take to get you," he implored.

BE CAREFUL ABOUT WHAT YOU ASK FOR

In a state of total dejection, I put a piece of stationery in my manual typewriter and started to write a letter with such extravagant demands that no one in their right mind would accept. It read:

What it would take for me to drop out of the doctoral program and join you:

1. $1,000,000 to play with.
2. A seat on the CBOE.
3. A salary of $100,000 a year.
4. One-third of the profits from my option trading.
5. None of the losses, if any.
6. A furnished apartment in Chicago paid for by you.
7. A round-trip airline ticket from Chicago to anywhere I might like to go every weekend (I don't want to spend any weekends in Chicago).

When I typed these ridiculous demands, there still was room for one more item on the sheet of stationery. What else could I want? I looked around my room and saw the treasure map that I had created while at Burklyn the previous summer. We had made treasure maps by leafing through dozens of magazines, cutting out pictures that appealed to us for any reason, and making a collage out of these pictures. My treasure map had piles of gold coins; exotic islands; pretty women; a picture of Jimmy Connors hitting an overhead; and right in the middle, a picture of a dark blue vintage Rolls-Royce. I finished my letter:

8. And as a signing bonus, I would like a Rolls-Royce.

I sealed and mailed the letter, not really expecting to hear from Marshall Thurber again. Three days later, Marshall called and asked what kind of a Rolls-Royce I had in mind. I had done a little homework in the off chance that he did call, and I told him about a 1958 Silver Cloud I had found for sale in Miami with 36,000 miles on it for only $25,000. We had a deal.

I dropped out of the doctoral program I believed I could never complete as long as I had that dissertation advisor, flew to Miami to pick up my Rolls, and drove to Chicago to start my new life as a stock options trader.

BE CAREFUL WITH MILLION-DOLLAR CERTIFIED CHECKS

Marshall sent me a certified bank check in my name for $1 million. I took the check with me to dinner with a few old friends my first night in Chicago. We fantasized about what wonderful and exciting things we could do with that kind of money. Maybe I should just cash the check and disappear to some romantic island and live the rest of my days in luxury.

My fantasies quickly disappeared when I got to my new apartment that evening and discovered that the check was missing. Only once in my life did I have a certified check for $1 million dollars made out to me. And I lost it! I felt like a real jerk when I called Marshall the next morning and said "oops."

In the next few days, I learned how to stop payment on a certified bank check and got back into business.

I took a required course on how to trade options, passed the test with ease, and found myself on the floor of the CBOE with a blue badge with the acronym SFO (San Francisco airport) and $1 million dollars to play with. There are two kinds of traders on the CBOE: (1) floor traders, who exercise orders placed with them by others (usually stock brokers from off the floor), and (2) market makers, who trade for their own account. I would be a market maker.

HAVING A PILE OF MONEY CAN BE A LIABILITY

I quickly learned that it would be impossible to double my money every 90 days, as I had been lucky enough to do the prior year. Having $1 million dollars to play with on the floor of the CBOE was actually a liability. Most of the market makers had about ½0th of that amount to invest. To put large amounts of money to work involved buying and selling a huge number of options. Word quickly spread on the floor that SFO had big money to invest. At one point, I walked into a trading crowd and overheard a broker saying, "Here comes size" (meaning I had large positions to put on). As soon as I revealed to the crowd whether I was buying or selling by placing my first order, the quoted option prices would suddenly shift against me. Everybody loved me. I was a naïve patsy with lots of money, and the other traders took advantage of me at every turn.

BULLS MAKE MONEY, BEARS MAKE MONEY, PIGS GET SLAUGHTERED

For the first five weeks in Chicago, everything was wonderful. Our account increased in value from $1 million to $1.3 million, and I was spending weekends in Bermuda; Charleston, South Carolina; or wherever else my whim drew me that week. Then, Marshall found a book about options entitled *A Great New Way to Make Money,* by Ralph Charrell. He asked me to spend a weekend in San Francisco to discuss the book. Marshall was most interested in a strategy called a *butterfly spread.* If you were lucky, you could triple or quadruple your investment in a single quarter with a butterfly spread. "Your system only makes 100 percent a year," he said, "and butterfly spreads can do much better than that.

I didn't like the idea of this spread because if the stock went up, or down, by 5 percent or more, you could lose your entire investment. With my time-spread strategy, you could never lose all of your money in a single quarter, no matter what the price of the stock did. Marshall argued that since I was right there on the floor of the Exchange, I could see if the market was going up or down and could make adjustments to our positions if a big market move began. I returned to Chicago and reluctantly put on a large number of butterfly spreads.

Shortly thereafter, the market took a sudden drop. I found that I could not get around the floor fast enough to make the necessary adjustments. We were just in too many stocks. When the market is falling quickly, everyone is trying to make the same adjustments at once, making it difficult and expensive to profitably trade out of a position. In a single day, we lost $280,000, and our account value dipped below $1 million. Marshall asked me to fly to San Francisco and explain what had happened.

FOUR GOOD REASONS WHY PROFITABLE OPTIONS TRADING IS DIFFICULT

I had learned many things in my first couple of months on the floor of the CBOE. First, having so much money was a real problem (as I discussed earlier). Much of our money was tied up in companies that did not offer us the profit potential I had discovered in the IBM time spreads.

Second, the Black-Scholes model was now in wide use on the floor, and the inefficient prices I had previously found were rarely available.

Third, it turned out that I was not a very good trader of stock options. Part of it was due to my inexperience, and part was due to my psychological makeup. A good trader needed to be less cerebral and more physically aggressive than I was. On many occasions, I got confused in the heat of battle and bought options when I meant to sell them. This was easy to do. When traders used the preposition *for* in front of a price quote, this meant that they were buying. If they said *at,* they were selling. I sometimes focused on the price quote and missed the preposition.

Fourth, short-term manipulations of the market are made by market makers, often acting in concert. They place large market orders to buy a stock on the New York Stock Exchange, for example, driving up the price by a point or two. Then, they quickly make a huge profit in an option position (a 1 percent change in the price of a stock may result in a 20 or 30 percent change in the price of an option). Finally, they close out their stock position, usually at a small loss, and the stock price goes back to where it was before the manipulation occurred.

The CBOE tries to monitor this type of illegal activity, but it is almost impossible to prove. Yet, I saw it happen many, many times, and any CBOE trader (retired at least) will admit that such manipulation is a common practice.

One proof of market manipulation on the option exchanges can be seen by the well-documented propensity of stock prices to close exactly on a strike price (e.g., $60, $65, or $70 rather than $63, $67, or $72) on the third Friday of the month when options expire. Market makers are usually short (i.e., have sold) both puts and calls at a particular strike price, and can make 100 percent profits in both positions if they can manipulate the price of the stock to close exactly on a strike price at option expiration. Of course, someone off the floor never knows which particular strike price they will choose to close the price at, so it becomes a guessing game for all but the insiders.

WHEN $1.7 MILLION DISAPPEARS, IT'S TIME TO SWITCH JOBS

While in San Francisco, I discovered that investors had entrusted Marshall with more than $2.7 million, thinking that all this money was being invested in the options market. Because I had been given "only" $1 million to work with, at least $1.7 million had been diverted elsewhere. (I later learned that most of this money had been invested in a large condominium conversion project in southern California.)

In any event, I did not want to be held responsible for the entire $2.7 million invested when I only had $1 million to start with. I immediately resigned from my position.

Marshall said nothing about the missing $1.7 million, and he asked me for two favors: (1) to stay on to teach at the next summer's six-week Burklyn Business School program, and (2) to teach him my system. I agreed to both requests.

SLEEP INHIBITS THE LEARNING PROCESS

To help Marshall learn about my system, I secured 10 hours of videotapes created by a CBOE clearing firm. These tapes explained everything (and more) that anyone would ever want to know about stock options and trading strategies. I sat down with Marshall to view the tapes, and he fell asleep before the second tape was finished—the same reaction that most people would have. Marshall's considerable personal skills surprisingly didn't help when it came to options trading. He would have to find someone else to manage the options portfolio, which he eventually did.

A year later, I sold my Rolls-Royce and used the money as starting capital to get set up on the CBOE once again. This time, I leased a seat (at the time, it cost about $3,000 a month) and hired a clerk to work full-time on the floor for me. Instead of making trades herself, she passed my orders on to a floor broker who exercised the trades.

In three months, my investment of $20,000 grew to over $220,000. Options now expired every month, rather than every three months, and extraordinary gains were possible (if you were lucky, that is).

IT IS NOT HEALTHY TO WANT SOMETHING TOO MUCH

I read in the *New York Times* about a house for sale. Located in South Pomfret, Vermont, this was the house of my dreams: a 1780 colonial on 200 acres with a four-bedroom guest house, a beaver pond, tennis court, maple sugar operation that yielded 700 gallons a year, and so on. It had an intimate library with a fireplace, where I sat with the owner, totally enthralled by the entire property. I wanted this house more than anything I can ever remember wanting. I absolutely had to have it. The price was $395,000, just about double what I had in Chicago.

I decided that the options market (now my only source of income) was so volatile that I couldn't depend on regular cash flow to make mortgage payments. I would have to pay cash for the property if I were to get it.

My plan was to put on an option position that was far riskier than normal, but would make it possible to buy the house of my dreams. Having a seat on the CBOE provided me with leverage that was not possible, or even legal, without a seat. I put my entire investment in Teledyne call options. The stock was selling for $132. In two weeks, if Teledyne closed at $130 or any higher, I would more than double my money and be able to buy the house.

On the downside, every dollar the stock fell below $130, I would lose $25,000. It was a gamble I was willing to make. The market in general, and Teledyne in particular, were both doing well. A week passed and the stock was still at $132. I had only five days to wait.

On Monday morning before Friday's expiration, a colorful stock market analyst at the time, Joe Granville, made a speech in London in which he said he believed the market would soon fall by 20 percent or more. Granville had thousands of followers, and they started dumping every stock they owned. The market, and Teledyne, crashed.

GO THE EXTRA MILE—OR LOSE YOUR SHIRT!

I didn't know about any of this, however, as I was out on my mid-morning run. I was training to run in a marathon, and usually ran 7 miles each morning. This fateful day, I decided to run only 4 miles and returned home early. The phone was ringing.

The call was from my clerk in Chicago. Teledyne was down to $120, and we were totally out of money. The clearinghouse wanted to close out my position, but they couldn't legally do it without my permission until I was in a deficit position at the end of the day. The market looked like it would be falling even more, and I would be losing $25,000 for every dollar that Teledyne fell. I gave my permission to liquidate the position, and the clearinghouse did the job in less than 20 minutes. I was stunned. At the end of the day, I owed the clearinghouse $11,000, and my dreams of the South Pomfret house were shattered.

Shortly after my position was liquidated, investors who didn't agree with Mr. Granville's prediction came pouring into the market, and prices started rising as fast as they had fallen in the morning. At the end of the day, Teledyne was back to $130. On Friday, it closed at $135. If I hadn't liquidated my positions, I would have had $450,000 in my account at the end of the week instead of an $11,000 deficit.

I have often wondered what would have happened in my life if I had run the additional 3 miles that morning.

IF AT FIRST YOU FAIL, TRY AGAIN AND YOU GET A CHANCE TO FAIL AGAIN

Two years later, after I had bought and sold All About Town, Inc. for a profit, I returned again to the CBOE. This time, I found a partner who leased a seat, and I shared the cost with him. He agreed to act as my clerk, passing orders to floor brokers for me. I put $30,000 of my own money into the pot and raised another $60,000 from friends, and I promised that I would reimburse their principal if I lost it (a mistake, of course).

In the first three months, I had almost doubled the investment once again, and then another fateful day came along. Before the opening, I placed a large order with my partner. It involved buying over $3 million worth of Teledyne stock and selling deep in-the-money calls. It was a very conservative trade, and I would lose only a very small amount of money if the stock fell significantly. My partner wrote down my orders and passed them on a piece of paper to a floor broker to execute. The floor broker called me at home before the market opened to confirm that I wanted to do exactly what was written on the paper.

I headed out for a root canal procedure and returned home in pain. The phone was ringing—the broker was calling with partial reports on my orders. He told me the prices he paid for the stock, and the prices he paid for the options. In my efforts to write down all these prices, I missed the fact that he was buying the call options rather than selling them. I told him he was doing a good job and to finish executing the order. At the end of the day, I discovered the broker's error, but by that time I owned the equivalent of 30,000 shares of Teledyne rather than having a neutral position (the equivalent of owning no shares whatsoever). Teledyne announced lower-than-expected earnings that night, and the next morning, I lost everything that I had—$170,000—before I could close out the position. I was broke once again.

The floor broker (foolishly, I thought) returned to my partner the piece of paper showing my orders to sell rather than buy the call options. I thought this evidence would be sufficient to sue the floor broker for his error.

Much to my surprise, the piece of paper counted for nothing in the rules of the CBOE. They have a tradition that oral statements are what govern trading disputes, and the floor broker had a recorded telephone conversation with me in which he told me he was buying (rather than selling) the options.

I contacted several lawyers in Chicago to get someone to represent me on a contingency basis (I would pay one-third of anything I could get from the floor broker). Not one lawyer would take my case. I finally agreed to pay a $10,000 retainer to a lawyer to represent me at a CBOE hearing. The day before the hearing, even though he had not done any real work on my case, the lawyer demanded another $5,000 or he wouldn't show up the next day. I got a cash advance on my credit card and paid him. Perhaps I was sending good money after bad, but I knew in my heart that I had been wronged and I wanted to be heard.

The lawyer's only advice to me was not to tell the CBOE resolution board that I was a college professor. "They'll think you're absent minded and won't believe a word you say," he admonished.

In the course of my testimony, I mentioned, almost by accident, the telephone call that I received from the floor broker before the market opened, and wondered if there was a tape recording of that call as well. The floor broker flagrantly lied and said he only made the one (recorded) call to me that day. The evidence I submitted to the board was my history of maintaining hedged positions, the piece of paper, and my partner's word. The floor broker's evidence was the recorded phone call. When we left the hearing, my lawyer said there was little hope that we would be awarded anything.

EVEN LAWYERS LEAVE MONEY ON THE TABLE SOMETIMES

While the board was supposed to render a decision in five days, none came. We waited three weeks. Then we got the good news.

They had checked the telephone company and learned that the floor broker had, indeed, called me before the market opened. If he lied about that phone call, they reasoned, he was probably lying about everything. They awarded me the $170,000 I had lost, plus $15,000 in interest. I was back in business. Several lawyers had turned down an opportunity to make over $60,000 for an hour's worth of work. I didn't feel sorry for any of them.

IF YOU FAIL A SECOND TIME, TRY AGAIN—YOU GET A CHANCE TO FAIL FOR A THIRD TIME

Three months later, I lost it all again. This time, it was all my fault. It would be many years before I could repay the friends who had put money into the options market with me.

A final note about my options trading. Today, I am still involved, every day. I trade through a discount broker, rather than with a seat. I maintain hedged positions, mostly time spreads on high-tech stocks. For the last five years, I have averaged over 50 percent return on my investments each year. In 1999, I made over 130 percent, but in 2000, when the Nasdaq fell by more than it ever had in its entire history, I lost a bundle.

Options trading is a tough way to make big bucks in the long run. You should only play with options after doing considerable homework—and then only with money you can afford to lose entirely.

Postscript

In 1982, feeling comfortable with $50,000 in my pocket, I reapplied to the doctoral program at the University of Virginia. To my utter dismay, the new head of the doctoral program was my old nemesis: my former dissertation advisor. Understandably, I was turned down flat.

I flew to Charlottesville and got an appointment with the newly appointed dean of the Darden Graduate School. I told him that I was planning to give a $20,000 retainer to the most adversarial lawyer in the state of Virginia (we both knew who he was) if I was not readmitted to the doctoral program. I believed that I had been unfairly forced out of the program by an envious and vindictive faculty member, and that I could prove it in a court of law. The dean asked me to give him three weeks to check out my allegations. He appointed a three-person committee to determine whether I would be readmitted, and included himself as one of the three members.

The committee unanimously voted to readmit me to the doctoral program. I was assigned a new dissertation advisor. Two years later, I finally got the doctoral degree I needed to become a full-time college professor. I never taught on a full-time basis again.

WHAT I LEARNED

- *The stock options market is a zero-sum game.* If you are lucky, you will end up with a zero sum. It could be worse.
- *You can stop payment on a certified check.*
- *Before committing large sums of money to any investment scheme, experiment with small sums first.* If I had started with $100,000, rather than $1 million when I leased a seat on the CBOE, I could have learned how difficult it might be to successfully invest large sums in options.

Chapter 13

Manufacturing Promotional Board Games

How to Start a Business with a Cash Advance from Your Credit Cards, and Sell It for a $350,000 Profit in One Year

In late January 1980, I found myself in what might be called an awkward financial situation. I had just lost my entire net worth by trading stock options. In addition, I still owed over $11,000 to the clearinghouse at the Chicago Board Options Exchange (CBOE). Most of my credit cards were up to their limit. I had no job or tangible assets other than my car and computer (on which I still owed almost $10,000). The child support payments I had magnanimously offered to pay to my first family were current, but there was little likelihood of my coming up with February's payment. And to make things all the more complicated, the prior month I had married a woman with a part-time job and four lovely children.

BE CAREFUL ABOUT YOUR DAYDREAMS— THEY JUST MIGHT COME TRUE

Many times throughout my life, I had daydreamed about moving to a strange town, probably in the Midwest, with no more than the clothes on my back. In these daydreams, I was escaping from the law (although I was innocent, of course), and I couldn't tell anyone my real name or anything about my education. I usually started out getting a job as a dishwasher in a restaurant (an easy job to get on the spot and you could eat the unfinished food on the plates). Then, I would move up to becoming a waiter on nights and weekends, and start some sort of business during the day. My goal was to accumulate $100,000 in less than a year, and in every daydream, I was successful.

In late January 1980, therefore, rather than feeling depressed, I suddenly realized how lucky I was! I had been given the opportunity to live out my dream for real. I certainly was broke and had just moved to a town where no one knew my name. Oh, what a challenge! I was deliriously happy! (I'm not so sure that my new wife shared the same level of joy that I did.)

ACCEPT EVERY OFFER
OF A NO-ANNUAL-FEE CREDIT CARD

The only tangible asset that I owned at this time was a pocketful of credit cards that I had accumulated over the years. I *never* refused an offer of a credit card with no annual fee, regardless of what the interest rate might be. You never know when you might need these cards to start a business. Of course, it's best not to actually use these cards until you need them for a business. I hadn't done so well on that score: For some reason, it's easier to get the credit cards than it is to not use them.

EVERY GREAT BUSINESS STARTS WITH A SIMPLE IDEA

I retired to my office/bedroom to plan a strategy. On my wall, I had posted my favorite inspirational words, "Your ultimate success depends on the amount of time you can get away from operations and contemplate what is important." Because I had no job, I had plenty of time to sit and think. And think I did, for almost two days.

The idea that I came up with was to capitalize on what I had just learned while losing all my money trading stock options. If someone had done just the opposite of what I did, they would have made a fortune! Surely, lots of people would pay me big bucks to show them how to get rich quick by doing what I didn't do.

I wrote the outline for a book entitled *How to Make 50% Profit Every Year on Your Investment, Even if Your Stock Does Not Go up One Penny*. I had my idea, but writing a book would not help me make the child support and computer payments next month. I needed money faster; therefore, I decided to run some seminars with the same title.

I quickly wrote up a business plan and made an appointment with the president of a small local bank. He had a reputation for sizing up an individual quickly and backing people he liked, even if they didn't have much collateral. I told him about my seminar plans and asked for a $5,000 unsecured loan to get me going.

Apparently, I didn't size up too well. He turned me down.

"I don't make loans to flatlanders," he said. (A *flatlander* is a pejorative term for a non-Vermonter who moves to Vermont, sort of like a carpetbagger headed north instead of south.) I sensed that he got a perverse pleasure from rejecting a Harvard Business School graduate who was down on his luck.

Feeling a little desperate, I looked in the classified ads of our local paper under "Money to Loan." There was one listing, a small-business investment company (SBIC) called Vermont Investment Capital, located in South Royalton, about an hour's drive from my home. I visited the company the next day.

Actually, it wasn't much of a company. There was only one man, Harold Jacobs, who sized up people much as the bank president had done. I hoped he liked my size better than the bank president had. We talked for two hours. I told him about my many businesses. We seemed to spend quite a bit of time talking about the straight-commission sales force I had supervised at Merchants Welcome Service.

ALWAYS BE READY TO SWITCH TO A BETTER OPPORTUNITY

While he was mildly interested in my seminar idea, he was really excited about All About Town, Inc., a game-manufacturing company in New Hampshire. He owned one-third of the company and had loaned them money. Even though they had a great product, they were on the verge of bankruptcy and still owed him $35,000. Perhaps I would be interested in buying this company with his backing.

The key to success in this business, he said, was selling advertising for the game with straight-commission salespeople. How funny, I thought, one of my early so-called learning experiences was coming back to reward me. While Merchants Welcome Service had ultimately ended up bankrupt, I had learned how to recruit and manage a straight-commission sales force.

I tried to hide my enthusiasm. I didn't care what kind of business it was. The words *with my backing* were all that I could think about. That, and how I was going to come up with $10 for gas to drive to New Hampshire to visit All About Town, Inc.

Fortunately, one of my credit cards wasn't totally maxed out, and I headed east with a full tank of gas and dreams of owning a new business, whatever that business might be. As I drove into the company's parking lot, a telephone company truck was parked at the entrance.

NEVER INVEST IN A COMPANY THAT DOESN'T HAVE A TELEPHONE

The phones were being disconnected. That's usually a bad sign. I sensed that the company was in the same financial shape as I was. I was greeted by a smiling receptionist (a luxury *I* could never afford). On the other hand, I could see three artists pretending to work in an adjacent room. At least, the electricity was still on.

I was ushered into the president's office, and Al Adams unfolded the story of how he had invented the game All About Town. In typical entrepreneurial fashion, while stuck in traffic in Manchester, New Hampshire, he came up with the idea of creating a board game with the actual street layout of the city. As you played the game, you would learn the best way to get around town. (If there was a one-way street, you would have to move your playing piece in the direction that that street went.)

IF THE COMPANY HAS A REALLY GOOD IDEA, FORGET ABOUT THE LACK OF TELEPHONES

His idea became a reality, every entrepreneur's dream. In the All About Town game, each player would draw a Shopping List, which required him or her to visit six businesses or civic sites, make a purchase at each, and return home. The player who could figure out the most efficient way to travel around town and make the six stops would usually win the game (it helped to throw high numbers with the dice, too).

Each of the stops on the game board was a pen-and-ink drawing of the actual business at that location. A player would learn how to get to that store, what it looked like, and get a card (much like the Monopoly property card), which told the story of that company and its products or services.

Inside each game, participating companies offered real coupons worth several hundred dollars. Because the game retailed for only $10, I could understand why people would buy it. Apparently they did. Al told me that the entire printing of 7,000 games in Portland, Maine, was sold out in three days.

Each merchant on the game board paid $400 for being included. It was a great form of advertising, especially if the business was located on a difficult-to-find side street. Additionally, each merchant who participated was entitled to purchase 100 games for $6 each. When he sold the games (usually in just a few days) for $10 each, his profit would cover his $400 advertising cost in full. Therefore, the merchant got valuable advertising for free!

Each game was cosponsored by the local chamber of commerce. In exchange for helping to solicit participation from its members, the chamber received several hundred games to give away or sell and 10 percent of all advertising revenues. The cover on the box of the game was usually an artist's rendering of local civic buildings, monuments, or other attractions, and it served as a high-quality promotional piece for the city.

Now, I could understand why merchants participated in the game, why chambers of commerce supported it, and why people bought it. But why had the telephone company just yanked the phones?

ONE OF THE THREE GREAT LIES:
"ALL WE NEED IS A LITTLE CAPITAL"

"Lack of capital," explained Al. "We were always behind the eight ball. We owed printers so much money, they wouldn't print anything more until we gave them cash for the last job. We could never catch up. But now we have produced successful games in twelve different cities, and we know how to do everything right. We are through the learning process and are poised for great growth. All we need is a little capital."

Then, he told me that a company in Rhode Island was talking about offering him $200,000 for the business. That scared me a little, but I decided to press forward. I didn't have too many alternatives.

"Do you have any financial statements?" I asked.

He reached into his top drawer and produced the report shown in Figure 13.1.

All About Town, Inc.

PREPARED WITHOUT AUDIT FOR MANAGEMENT USE ONLY

BALANCE SHEET
Period Ending 12/31/79

ASSETS

Current assets

Cash—Bank of New Hampshire	(448.35)
Cash—Depositors Trust	4.96
Accounts receivable	46,230.07
Accounts receivable—employees	1,756.57
Inventories	6,286.84
Deposits	530.00
A/R Stockholders*	11,170.46

Total current assets		65,530.55
Office equipment (net)		6,158.72
Total Assets		71,689.27

LIABILITIES AND EQUITY

Current liabilities		
Notes Payable—Shareholders	6,000.00	
Taxes Payable—FICA & W/H	3,995.82	
Accounts Payable/Production	131,143.49	
Total current liabilities		141,139.31
Long-term debts		
Notes payable—VT Investment Capital	29,630.20	
Notes payable—Comm. Credit	2,073.86	
Notes payable—sales mgr.	6,157.20	
Accrued commissions	3,487.65	
State Scale Company (secured by receivables)	38,761.68	
Long-term debt		80,110.59
Total liabilities		221,249.90
Equity		
Capital stock	23,000.00	
Retained earnings	(81,333.06)	
Net (loss) income	(91,227.57)	
Total equity		(149,560.63)
Total Liability and Equity		71,689.27

---

*Note: *A/R stockholders* is uncollectable but has to be shown, bringing the *net loss* to $102,398.03.

Figure 13.1   All About Town, Inc.'s balance sheet.

THE SECOND GREAT BUSINESS LIE:
EVERY FINANCIAL REPORT THAT IS CREATED
BY A SMALL COMPANY (ESPECIALLY IF IT'S FOR SALE)

I have always loved to read financial statements of small companies. I find them entertaining, even comical. This one was perhaps my most favorite of all. From my experience, they are all lies. If the company is planning to sell itself, the financial statements are designed to make the company look great. If they are presenting themselves to the Internal Revenue Service, the statements will look awful. The trick is to figure out which way they are lying.

Al assured me that the statement was prepared by an outside accountant who told him it was "absolutely accurate." (Sure, Al, whatever that means.)

While my guess would be that this statement made the company look better than it really was, it was hard to imagine the real condition being any worse than what was written down. They were overdrawn at their bank, and their negative net worth was more than twice their total assets.

I asked Al about the A/R stockholders asset ($11,170.46). At the same time, I also wondered about the qualifications of the outside accountant who put in a footnote that it "was uncollectible, but has to be shown." It seems that when Al got his loan from Harold Jacobs, he spent almost half of it on a new car for himself. Before he had a chance to purchase insurance, he ran the car into a tree. It was a total loss. Of course, he was not in a position to pay the company back, but the $11,000-plus asset remained on the "absolutely accurate" balance sheet.

MANAGEMENT IS ALWAYS MORE
IMPORTANT THAN CAPITAL

When Al told me how he spent his borrowed start-up capital to buy himself a car, and then I looked at the four employees who were doing nothing, I decided that poor management, not lack of capital, was the underlying problem at All About Town, Inc.

As I left the building to head home, Al told me that he really liked me and would consider selling the whole business to me for only $150,000 since I was such a nice guy. I told him I would get back to him.

"By the way, what's your home phone number?" I remembered to ask.

Later, I confirmed that the largest asset on the balance sheet (accounts receivable—$40,000) was actually worth less than $20,000 and had been pledged for a loan of over $38,000. The value of the inventory was vastly understated, as was the amount owed to Harold Jacobs. As bad as the financial statement was—and it was *really bad*—the real condition of the company was far worse.

IF YOUR FINANCIAL SITUATION IS *REALLY* BAD, TELEPHONES ARE NOT A GOOD IDEA

On my way home, I thought about the $131,143 that Al owed to local suppliers and figured he was probably feeling better now that the phones were cut off.

I had two hours to think before I got back to Harold Jacobs at Vermont Investment Capital. Clearly, there had to be a great business opportunity here someplace, and I had to figure a way to structure a deal that would be a win for everyone involved.

I guessed that I would need about $20,000 to get this business off the ground. I had no interest in buying the stock of the corporation because I would inherit all that debt (and probably a lot more that wasn't recorded). But maybe I could license the concept (and the name, which Al said had been registered—another lie, as it turned out). The only things that I wanted from the company were some of the incomplete games to use as samples, and the page of testimonials from chamber of commerce executives who said that All About Town was a truly wonderful promotional idea for any city.

I stopped in South Royalton on the way home, and made an offer to Harold Jacobs. If he would loan me $20,000 to get a company started, I would repay him the $20,000 plus the $35,000 that All About Town, Inc., owed to him, both loans with interest.

I told him that less than a year before, I had been driving a Rolls-Royce (fully paid for), and that I would surely accumulate some assets again soon. For sure, if he didn't lend me the $20,000, he could kiss the $35,000 loan good-bye. He agreed to my offer. (Desperate men grasp at straws.)

I drove home with dollar signs in my head. I was back in business! If only I could strike a deal with Al Adams. I had set out in the morning to get $5,000 to start a seminar business, and come home with a $20,000 loan for a new business I had never heard of. Isn't life great?

DON'T FRET OVER THE INTEREST RATE—GET THE LOAN

Of course, the interest on my loan was a little steep, but I didn't let that dampen my spirits. I'm not even sure how you calculate interest on a $20,000 loan where you promise to pay back $55,000 plus 10 percent interest on the whole $55,000. I figured that if I paid the loan back within three years, the interest rate would be more than 100 percent per year. That's more than four times what my credit cards were costing me, but I didn't have enough credit left on them to start this, or any, business.

To me, the interest rate is almost meaningless. Getting the capital is absolutely everything. You only pay interest for a little while. If your new business is successful, you pay off the loan and the interest stops. If your business fails, the worst that can happen is that you declare bankruptcy and the interest stops. So don't fret about the interest rate. Get the loan.

Next day, I drove back to New Hampshire and found Al still at his desk, along with the receptionist and the artists. They did not have any games to work on. To this day, I have wondered why they were there, what they were doing, and how they were being paid—if they were being paid.

I told Al that I wouldn't pay him the $150,000 he was asking, but my proposal might work out to be much more than that if I were successful. I offered to pay him 5 percent of my gross receipts, with a minimum of $30,000 a year.

THE THIRD GREAT BUSINESS LIE:
THE EXISTENCE OF A PHANTOM BUYER

He didn't like the offer much, but had about as many alternatives as I did at that point (the Rhode Island buyer had apparently vanished overnight). He asked for some money in advance, say $10,000. Fortunately, I didn't have it, so I couldn't agree. Finally, he begged for $1,000 up front so he could go on his honeymoon in two weeks. I agreed, and we hand-wrote a purchase and sale agreement on the spot. (I got a cash advance on one of my credit cards to pay him the $1,000; the $20,000 Vermont Investment Capital loan didn't come for several weeks.)

ALWAYS PERFORM DUE DILIGENCE BEFORE YOU
BUY A BUSINESS (UNLESS YOU ARE DESPERATE)

Under normal circumstances, when a person buys a business, he or she performs some sort of due diligence. This involves contacting customers, suppliers, employees, or anyone else whom you can find, and asking them what they think about the company and its product.

In my case, I didn't have the luxury of undertaking due diligence. First of all, I was broke, and had found someone willing to stake me. If Harold Jacobs had a few days to think it over, maybe he would change his mind.

Second, we were almost into February, and I had very little time to get games accepted by chambers of commerce, advertising sold, and games manufactured by Thanksgiving so that they would be in the stores for the Christmas selling season. I didn't even have one chamber lined up to cosponsor a game for their city.

If I had, indeed, performed due diligence, I probably wouldn't have bought the business. I would have found out that the biggest asset, the testimonials from the chambers of commerce, were totally bogus. Some were solicited by cash being paid as a bribe. Others were overridden by subsequent letters from the same executives after they had gained experience from working with the company.

Several executives on the list had specifically requested in writing that their testimonials not be published.

Months later, I visited one of the chambers on the testimonial list. I wanted to buy some of their excess games to use as samples for salespeople in several cities. The chamber executive asked if I planned to continue the same testimonial procedure that Al Adams used. "What is that?" I asked.

"Well, whenever another chamber executive calls me, I give a glowing recommendation. I get $50 for the call, and another $50 if he eventually agrees to cosponsor the game for his city."

"What do you really think of the game?" I asked.

"Well, it's a cute idea, but playing it is as boring as hell. No one plays it more than once. And the company rarely if ever does what they promise. Half the chambers Al Adams worked with are suing him."

Fortunately, I didn't know these things in early February when I wrote to every chamber east of the Mississippi, asking if they would like to cosponsor a game of their city. I enclosed the testimonial page with each letter. I also wrote to several other chambers in the West who had earlier contacted Al Adams and expressed interest in All About Town. All together, I got responses from about 60 chambers.

SUBSTITUTE CREATIVITY FOR CAPITAL

I set up my business in a spare room (my good luck—one of my new wife's four children was away at school). I set up my computer on a card table and made my first purchases—some stationery and an 800-telephone number. As soon as my $20,000 loan came in, I paid down my credit cards to lower the interest payments and maintain my credit rating.

My next move was typical of creativity used by entrepreneurs when they have little or no cash. USAir had a promotional special at the time: For 21 days, you could fly to as many cities as you wanted wherever USAir flew. The total cost was only $476. I got out a USAir route map and my list of 60 interested chambers, sticking a pin in each city where they flew. I was able to arrange visits to 17 cities in 21 days.

By the middle of March, I had commitments from 13 chambers, as far west as Colorado Springs and south to Columbus, Georgia. The cities ranged in size from the largest, Cleveland, to the smallest, Rome, Georgia.

When I returned from my whirlwind trip around the country, two urgent telephone messages were waiting for me. The first was from the executive director of the Portland, Maine, Chamber of Commerce. His quotation on the testimonial page had been "We sold 7,000 games in three days, and placed an order for 3,000 more." What I didn't know was that he had sent $6,000 to Al Adams as a deposit on the additional games, and Al never delivered. (Actually, Al Adams had taken the money personally and signed a note to the company for $6,000, which was listed under liabilities on the balance sheet.) Because I now owned the company, the Portland executive was holding me responsible for delivering the missing games. If I didn't, he threatened to tell every chamber executive he could find that I was a fraud.

The second call was from a former salesman for All About Town, Inc. He was owed over $2,000 in back wages and wanted me to pay up. In the course of our conversation, he told me that he owned 20 percent of the stock of All About Town, Inc., received in payment for over $6,000 in wages the company couldn't afford to pay him. He wondered (as a stockholder) how he would benefit from my owning the company.

NEVER SELL AN OPTION UNLESS
YOU GET VALUABLE CONSIDERATION

I had a sudden brainstorm, and asked him if he would be interested in selling his stock. "The company is worse than worthless," he volunteered. "Why would you want to buy my shares?"

"Would you sell them to me for the $2,000 you are owed?" I asked.

"Of course," was the answer. I didn't agree to buy his shares, but now I had at least a verbal option to acquire them for $2,000.

I then called my benefactor, Harold Jacobs, and inquired if he would sell me his 33 percent of the company for $5,000. He said he would. Of course, I didn't have $5,000, so I asked if he would sell me an option instead. The option would last for only a year, and I offered to speed up the repayment of the $35,000 All About Town, Inc., loan. Instead of paying it over seven years as the original agreement called for, I agreed to pay him 5 percent of our gross receipts if this would liquidate the loan faster. He agreed to give me the option on these terms.

ALWAYS BUY AN OPTION
IF THE CONSIDERATION IS MINIMAL

I love to buy options. They usually cost very little, and sometimes can become extremely valuable. (The best thing about buying an option is that you don't have to exercise it unless it's in your own best interest.) In this case, the option really didn't cost me anything because I planned to pay off both loans as fast as possible, hopefully within one year.

I called Al Adams and set up a lunch date at the Holiday Inn in Manchester. I was paying, but this lunch cost him a whole lot more than it did me. On the way down, I stopped at Vermont Investment Capital and had Harold Jacobs sign the option agreement I had typed up.

ALWAYS THROW A DOG A BONE,
EVEN IF YOU DON'T HAVE TO

After we exchanged some pleasantries, I told Al Adams that I would like to renegotiate our arrangement. I did not mention the phone call I had received from the Portland Chamber executive, but in my mind it gave me the justification for what I was about to do to him.

"Instead of paying you 5 percent royalties on all my receipts, I would like to pay you a flat $10,000 for the rights to All About Town. I will give you $1,000 today, and $9,000 on or before Labor Day."

"No thanks," he said, "I think I'll take my chances with the 5 percent royalties and a minimum of $30,000 a year."

I then went on to explain that things had changed. I showed him my option to buy 33 percent of his company for $5,000 from Harold Jacobs. Then, I told him that his former salesman had offered his 20 percent of the company stock for only $2,000. The two options meant that I controlled 53 percent of the company (if I decided to exercise the options); therefore, I got to call all the shots.

"So, I have two choices," I said. "One choice is to pay you $10,000 for the rights to All About Town. The other choice is to spend $7,000 and buy control of the corporation. Then I would elect my own board of directors and appoint new officers. Our first business decision would be to tear up the royalty agreement to you and execute a new one calling for payments of $1 per year. Then we would declare bankruptcy and let the whole corporation dissolve. In this scenario, you would not get one cent."

Al Adams squirmed, squealed, steamed, and stammered, but before he finished dessert, he signed the purchase and sale agreement I had brought along. He left the restaurant with a $1,000 check. (I had hit my credit card again.)

I clearly had Al Adams at a disadvantage and could have offered him even less than I did. In cases like this, I think it is best to offer more than you could get away with so the other guy doesn't feel absolutely exploited. Al was at least able to walk away with $1,000 in his pocket.

As luck sometimes has it, Al never got the other $9,000. The federal government came after him for unpaid payroll taxes (also missing from the "totally accurate" balance sheet prepared by the honest accountant), and put a lien on me. When the money came due, I had to pay the entire $9,000 to the Internal Revenue Service on Al's behalf. In the end, he received a total of $2,000 for his company, exactly 1 percent of the $200,000 he first tossed out as the asking price.

ELIMINATE POTENTIAL COMPETITION
BEFORE YOU START

Driving home from New Hampshire on the same highway where years earlier I had come up with my brilliant idea to write a book about rental stores, I had another brainstorm. I had learned that several chambers of commerce had sent copies of the All About Town game to a company in California called Windsor Publications with the suggestion that Windsor publish a similar game.

Windsor Publications would have been a formidable competitor. They spent almost a million dollars a year entertaining chamber executives at trade shows throughout the country. They had 80 full-time salespeople who specialized in selling advertising for chamber of commerce publications. In fact, they had published a glossy brochure of Rutland, Vermont, 12 years earlier when I was president of that chamber. I knew the company to be of the highest integrity. If they decided to do an All About Town game, I would be toast.

So, I called the president of Windsor Publications. "I just bought the rights to this game," I told him, "but it's a product that your company should be selling instead of me. Why don't you buy the rights from me?" I even offered a price—5 percent royalties on gross receipts, just what I had first offered to Al Adams.

He said that he would like to see how I did with the game before they got involved. I then offered to open my books to him, and send him a monthly report for the first year, telling him how I was doing. As consideration for this information, all he had to do was to agree not to go into competition with me in the game business. In short, I sold him an option, even though we didn't specify a price. I outlined an agreement in a letter, which he signed and returned.

I was delighted. I had eliminated the most likely serious competition I might have, and possibly found a buyer for my business before I even sold a single game.

MATCH SALESPEOPLE TO THE SELLING TASK

Now that I had settled the score with Al Adams and eliminated some potential competition, I could return to the task of creating a sales force to sell advertising, and games in 13 cities scattered across the country. Where could I find and train good people who would be willing to work for just a few months and then be laid off?

I decided to hire MBA students as a summer job between their two years of schooling. I offered $500 a week base salary plus commission, which was an excellent rate compared with most summer positions. I wanted hungry kids who needed money and who would work hard by themselves. I didn't want students who could accept an internship paying little but yielding more management experience.

I interviewed at Dartmouth's Tuck School because it was only one and a half hours away, and at the University of Virginia's Darden School where I often visited because my three sons still lived in Charlottesville. I hired two students from each school and hoped that each one could do all the selling in three or four cities during their summer break. In two cases, I hired students because they had a free place to stay in the cities where I needed them to work. Creativity substituting for capital once again.

As we prepared for the big selling push, I had the most confidence in a Darden guy who was handsome, articulate, and personable. He had been a successful IBM salesman for six years. I gave him our biggest city, Cleveland. I had the least confidence in a Darden woman who had never sold a thing (she had worked in a bank). However, her family was from Lancaster, Pennsylvania, one of our cities slated for a game, and she could do York, Pennsylvania, at the same time. I was mostly impressed by her enthusiasm. She asked if she could sell in Charlottesville as well, between classes. This offer reminded me of me, and I liked her even more.

I wrote up a sales manual, and created order forms and selling aids (mostly testimonials from dozens of merchants who had participated in All About Town and sold their allotment of games in short order). I spent one full day with each salesperson in the field and made sales calls with them. In almost every case, I made a sale on the first visit to a prospect. I think I was a good model. That single day, however, was the entire training program. After that, they were totally on their own. When I look back, I think it was a miracle that we sold anything.

Things started off with a bang in Cleveland. My former IBM guy made a big splash in the city. He appeared on local television twice and was wined and dined by many of the most significant executives in Cleveland. Everyone loved him.

He was a flash in the pan, however. Halfway through the summer, his mother offered to send him on a Colorado rafting trip for his birthday, and he accepted. He had not sold one single contract. He spent half a summer building wonderful relationships but apparently never asked for the order.

On the other hand, my lady in Pennsylvania was an absolute dynamo. She got married in July, hired her husband to work for her, and offered to finish up Cleveland for me. She earned over $30,000 in commissions and salary during the summer. I don't know where she is now, but I hope she's running her own business instead of wasting her wonderful energy working for some big anonymous corporation. She saved my life that summer, and I shall always be grateful to her.

I should have realized that the nature of our selling task was a one-call close. Each sale was small, and hundreds of sales needed to be made in a few short months. There was no time to create a personal relationship with the merchant; the order form needed to be filled out and signed at the first meeting.

EVERYTHING HAS A COST—FIXED OR VARIABLE

The economics of manufacturing games is typical of most printing businesses: high fixed costs and low variable costs. The first game might cost $6,000 to produce due to the one-time costs of creating the board and box cover, setting up the advertising, and other customized game materials. I considered the first game to be a fixed cost. The second game cost only $3, a variable cost. It is important to totally understand which costs are fixed and which are variable in any business.

We set 2,000 games as the minimum number we would manufacture. This was our break-even level. At this minimum level, our total manufacturing costs would be $12,000—the setup fee of $6,000, plus 2,000 games costing $3 each. We would sell these 2,000 games for $6 each and collect $12,000. We would have to depend on advertising revenue to make a profit.

In theory, our cities would range in profitability from $4,000 (2,000 games sold and 20 participating merchants) to $26,000 (8,000 games sold and 50 participating merchants).

LIVING ROOMS MAKE FOR LOUSY PRODUCTION FLOORS

Once the salespeople were trained, my energies shifted to manufacturing the games. At first, all of our work was done in the living room. Three artists came each day, bringing their paintbrushes and cigarettes. Even though we didn't allow smoking in the house, the rules soon became no smoking in the house while the owners are around. At least, that's what we concluded as the entire house smelled of cigarette smoke when the artists left each night.

One day, we came home to find drawings in process hanging up on every wall of our living room, affixed by common pins or scotch tape. Starting a business in your home keeps fixed costs low, but it sometimes results in exorbitant psychic costs.

If my five-month-old marriage was to be saved, we would have to find somewhere else to design and manufacture the games. I couldn't find anything to rent within 10 miles of our house, at least in my absolute minimum price range.

SOMETIMES, IT PAYS TO BE IGNORANT

There was an old abandoned building not 300 yards from our house. It was about the size and shape of a two-room schoolhouse and had served as the meeting hall for the local farmers' grange, a long-dissolved organization in this town.

Clearly, the grange hall had not been used for years. It featured a three-hole attached outhouse. I never could understand why outhouses were built with two or three holes. In the old days, was this a community activity? Some things will always be a mystery to me.

It was no mystery that I really wanted that building. It was close by and surely cheap. I stopped by an old farmer's house, got some names of former grange members, and a dozen calls later found someone 100 miles away who was in charge of selling no-longer-used grange halls. Twenty thousand dollars would take it, he said.

Fortunately for me, my salespeople were taking deposits on games throughout the country, and I had real cash in the bank. I also found a banker who was amused by my game venture and thought $20,000 was a cheap price for any commercial building. He loaned me $15,000 and I had my manufacturing facility, complete with thousands of dead bugs, dozens of dead rats, and three holes.

On the day we moved the artists to our new home at the former grange, I was visited by John Hart, the next-door neighbor, who owned the only gas station in town.

"What are you doing here?" he asked incredulously.

"I bought the grange hall to make games," I replied.

"You can't buy this building," he said with a great deal of emotion, "I have been trying to buy this building for 15 years. It isn't for sale."

"Well, lucky for me, I'm new in town and I didn't know it wasn't for sale," I explained. I would rather be lucky than smart any day.

The story has a happy ending for both of us. When my game-making days were over less than a year later, I sold him the building for $25,000. I made a nice profit, and John got his building.

A GOOD ENTREPRENEUR OFTEN MAKES A LOUSY MANAGER

Now that I had a building, I had to figure out how to manufacture the games. Ideally, especially in the first year while you try to figure out if you really have a viable business, it's best to farm out as much as you can to other companies. This serves to make all costs variable instead of fixed. Let your suppliers incur the fixed costs, even though it might be cheaper to make it yourself in the long run. If you discover that you have a successful business, then you can bring all the activities in-house. That's the long run, however, and starting a new business is, first of all, a short-run survival test.

I was able to find an outside color separator, four-color printer, box maker, and game board laminator (these latter two in Connecticut).

I decided to perform the one-color printing and game assembly in the former grange hall, rather than farming it out. We needed to print the cardboard parts (Travel cards, property-like cards, and Shopping Lists) on a letterpress rather than an offset press (so they could be perforated). There was only one letterpress available in the area—a man working out of his garage—and he couldn't promise the fast turnaround time that we needed. Letterpress is sort of an obsolete printing process, but I was able to find a retired operator who agreed to work part-time on our project.

ALWAYS MEASURE THE DOOR OPENING BEFORE ORDERING A LARGE PIECE OF EQUIPMENT

I went to Boston and bought most of the equipment of a printer who had recently gone bankrupt—including a letterpress, offset press, platemaker, and paper cutter. Everything arrived in Vermont on a big truck on a Sunday.

Unfortunately, the letterpress was 6 inches wider than our front door. I called a nearby farmer who had a chainsaw, and I decided that the old grange really needed a loading dock anyway.

We had just succeeded in cutting a large hole in the side of the building, when the local building inspector screeched to a stop in front of our building and leaped out of his car. "Do you have a building permit for this construction?" he bellowed.

I told him that I had never even given it a thought, because we were not changing the footprint of the building (that came later when we added the loading dock).

"There'll be a $200-a-day fine until you get the permit," he admonished and drove off in a huff.

Because it took 60 days to secure a building permit, I felt certain that All About Town would most likely not make a profit the first year. We had to move forward, though. We started by moving the 2-ton letterpress through the newly chainsawed hole in the wall. It took four men, several round logs, a winch, and a tractor to do the job. We all had a beer afterward and toasted the building inspector.

I figured that we would have to assemble the games ourselves because we needed to make about 50,000 games, each with hundreds of unique parts, and our entire production season would have to be squeezed into a period of about six weeks just before Thanksgiving. What outside company could tool up for such a project and then shut down?

I also wanted to prove to myself that I could be a good manager after all. I had already demonstrated that I was a good entrepreneur—I had started a dozen businesses, always with no outside (or inside, usually) capital. Now would be my chance to finally prove that I could manage a workforce as well.

USE EXTREME CREATIVITY TO FIND WORKERS, AND EXPERIENCE EXTREME RESULTS

Where would I find lots of workers (unskilled would be fine) full-time for only six weeks in a rural town with virtually no unemployment? I lucked out by finding a wonderful man named Tom Hart (John's brother), who ran the Life Program, a place for teenagers who couldn't handle the traditional high school experience. If they weren't in the Life Program, they would probably be unemployed dropouts, perhaps committing crimes and abusing drugs or alcohol. For over 20 years, Tom had made good citizens out of troubled kids, teaching them social and practical skills that would enable them to get and keep jobs after graduation. Tom loved the idea of having his kids assemble the games as a class project. And I even agreed to pay them!

When we started assembly production in full, we needed to expand to a second and a third shift. The most readily available source of labor turned out to be the parents of the Life Program kids. In addition, a man from the State of Vermont Alcohol Rehabilitation program stopped by and offered several recent graduates (they were willing to work for little money, and we got a small subsidy from the state as well).

HIRING ALCOHOLICS TO SAVE MONEY CAN BE EXPENSIVE

In total, when we started assembling the games, we had three shifts of virtual misfits, all trying to get the right pieces in the right boxes. Most of the time, they were successful. Some of the time, they were almost successful. The coupons for merchants in Little-ton, Colorado, were put in the Colorado Springs game boxes ("What the heck," they said, "it was all Colorado.") This slight error resulted in my paying the Littleton Chamber of Commerce a refund of $5,000. At least they accepted the games. I felt blessed by their generosity.

Once, near the end of our production crunch, I left a camera fully loaded with film in the grange. Someone took pictures during the third shift. After Christmas, when I had the film developed, I real-ized that some of the alcoholics weren't fully rehabilitated. Empty liquor bottles were everywhere, and several workers had passed out on the floor. In business school, I remembered reading that third shifts were notorious for low productivity, but I think we set some sort of record at All About Town.

SOMETIMES, HAVING A LARGE FAMILY IS A GOOD IDEA

For the four-day Thanksgiving vacation, my entire family (my three sons plus my new wife and her four children, plus a foreign friend who unwittingly came home from prep school with my stepson) assembled All About Town games. We took a short break for dinner on Thanksgiving Day.

I was thankful that the honeymoon was still on, and for once I was thankful for all those kids—and they were trying to be good. (A year later, they wouldn't have moved from the couch in front of the tele-vision set.)

At one point, we were madly assembling games when I realized that at the front of the two assembly lines were two 7-year-old kids—my youngest son, Jared, and a neighborhood urchin affec-tionately called Mud. They were in charge of putting two dice in each game box and making sure the right box went into the right assembly line. I never thought about the child labor law implica-tions, but I did resolve never to try to manage production workers again. It was my final acknowledgment that I would never make it as a production manager—significant revelation in the middle of mad-ness on Thanksgiving Day.

By the week after Thanksgiving, all of the games had been shipped to the 13 cities across the country. Now came the most difficult part: collecting the balance of the advertising money and payment for the games. A full 10 percent of the retail merchants we had signed on during the summer had gone out of business by the time we delivered the games in the fall.

My experience with selling All About Town games was a microcosm of most entrepreneurial efforts: lots of lows, lots of highs, and not much in between. Our worst experiences occurred in Cleveland and Westchester County, New York—our two largest metropolitan areas. In Cleveland, our fair-haired IBM salesperson who never made a sale also failed to learn that a similar game had been proposed in Cleveland two years earlier. Advertising deposits had been taken from many retail merchants, and the game company had absconded with the money without producing a game. That event created some wary, hard-to-sell, potential participants. (I have long believed that some of Al Adams' former salespeople were behind the scam.)

In the end, we sold fewer than 500 games in Cleveland, and we lost more than $25,000. So much for our theoretical minimum profit of $4,000 per city.

In many respects, our experience in Westchester County was even worse. We created games in White Plains and New Rochelle. When it became apparent that only a small number of retail merchants were signing up for the game, I approached the two chambers and suggested that we create a game for the entire county instead.

The New Rochelle executive refused. I offered to give all advertising deposits back in his city and not produce the game because we couldn't come close to breaking even. He got angry, and said he would sue us and complain to every chamber of commerce in the country if we didn't produce a game as we had promised.

When the Portland, Maine, Chamber of Commerce executive threatened to sue us for the $6,000 that Al Adams had stolen from him, I was able to convince him that I had not bought the company but only licensed the idea. The New Rochelle threat was a different story, as this was indeed my company. I couldn't afford the publicity or cost of a lawsuit and agreed to finish the game.

Because we only made 1,000 games in New Rochelle, our loss was under $10,000. This was the cost of learning that our contract with the New Rochelle Chamber of Commerce should have stated that we would produce a game only if at least 20 of their members signed up. This would help us only in subsequent years, and as luck would have it, there were no subsequent years for us.

Our experience in White Plains was even more painful. Even though we had a minimum number of participating merchants, we had sold Macy's, and surely we would sell many thousands of games at Macy's. We manufactured 5,000 games, 3,000 of which were slated to be sold at Macy's, even though they agreed to pay only $5 per game rather than the $6 everyone else paid. Of course, we had to provide the games on consignment.

When our truck carrying 3,000 games arrived at Macy's, they refused to take the games. Instead, I got a call from the buyer, who said:

- They would take only 100 games for inventory at first. We would have to find a local warehouse in which to store the games, and deliver them on two hours' notice when they ran out of inventory.
- The games would only be displayed in the stationery department (a dead area at Christmas) and not in the games section (which was crawling with buying customers).
- They would only display the games if we provided a full-time demonstrator (at our expense) to be in the stationery department at all times.

What could I do but agree to her terms? After all, there had to be some costs associated with dealing with such a prestigious institution as Macy's.

I calculated that our demonstrator would have to sell three games every hour just to cover her costs (through a temp agency) of $12 an hour. To cover our total costs, she would have to sell 24 games per hour.

As it worked out, she sold less than one game each hour, and we let her go after two weeks. At the end of the Christmas selling season, we received a certified letter from Macy's stating that they were charging us rent for our remaining inventory in their warehouse until we picked it up.

Macy's never paid us one cent for all our efforts. I have never walked into a Macy's store since then.

On the other hand, things were a bit different in small towns like Lancaster, Pennsylvania (over 50 participating merchants, 9,000 games sold in a single week—we made over $40,000 profit), Charlottesville, Colorado Springs, Rome (Georgia), and Ithaca (New York). There was almost an inverse relationship between a city or town's population and the number of games we sold. We sold four times as many games in Rome, Georgia, than we sold in Cleveland, for example.

What I learned—and the first year in business is primarily one big learning experience—was that the game worked best in medium-sized or smaller cities where there was a lot of community pride. I felt confident that I could do 10 times better in my second year, but as I said, there was not to be a second year for me.

SOMETIMES YOU CAN, INDEED, FIGHT CITY HALL

I did experience some high points along with the disappointments. One was facing the board of selectmen concerning the lack of a building permit for cutting the hole in the wall of the old grange hall. A full 120 days had transpired since my transgression, and I faced a potential $24,000 fine, far more than I had made making the games.

The town hall was packed the night of the hearing, not because of my case, but because someone was proposing to build a topless bar in our small town. Fortunately, I was first. The building inspector, seemingly as irate as the day he discovered us making the hole in the side of our building, demanded that I pay the entire $24,000 fine that the law provided.

After his statement, one of the selectmen (a woman, she was still called a *selectman*) asked, almost innocently, "Aren't you the person who has hired all the Life Program kids? And anyone else in the area who is willing to work? What is the starting wage rate you offer for these unskilled assembly jobs?"

Of course, she knew the answers to all these questions. Her son worked for us every day after school, and on weekends, and earned more money than he could at any other job in the area.

After hearing testimony from several other townspeople, all of it favorable to my project, the selectmen excused themselves to consider my fate. They returned to render their verdict—a $5.00 fine. The chief selectman winked at me as he announced the news. The audience applauded, and the building inspector stormed out of the building.

Windsor Publications contacted me early in January. I had sent them regular monthly reports as promised. They saw that while I lost money in many of the cities, I also made a nice profit in others. They believed that by getting a stronger commitment from the chamber of commerce before starting a game in that city, they would make a profit in every city they worked.

Windsor offered me $10,000 up front and 5 percent of their revenues for 10 years, with a minimum of $50,000 each year. Once they had made $300,000, they could discontinue making the games and give me back the rights to All About Town. I accepted their offer.

I never really made money running the business of All About Town (I *was* able to pay off my loans to Harold Jacobs and all my credit cards). The only real money I made was selling the business, eventually collecting $350,000 over the next three years. So my daydream had come true. I had arrived penniless in a strange town and made over $100,000 in a single year.

THE BEST PLACE FOR YOUR CREDIT CARDS IS IN YOUR OWN POCKET

In the middle of January, I received invoices from two of my credit card companies. I was puzzled to see the balances owed nearing my credit limit even though I had paid off the entire balance in December. It seems that I had bought an expensive guitar, bifocals, and an airline ticket to Las Vegas, plus taken out cash advances on almost a daily basis. Because none of these activities were anything that I remembered, I called the banks and reported my credit cards as stolen.

Two hours later, I received a call from one of the banks: "Is this Terry Allen?"

I answered, "Yes."

"Are you in our Shelburne Road branch right now making a cash advance?" the caller asked.

"No," I said, "I'm at home where you called me."

"Oh, then we have a problem. We'll send the police."

The culprit was one of my employees. This man had made a trip every day in a rented truck to pick up game boards and boxes in Connecticut, and get them back in time for our second shift to start assembling. I had given him two of my credit cards to buy gas on the way. In all the confusion around Christmas, I forgot to get them back.

The judge sentenced him to a week in jail, plus restitution, plus probation. At least I would get my money back, I figured. But crooks are smarter than honest people. He violated probation, spent six months in jail, and was legally absolved from paying me back. Some things, like our legal system and three-holed outhouses, will always be a mystery to me.

Once Windsor Publications had paid me the $350,000, they decided not to continue any longer. Competitors had come along and offered an inexpensive Monopoly-like game of local cities. Although this game was of far inferior quality, the merchants felt that they had already been on a game board, and All About Town proved difficult to sell.

I now own the rights to All About Town. Will I start it up again? I don't think so. I'm with Beverly Sills, who wears a necklace with the letters *IADT* (I Already Did That). Every day, I'm looking for some new business to start. Some are irresistible. If you want to check up on my newest venture, log on to my website at **www.terrystips.com.**

WHAT I LEARNED

■ *Starting your own business can result in some truly staggering profits.* I started All About Town with cash advances from two credit cards and an unsecured loan (with a 100-plus percent interest rate). In less than a year, I made a $350,000 profit.

- *Having your own business will inevitably result in your experiencing both the ecstasy of victory and the agony of defeat.*

- *The business world is crawling with snakes.* Be wary. Everyone is not as honest as you. If you discover that someone has not been absolutely honest with you, be totally skeptical about everything that person says to you.

- *Large retail department stores are the most ruthless and difficult to deal with of any business organizations.* You may think that you need them to succeed, but don't count on it being easy. They will haggle over everything, squeeze you in every way possible, and if they ever pay you at all, it will be very late. In addition, they will take a cash discount even if you didn't offer one or they are not entitled to it. You may feel a sense of pride in having your product for sale at one of these prestigious retailers, but you will pay a steep price for the privilege.

Chapter 14

Information Industry
Déjà Vu

How to Survive Bankruptcy and Prosper the Second Time Around

Sometimes, the most insignificant events end up resulting in major life changes. One of these events happened to me in the spring of 1983 while I was in Boston doing research for my dissertation. I had an appointment with a food broker to discuss that industry. The insignificant event was that the food broker's wife's car broke down, and she had called to ask him to come pick her up. When I arrived at his office for our appointment, he was out on his errand of mercy.

I now had two hours of free time on my hands with no planned activities. I sat in my car and thought about what I might do. My thoughts turned to my old company, Auto-Data Systems (renamed Colonial Publications by the new owner). I wondered if they were still in business. Last I knew, they were on the brink of bankruptcy. I called their number in Natick and asked if Suzanne Miller, my former office manager, still worked there. She did, and "would love to have lunch" with me.

At lunch, Suzanne reported that the real estate business had turned around, and the company was doing very well financially. The quality of their service, however, had deteriorated significantly.

Their monthly reports were going out two months late, and although their customers were complaining, they didn't cancel their service, because they couldn't get the information anywhere else.

Suzanne was upset about how she was being treated. She told me that the owners had brought in a young friend of the family's and named him president. They gave him a company car and paid him triple her salary. She was still running the company while he went out and played golf every afternoon. They wouldn't give her the small resources she needed to improve the service. Suzanne was ready to quit.

PAY ATTENTION TO WHAT YOU SAY WITHOUT THINKING

I told her that they had not paid me as they had promised, and I had no love for them, either. "Maybe we ought to start a company and go into competition with them," I said without even thinking about it.

"I'll give them a month's notice," she said, and our new company was born.

We named the company County Comps. In the real estate industry, *comps* are comparable real estate sales, which are used to help determine the asking price for a new listing. We expected that our only product would be a comp reference service—a monthly listing of all real estate sales, sorted by street within each town, with quarterly cumulative directories.

HAVING YOUR COMPETITOR'S ENTIRE CUSTOMER LIST IS A GOOD THING

Suzanne and I understood this business much better than the new president of Colonial Publications. We knew exactly what the customers wanted and how to deliver it. Best of all, we knew all their customers' names. (Having your competitor's list of customers is a major advantage for any company, and it is worth most any legal effort to secure.)

No sooner had we opened up for business, when Colonial sued us, saying that Suzanne had stolen their customer list. Actually, she hadn't. Having worked with these customers for more than 10 years, however, she had a pretty complete list of them in her head. They couldn't sue us for what she had in her head, and she had never signed a noncompete agreement. In court, she went through a Yellow Pages listing of real estate brokers and correctly identified Colonial's subscribers from memory. The court threw out their claim.

I started County Comps with the sum total of $13,000, which I had just received as a quarterly royalty payment from my sale of All About Town. I didn't even have incorporation expenses. The All About Town, Inc., corporation shell still existed, and I simply changed the name to County Comps, Inc., for a $25 fee.

Our largest expenditure, $7,000, was for an IBM XT personal computer with an external 10-megabyte disk drive. I calculated that this would be sufficient computer capacity for our company for at least five years. Today, many personal computers come with 2,000 or more times this much memory, but in July of 1983, we thought we were on top of the computer world. (Just a few years earlier, we were renting a far less powerful IBM computer for $3,000 every month.) The rate of technological change in the computer industry is absolutely miraculous.

DON'T JUDGE AN OFFICE BY ITS SMELL

We rented a small three-room office over a beauty salon in Framingham, Massachusetts, furnishing it with used office furniture. There were two employees in addition to Suzanne and me—a data entry woman and a salesman. All were heavy smokers, except for me. Our little office reeked with smoke every day except Thursday when it smelled even worse—that was the day the beauty salon downstairs did all their perms.

I was living at that time in Peterborough, New Hampshire, still working on my dissertation, and teaching marketing full time at Northeastern University in Boston. All of my classes fell on two days, so I had five days left to do my part in building our fledgling business. Most nights I would pack a blanket and pillow, work until midnight at the "Blue Cloud" (the name I had for our office because of the smoke), and sleep on the floor until 6 A.M. The wall-to-wall carpeting made for a soft covering to a very firm bed. I never minded sleeping on the floor, but the smoky atmosphere was dreadful. Usually, I had a tennis match at 7 A.M. at a nearby health club, where I could shave and shower before the workday began.

BE EVER VIGILANT FOR CUSTOMER LISTS OF ALL KINDS

My first job was to arrange for getting the real estate sales data from the county registries. I visited each one in person. In Norfolk County, I was directed to a back office, where the woman in charge of the daily transactions lists had her office. To get there, I passed through the copying machine room. I noticed a list of company names tacked to a wall. Returning the next day at 12:30 (when everyone else was out to lunch), I copied down all of the names. I had correctly guessed that these were the companies receiving the list of deeds. It was almost as valuable as having my competitor's customer list.

One of the companies listed on the wall was Home Data in New York. I soon learned that Home Data purchased lists from every county in Massachusetts, keypunched the names, and sold them, along with new homeowner names from many other states. Because we were also entering these same names into our computer, I was able to sell Home Data every name we had for slightly less than their data entry cost. It was a great deal for both of us. They no longer had to buy lists from the courthouses, and I had almost my entire data entry cost covered.

A second name on the wall was Marketing Concepts of Sharon, Massachusetts. This company had been formed when two of my former Merchants Welcome Service franchisees joined forces. They were still a little angry with me because, after I sold Auto-Data Systems, the new owners had dropped their support of the welcome service. However, when I agreed to substantially lower their data acquisition costs (and also promised not to compete in the new homeowner welcome business), they became major customers.

Thanks to my noticing the list of names on the Norfolk County copy room wall, I now had an absolutely free list of every real estate transaction in the state of Massachusetts. (In fact, I actually made a profit on every name I collected.) Every time I sold this same data to the real estate industry, I only needed to cover the variable costs of printing and mailing the information.

We got very aggressive with marketing County Comps. We charged one-half the prices charged by Colonial Publications (our only competitor) and guaranteed that our list would arrive sooner than theirs. At first, we were a full two months more current. Eventually, they speeded up their delivery, but never got better than being one month behind our list. Even at our low prices, our average variable cost of delivering the data was only 15 percent of the subscription price.

Every month, we sent a free list of our data for one town to every customer of Colonial's who had ordered at least a full county from them. We invited these customers to compare the accuracy and timing of our list, and asked them to subscribe to our service at one-half of what they were currently paying. If they sent us a copy of their invoice from the competitor showing what towns and counties they subscribed to, we offered our faster service absolutely free until their subscription with Colonial expired. Many agencies took us up on this offer.

PAY ATTENTION TO YOUR BIGGEST FEARS

My biggest fear at this time was that the information we were selling might no longer be public. Consumers were clamoring for more privacy, and what could be more sensitive than the price they had paid for their home?

Once, I had been waiting in line to buy a ticket for a play in London, and started a conversation with a nice British couple. I told them that my business was selling a list of what people paid for their homes. "No wonder you're wearing dark glasses," the gentleman said. This information is not public in Great Britain.

A related fear was that I could not get access to the information in a timely manner. The older the data, the less valuable they were for real estate sales comparables. Middlesex County, the largest county in Massachusetts, got two months behind with their daily list. My customers started to complain, although they understood that no one else had a more current list.

I decided to bite the bullet and hired a full-time person to go to the registry and copy down all of the real estate transactions. My costs went from $80 a month to $1,000, but I now had more current information than anyone. Once again, I offered a daily list to fuel oil companies and soon recouped my extra costs. (Eight years earlier, we had used the U.S. Post Office to deliver our daily list. Now, fax machines were widespread, and we could fax the data for less money and have them arrive a day earlier.)

TURN CRISIS EVENTS INTO WINDFALL GAINS

Then, the Middlesex Registry threw us a real curveball. My full-time employee was getting in their way, and they wanted her out of there. Instead, they offered to publish a current list every day (actually, it was not a list, but a Xerox copy of every deed and mortgage). The price—a cool $2,000 a month! Paying it would have put us out of business.

I went to the Registry and asked for the names of all of the companies who were subscribing to their old daily list for $80 a month. Surely, these companies were a little angry that the price had soared to $2,000, even if it was more current. I told the registrar that I would offer these companies a daily list for far less than $2,000, and it would be far more current than what they had been receiving from him.

He gave me his list of subscribers, relieved that they would not be descending on him for jacking up the price. Once again, I owned someone's customer list. I offered a daily list to the Registry's former subscribers for $120 a month, and most of them agreed to buy this list from us.

In the end, only Banker & Tradesmen and our company bought the daily copies of the deeds and mortgages for $2,000 a month, but we resold the information for over $2,500 a month to the county's former subscribers. We were able to maintain our advantage of having a zero cost of data, and we now had current information. The $2,000 monthly nightmare news had turned into a major victory for us.

IF YOU HAVE A BETTER PRODUCT AND CHARGE ONLY HALF AS MUCH, YOU STILL WON'T GET ALL OF THE BUSINESS

After a year in business, we had taken over about 40 percent of Colonial's business. Actually, I was disappointed that it wasn't more. There is a lot more inertia in business than most people think.

At this time, Bill Bornheimer, co-owner of Marketing Concepts, approached me with the idea of buying out his partner and merging our businesses. By luck, I had just inherited (a loan of) $30,000—not from a rich uncle, but from a friend whose father had died, leaving her the money. She asked me to invest it for her, and she said that she would be happy with 12 percent interest. I agreed to pay the interest.

ALWAYS SIGN A PRENUPTIAL AGREEMENT

Bill and I set up our joint venture with each of us owning 50 percent. We made an agreement that I call the "cookie-cutter" arrangement. Remember when there was only one cookie for two kids? One kid would cut the cookie in half, and the other kid would pick the half that he or she wanted (usually the larger piece, but maybe the one with the most chocolate chips). The point is that the kid who cut the cookie learned to cut it as evenly as he or she could. Even so, it was always an advantage to be the chooser rather than the cutter.

In our case, if either Bill or I became disenchanted with our partnership, that person could set down a price for his half of the business. The other partner then had two weeks to decide whether he would be the buyer or the seller at that price. There would be absolutely no negotiation, unless the second person suggested a second price. But then, the first person would have the right to choose being the buyer or the seller at the new price.

This arrangement is absolutely the fairest way to dissolve a partnership. It is essential to set up something like this for anyone who is in a partnership or equal ownership venture *at the beginning* (when everything looks rosy and the partners are sure they will love and respect each other forever).

I can think of only one caveat for the cookie-cutter arrangement. It must be reasonably possible for either person to be the buyer. It wouldn't be fair if one partner is much richer and set a $500,000 price tag on the business, knowing that the poorer partner couldn't come up with that much money. A price can't be set that would preclude the partner with fewer resources from being the buyer. In these cases, a price that is payable over several years, perhaps out of profits, would be an acceptable proposal. It would then be possible for either partner to be the buyer.

After signing a cookie-cutter arrangement, Bill and I merged County Comps and Marketing Concepts into a new company, which we called County Home Data. The combined companies had a positive cash flow, even after making monthly payments to Bill's former partner to buy out his interest. A major benefit to me was that I was taking out a salary for the first time. Since I now had an equal partner who was taking a salary, it was only fair that I should take out an identical salary.

There were a few other benefits to the merged company. Most important was the common database. County Comps was compiling real estate sales information and selling it to any willing buyer (including some competitors of Marketing Concepts). We quickly doubled or tripled the price we were charging these competitors. Two of them eventually decided to sell their companies to us at an attractive price rather than paying the exorbitant fees we were asking for our data.

CPAS, LIKE ENTREPRENEURS, ARE OFTEN LOUSY MANAGERS

Bill's wife, Carol, was a CPA and, in addition to handling our accounting needs, became the general manager of the merged companies. We also decided to move both companies to a building that she owned in Cambridge Square. My employees (there were now 10) rebelled. They did not like their new boss (or Bill), nor did they want to commute from Framingham to Cambridge. They all gave two weeks' notice.

I hate personnel problems. They were bad enough when I owned the entire company, but now they felt even worse since I owned only half the company. Worse yet, I believed that my partner (and his wife) were the cause of most of the problems. I had just completed my doctoral program and had several offers of full-time tenured teaching positions. Owning half of County Home Data was no longer fun for me. I resorted to the cookie-cutter arrangement and set a price of $200,000 for my share of the business, payable over five years. That would give me a good return on my $13,000 investment of a year earlier.

IF THE PARTNERSHIP ISN'T WORKING, COMMUNICATE YOUR FEELINGS QUICKLY AND CLEARLY

Bill and Carol asked me to sit down and discuss my concerns. I said that Carol was the biggest problem and the move to Cambridge was second. Carol was delighted. She didn't like being manager, either, and wanted to return to her CPA business. She could also get more rent for her building from someone else. I agreed to continue on in Framingham with a new general manager. My employees were happy to stay on board.

The honeymoon lasted only a few months. Even though we found a new general manager, an MBA who was doing a good job, Bill often verbally abused him and the workers. His favorite expression was, "It's not brain surgery," while he castigated them for some minor typographical error that they had made.

Most important, I had decided to move back to Vermont and start a new life. Because all of our customers were in Massachusetts, it would be silly to move the operation to Vermont. And I certainly did not want to commute to Massachusetts, even on a part-time basis.

YOU CAN NEVER PREDICT WHAT OTHERS MIGHT DO

Fortunately, the cookie-cutter arrangement offered me a clean way out. All I would have to do was set an even lower price for the business, so low that Bill would buy me out. A few months earlier, he had passed up on the opportunity to buy or sell the business for $200,000. I put out a new price of $150,000 over five years, feeling certain that at this price he would surely buy me out. After all, if he were indifferent to a $200,000 price (he hadn't been able to decide whether to buy or sell at that price), he would surely be the buyer at $150,000.

Two weeks later, Bill said he would be the seller. So much for my business instincts. He said that I was capable of running the business, but he wasn't. I was stuck. I had already signed a year's lease on a condo in Vermont, and now I owned a business that only had customers in Massachusetts. I would have to move the business to Vermont, even though such a move made no sense at all.

I also felt that I had a problem with my newly hired general manager. I had lured him away from a nice job, and he had done a great job for me. He had a wife and two small children and did not share my love for Vermont. I decided to offer him a $10,000 severance bonus, an amount that would severely deplete our cash position, but which I felt was a necessary settlement offer.

TIMING IS EVERYTHING

The evening before I planned to drive to Framingham and tell everyone about the move to Vermont (and offer each person his or her severance bonus), I got a call from my manager. "Are you sitting down?" he asked. I told him I wasn't sitting, but I could handle his news. "I'm quitting," he said, "I'm sorry, but I found an opportunity too great to pass up."

I was soon not only not sitting, but I was jumping up and down with joy. That phone call may very well have been the difference between our success and failure in the next year. With an extra $10,000 gone, I doubt if we could have survived.

In December 1986, I moved the Massachusetts business I didn't expect to own (nor did I especially want to) to the basement of an old Victorian house in Shelburne, Vermont. I hired only three employees to replace eight who had worked in Framingham, and I hired two people to do data entry in their homes in Lowell, Massachusetts. Each Thursday, they would overnight a computer disk with a week's data for us to process and mail out on Friday or Saturday.

For the first two years, just keeping our operation going was a major challenge. The accounting data that I had from Marketing Concepts were a disaster. It took us a full year to figure out who our customers were, how much they had paid, and how much they owed. Oftentimes, we had to take their word for it if they told us that they had paid a salesperson cash for a full year's worth of service.

I suspended all new sales activities for the welcome program until we got the mess straightened out and only made a few mailings to sell County Comps.

KNOW WHEN IT'S TIME TO MOVE OUT OF THE BASEMENT

Late in 1986, I sold 70 acres of land in southern Vermont, which I had bought for $365 down 23 years earlier. The net proceeds were $28,000, and all but $10,000 went toward paying our overdue payroll taxes, penalties, and interest. I used the rest as a down payment on a small, single-level prefab house that was two blocks away. The employees, now five in number, felt depressed working in the basement.

Although the company was now out of the basement, I was not—figuratively or literally. I set my new office up in the basement of the house so that my employees could have the first floor offices with windows. (I have always believed that real entrepreneurs do not care in the least about fancy office trappings.)

BEWARE OF PYRRHIC VICTORIES

Our aggressive sales and pricing of County Comps finally paid off—Colonial Publications gave up. The bad news was that they gave what was left of their business to Banker & Tradesmen, the 105-year-old company with 7,200 subscribers to their weekly real estate data publication. Soon, four full-page advertisements were appearing in every edition promoting their new comps service, which competed directly with ours.

While I was proud that we had put my old company out of business, I was scared to death that Banker & Tradesmen would soon gobble me up, especially now that we had moved to Vermont. They were closer to their customers in all respects, and they already had a relationship with them with their popular weekly publication.

WHEN YOU EXPECT TO LOSE EVERYTHING, TRY TO SELL IT FIRST

I called Tim Warren, president and grandson of the founder, and asked to meet with him in Boston. I offered to sell him my County Comps business with no money down. At the time, we had about 1,000 customers, and our annual revenue was about $300,000. I offered to turn over all my accounts for 40 percent of the cash that came in on these accounts for five years. Because the fulfillment cost was only 20 percent (by his calculation), he would be making a 40 percent profit on all of the sales from the very beginning. Furthermore, he could raise the prices to the customers substantially because without me, there would be no competition. In Connecticut, where he had no competition, he was charging more than double what he was charging for an identical service in Massachusetts.

"Why should I buy your accounts when I'm just going to take them away from you anyway?" he responded. "I believe that after 105 years in the business, our family sort of has a divine right to all the real estate data business in Massachusetts. Sooner or later, we will have it all."

I returned to Vermont, wondering how long it would take for him to take away my business. If he had accepted my offer and been able to retain my customers, I would have earned $600,000 over five years, four times the value that I had put on the business a few months earlier. But it was not to be, at least for now.

BUSINESS AXIOM NUMBER ONE:
CASH IN MUST EXCEED CASH OUT

Cash flow was a major problem, ranging from really bad to nearly hopeless. We did not make our payroll withholding payments to the government, accruing penalties and interest every quarter. I did not have a credit line at the bank. There was no money for me to take a salary (I was driving three hours each way to teach two days a week at New Hampshire College to keep food on the table). To make matters worse, the stock market crashed in 1987, and my leveraged option position on the CBOE caused me over $60,000 in losses. I declared personal bankruptcy. My only creditors were the CBOE clearinghouse and a few credit cards, but they were threatening to attach my teaching salary, and I felt that I had no choice. The bankruptcy court allowed me to keep County Home Data because it was worthless—it had a negative net worth and had never shown a profit.

FEAR OF LOSING BUSINESS THAT YOU ALREADY
HAVE IS A WONDERFUL MOTIVATOR

I was determined to move forward, particularly with County Comps. To postpone the day when Banker & Tradesmen took over all of our business, we had to offer a better service. We did the following:

■ *Kept our prices less than theirs.*
■ *Guaranteed faster delivery of the data.* We printed, collated, and mailed our subscriptions on the last weekend of each month. B&T farmed the work out to others, and it took a minimum of two weeks to get out.
■ *Offered better statistical information.* For more than two years, B&T published the mean average selling price in each town, a meaningless average in the real estate industry, whereas we published a median average—I wrote the median program myself. (The *mean average* is the total sales prices added up and divided by number of sales. For example, if there was a city with nine houses that sold for $100,000 each and

one mansion that sold for $2,100,000, the mean average price would be $300,000. The *median average* is the price in the exact middle range of prices, in this case $100,000, which would be a far better indicator of the average house sale price in this town.)

■ *Offered extended payment terms.* Real estate agencies often have irregular cash flows. B&T would suspend their customers' service if they didn't renew, whereas we would continue serving them until the agency made its next big sale.

■ *Offered a free 800-number.* Most calls to B&T were toll calls. Even though we were in another state, it was cheaper for customers to call us than to call B&T.

■ *Provided higher-quality data.* In all cities with a population of more than 10,000, we purchased a copy of the city assessor's property records so that, in addition to reporting a real estate sale, we could also include assessed value, the architectural style, number of bedrooms and baths, lot size, and so forth.

■ *Delivered more than we promised.* We gave away several thousand three-ring binders (with our 800-number prominently displayed on the spine) and divider tabs for each city, two features that our competitor did not offer.

■ *Maintained close contact with customers.* I wrote a personal note of thanks to each new subscriber, and we conducted a customer satisfaction survey every year in which we asked how we could improve the service. We also sent greeting cards to subscribers on Christmas, Halloween, and other holidays.

In short, we did not give potential customers a single reason to buy our competitor's service rather than ours. We gave them *eight* reasons why our service was better. We were ruthless in upholding our superior standards.

Our efforts paid off. We enjoyed a 90 percent renewal rate, which was extraordinary because each year nearly 10 percent of real estate agencies either went out of business or merged with another agency. For each of the next five years, our customer base increased by an average of 25 percent.

USE CASH FROM ONE SERVICE TO EXPAND A MORE PROMISING SERVICE

We put all of our marketing efforts into expansion of the data products, rather than the welcome program. The number of welcome program customers declined each year, but the service still provided us with a nice cash flow to underwrite geographic expansion of the real estate data service. I chose to focus on the real estate data service because of the considerably higher renewal rates, and because we could sell the service by direct mail rather than with straight-commission salespeople (who had burned me so badly earlier in my career).

When cash flow allowed it, we expanded our coverage to include four new states (New Hampshire, Rhode Island, Vermont, and New Jersey). In each state, we duplicated our insistence on highest quality and lowest prices, and generally won most of the business from the competition (if it existed).

We also dramatically increased the number of services that we offered, using the real estate sales data we already had stored in our computer. Five of these new products included:

1. *Bank market share report.* We reported each bank's share of all of the mortgages written in each city or county.
2. *Expires report.* Because a homeowner's insurance policy was up for renewal exactly one year from the date of the house purchase, we published a list of soon-to-expire homeowners' policies for insurance agents.
3. *Delivering data on disk or magnetic tape rather than on paper.* Two of our largest customers were the IRS and the tax department of the Commonwealth of Massachusetts, both situated within a block of our competitor in Boston. (We absolutely loved these sales, not only for the revenue we earned, but because they were proof that we were outfoxing B&T.)
4. *Lists of high-net-worth individuals.* We knew the sales price and mortgage amount of every home sale, so we could calculate how much equity a family had in their home.

5. *Special reports.* Mortgage companies bought names of people who had borrowed from finance companies or other high-interest institutions, or who had taken out a mortgage at a time when interest rates were unusually high. Governmental agencies used our data to determine whether banks were red-lining (not making mortgages in lower-income areas). Divorce lawyers used our data to find out if certain people had purchased real estate anywhere in the state for the past several years.

DON'T VALUE A SEMINAR BY HOW MUCH IT COSTS

In 1989, the U.S. Post Office offered a seminar on direct mail. The cost was $10, well within my budget. Halfway through the day, I had a really significant revelation: I was in the direct-mail business! Somehow, before this seminar, this thought had never really occurred to me.

Now, I embraced the idea with a vengeance and vowed to become an expert in the field. I read everything that I could get my hands on and ran test mailings every single month. I agreed to give a lecture on business-to-business direct marketing at a national convention because I believed that having to teach something is the fastest way to learn it. Teachers always teach best what they learned last. When I agreed to give the lecture, I hadn't even learned it yet, but *now* I had an even greater incentive to become an expert. (At the end of Chapter 15, I have included a list of ideas that will tell you 90 percent of everything that you will need to know about direct mail. Of course, it will take you a lifetime to learn the other 10 percent.)

SEARCH FOR PROFITABLE SEGMENTS

Each year, we made several mailings to every real estate agency in all five states where we offered County Comps. We felt lucky if we sold to 1 out of 200 of the recipients of our mailing. One segment of the list always yielded double-digit response rates, however. This segment was the new agencies who had never received mail from us before. I wondered where we could find a list of newly established real estate agencies. No one I knew of offered such a list.

Our solution was to keep close track of when new telephone directories came out. As soon as a new one was published, we compared the Yellow Pages listings with last year's directory, and we compiled a list of new agencies. This list, although it was small, was a goldmine for us.

Imagine my relief when I discovered a company in Framingham, Massachusetts (our former city), called The Lead Sheet, which published a monthly list of every new company formed in seven states (including four of the five states that we covered.) I called the president and said I was interested in buying his names.

That phone call was the first in a series of developments that changed the nature of our company dramatically—so much so that we changed our name from County Home Data to County Data Corporation. Although this may seem like a minor change, it reflected a significant shift in our focus: out with *home* and in with *data*. A paradigm shift had begun.

WHAT I LEARNED

- *It is possible to win out over a better-positioned competitor.* Focus all of your energies on providing a higher-quality product or service, and you will ultimately succeed. (Just like in sports, the winning team usually wants to win the most.)
- *Timing is everything.* Of course, you can't usually influence timing. Sometimes, the most insignificant event becomes overwhelmingly meaningful because of timing. Even though it's always best to be in the right place at the right time, there is no way that I know of to know just where and when it will be.
- *There is life after personal bankruptcy.* With a positive attitude, bankruptcy can be a new start rather than a bad ending.
- *Cash in must exceed cash out.* No matter how good the profit and loss statement might look, positive cash flow is the ultimate goal for any new business.

Chapter 15

Selling New Business Names

How to Use a Cash Cow to Finance Your New Business

Ninety Percent of Everything You Will Ever Need to Know about Selling by Direct Mail

W hen I called the president of The Lead Sheet in 1990, I offered him $10 for every newly established real estate agency he could find. "We don't sell our names that way," he said. "You have to buy the whole list and search through it for the real estate agencies."

I offered to try his service in Massachusetts for three months for one-quarter of his $2,400 annual subscription price. That way, I could find out how many useful names I could find, and I would know better whether I wanted to sign up for a full year. He refused. "The only way you will see our list is to pay $2,400 up front for a year's subscription. Or go to our competition." Wow, he was tough, I thought. We both knew there was no competition—yet.

After that, every month or so, the president of The Lead Sheet called me and tried to sell his service, but never relented on his demand for $2,400 up front. During one of these calls, I said to him, "You know, we have similar business challenges—I have to send someone into the county clerk's office to collect recently filed deed information much like you send someone to the secretary of state's office to get data from new incorporation papers."

Then, he made a statement that would yield me millions of dollars in a very short period of time. Millions! Really! And I can't to this day understand why he said it.

"Oh no, I don't have to send someone into the secretary of state's office any longer—they send us all the filings on microfilm."

Microfilm? Really! I soon headed for Boston and returned with my first reel of microfilm—with every new corporation filing papers in the last month. Now, I could test the list for the state's monthly charge of $40 rather than The Lead Sheet's $2,400.

At this point, my stepson, Brian O'Connell, who had been general manager of County Home Data, came to me and said that he really wanted to start a business of his own. His idea was to go into competition with The Lead Sheet, selling a list of new incorporations. He planned to keypunch the entire Massachusetts microfilm. I would be his first customer, buying the new real estate agency names for $10 a pop.

I totally understood his need to scratch his entrepreneurial itch and encouraged him to do it. I offered him use of our laser printers and copiers at night so that he would not have to buy them until the business got up and running.

Brian set up Data-Biz in his condo to keep overhead low. His understanding wife, Kathy, did all of the data entry at nights and on weekends while she held down a full-time job as a high-level executive at the largest bank in Vermont. Brian made sales calls all day.

Three months later, Brian asked for his old job back. The new business was becoming a real strain on his marriage, and he really didn't like selling on the telephone. Because I hated being a general manager as much as he hated selling, I welcomed him back. I offered to pay for the computer he had bought to set up Data-Biz. I also agreed to fulfill the 20 or so subscriptions for new incorporation names he had sold. At some point, maybe we could figure out how to sell that service by direct mail, I thought.

A month later, we made our first mailing to prospects in Massachusetts. I got one significant call from the mailing: from the president of The Lead Sheet. "So, you're in competition with us?" he asked. I told him that if I ever could choose a competitor, it would be him. He made it so difficult to buy his service that anything I did would look good to the customers out there.

Two weeks later, he called me and offered to sell his business to me. He had about 150 subscribers in seven states who paid a total of about $300,000 a year. We negotiated a price of $10,000 down, payments to him of 25 percent of all the cash collected from these 150 accounts for a period of three years, and we would fulfill the subscriptions that he had sold with money paid up front (these added up to about $75,000).

I paid the $10,000 to buy The Lead Sheet with cash advances from three credit cards.

In most businesses, the newest product or service gets most of the attention. Our The Lead Sheet business was no exception. I fell in love with this business. From previous experience, I knew that falling in love with a product or service is a dangerous thing, but perhaps such a level of passion is necessary to make a real success of it.

When we took over The Lead Sheet, no one offered a national list of new business names. The closest thing to such a service was American Business Information's (ABI's) list, compiled from the Yellow Pages. However, the most current of these new businesses had been formed 10 months earlier, and the least current had been formed 22 months earlier. We could deliver a new business name within a week or two of its filing organization papers, often before the doors were open for business.

To expand our list from 7 states to 50 in a short period of time, which was my goal, would take lots of money—more than we had, of course. Some of the new business names, corporations, were fairly easy and inexpensive to compile, because they were filed at the secretary of state's office in each state. Most states made this list available on paper, microfilm, or magnetic tape—for a fee, of course. Except for the five or six states that did not sell a list of new incorporations, we could purchase a large number of new business names from a single source in each state without visiting the state in person.

New corporations made up about 40 percent of all new businesses. The other 60 percent were unincorporated sole proprietors or partnerships that were called by several names: *trade names, doing-business-as (DBAs), or fictitious names.* In almost all cases, these businesses filed papers at the county level, and almost no counties sold a list of these filings. In other words, if we were to compile a complete list of new business formations, we would have to hire part-time collectors in every populous county in all 50 states. This would be very expensive.

Where would I get the money to finance this expansion? I did not want to raise money from outside investors, both because I did not want to share the profits and because I was afraid they might lose all their money. I was still scarred from my Auto-Data Systems days when my outside investors lost everything. I was not willing to risk this happening again. (I understand that this is a personal and slightly weird preference of mine—I think it's totally appropriate for other entrepreneurs to seek outside capital to help get started or expand.)

We were not eligible for bank loans. We had hardly any accounts receivable because most of our subscribers paid in advance. In fact, we had built our entire company using these payments in advance as start-up capital. While we enjoyed the cash, they were listed as a liability on our balance sheet (until we delivered the service). Banks only loan on assets, and we didn't have much in that department. Even our computers were leased.

What we really needed to finance our expansion was a cash cow, and lo and behold, we found one right inside our little company. A cash cow is a product or service with two characteristics: (1) slow growth and (2) you already dominate the market segment (i.e., you sell more of the product or service than any other company).

Our County Comps service met these tests: Over half of the real estate agencies in Massachusetts, Vermont, New Hampshire, and Rhode Island subscribed to our service, and the industry was actually declining as more agencies merged with others, and few new independent agencies were created.

To milk a cash cow, you have to make a conscious choice not to try to grow the business. In other words, you completely eliminate all marketing expenditures for the cash cow product. It's a common business principle that an easy way to increase short-term profits is to eliminate advertising. It almost always works. The benefits of advertising are only achieved over the long run. In the short run, advertising loses money.

We made the decision to cut back (almost eliminate) marketing expenses for County Comps, learn to live with flat or declining sales, and use the cash we generated to invest in making The Lead Sheet a national company.

POOR JOB MARKETS PRODUCE THE BEST EMPLOYEES

In the same year that I bought The Lead Sheet, a poor job market for recent liberal arts graduates encouraged all three of my sons to (reluctantly) join the company. My oldest son, Seth, came first, giving up his job repairing bicycles at a local sporting goods store. Seth was blessed (if that's what it can be called) with my selling skills. Even more important, he could focus all day on just selling, and he soon became our top salesman. Five years later, we had over 15 salespeople, and he was still the top producer.

Andrew, my second son, had been captain of the Williams College football team (which had won 26 straight games—a national record—while he was there). Only, he couldn't get a job on graduation. It could have been the best thing that ever happened to my business. Between job interviews, Andrew agreed to join a construction crew that was remodeling our building for the anticipated expansion. His job was to sandblast white paint off all of the old wooden beams in the 100-year-old building. It was the grimiest of all work— black sand invaded every pore of his skin and hair. Even though he never complained, I sensed that it would be a good time to offer him alternative work.

"How would you like to come to work for County Data?" I asked.
"What would I do?"
"How would you like to start as president?"

Unbeknownst to him, Brian had left for a second time to scratch his entrepreneurial itch in another arena, and I desperately needed someone to run the company. I sure couldn't do it. Andrew soon became the manager that I never was. We became a professional, highly effective company. Of course, Andrew did not do it all by himself, but he did help build an unbelievably high-quality crew of productive and loyal people. I will always be grateful to him, and them, for the job they did.

My third son, Jared, was a sophomore at the University of Vermont, living with me in my condo. I knew he was working for County Data on a part-time basis because I often saw him in the shipping department downstairs from my office. Each morning, we would have breakfast together, and he would leave for school while I headed for the office.

DON'T ASK A QUESTION IF YOU DON'T WANT TO HEAR THE ANSWER

Every year, I had been asked to speak to a class or two at the University of Vermont about entrepreneurship or direct marketing. This year, in front of a large lecture hall full of students, I started off by telling them that my oldest son had enjoyed UVM so much that he took five or six years to finish. "And maybe some of you know my youngest son, Jared," I said.

"Yes," one of the students said, "He used to be in my history class."

"What do you mean 'used to be'?" I responded. As soon as I blurted out this question, I had a funny feeling that I didn't want to hear the answer.

"Oh, he dropped out of school," he said hesitatingly.

For once in my life, I couldn't think of anything to say.

That evening, I asked Jared if there was something he needed to tell me about school. Sensing that I knew, he confessed. He said he had been saving up his money to repay me the tuition before he told me. Right!

"Where do you go when you leave in the morning?" I asked. His response shocked me a bit. Seems that he had been working about 60 hours a week for County Data for a couple of months. He was earning so much in overtime pay that Andrew had put him on salary to save the company money. So much for aware and observant fathers.

CREATIVE ALTERNATIVES ALMOST ALWAYS SAVE MONEY

In the information business, it is critical to minimize the cost of getting the data from their raw form, wherever it might be, and into your computer so that they can be sold. For us, trade names presented the greatest challenge because they were recorded in the 3,117 counties throughout the country. This might mean that we would need 3,117 part-time data collectors—an administrative and hiring nightmare and a recurring large expense.

We were lucky not to have a large pile of cash sitting in the bank. If we had, we might have taken the easy route of placing ads for part-time collectors and paying $1 per trade name (a fair price to pay for someone's time to travel to the county courthouse once a week and send us a list of trade names filed). Because we had only a small amount of free cash, we had to be more creative.

(I think our situation was analogous to the millions of dollars thrown at dot.com start-ups recently. In many cases, because they suddenly had all of this money, they spent it quickly and unwisely in an attempt to be the first ones in their particular market. Soon, many dot.coms were out of money, and still a long way from profitability. They were forced to either give away more equity for more cash, or cease being—by closing down or selling out to another company.)

Our first step in setting up our trade name data acquisition was to subscribe to a national newspaper clipping service. For $1.25 per clipping, this company sent us every listing of trade names printed in local publications throughout the country. Sometimes, the clipping would have just 3 names (costing us about 41 cents each), but others might have 30 names, reducing our cost to about 4 cents each. Either alternative was a whole lot better, and cheaper, than the hassles of hiring, training, supervising, paying, and ultimately replacing a part-time person in that county.

We did not intend to use the clipping service for long. Our real goal was to identify the local publications that printed trade names. We then subscribed to each publication directly. Most of them were weekly or monthly business publications costing about 50 cents per issue. We consulted *Editor and Publisher* and directly contacted every business publication to determine if they had lists of newly filed trade names.

In counties where there wasn't a local publisher of trade names, we contacted the county itself and asked if there might be someone working there who could earn some extra money during their lunch hour by copying down trade names and mailing them to us. We only had to pay 50 cents per name because no travel was required, and we found dependable workers at many counties.

Massachusetts and Rhode Island presented special problems (and coincident opportunities) because trade names were filed at each city or town instead of at the county. In these states, we paid our collectors $1 per trade name, plus travel costs. Although our ultimate cost was extremely high—$1.75 per name—we were the only company to have these names, and we were able to collect a premium price for them.

In many areas, we encountered potential competitors who collected trade names and sold them, much as The Lead Sheet did in seven states. At first, we would make an arrangement with these companies whereby we would buy their names and agree not to compete with them in their local area. Because we were primarily interested in compiling a national list, it was not much of a sacrifice for us to forgo selling the names in a few isolated areas.

INVENT CREATIVE WAYS TO GET YOUR COMPETITOR'S CUSTOMER LIST

Eventually, when we succeeded in covering the whole country, we terminated these arrangements and gave notice that we intended to compete with them. Our strategy was to contact a newly formed company and offer the owners $5 for a copy of every piece of mail addressed to them that they received in their first 60 days in business. The senders of this mail had either bought the new business name from our local competitor, or secured the name directly from the county. We have already established how important it is to have your competitor's complete list of customers. In our business, it was this easy to obtain for $5 per customer.

Once we had the name of every company that was soliciting business from newly formed companies, we went after them with a vengeance. Our prices were usually less than half of what our local competitor charged. We were in the enviable position of not having to make a profit in any local market. Most of our money came from national accounts that bought our names for the entire country. The local competition eventually melted away. Many of them sold their remaining accounts to us.

There were unique opportunities and challenges to collecting new business name data in Pennsylvania. The state had passed a law that every piece of data in the public domain could be purchased for 25 cents per record. Once a month, we received a printed list of every corporation and every trade name that was filed in the entire state. It was a fantastically cheap and complete list—for as little as $1,200 paid in advance, we got about 5,000 names each month.

However, Pennsylvania's policy scared me. If every state offered data on this basis, we would be out of business. Anyone could easily compile a national list simply and inexpensively. The value of our list depended on its difficulty of being replicated. Our rag-tag collection of local publishers, courthouse employees, and part-time retirees was our most important asset because it represented the greatest barrier to entry. (One of the greatest challenges of making money on the Internet is this curious feature of information: If it's easily attainable, it's essentially worthless as a business asset.)

One night, I was thinking about the possible threat to my business that Pennsylvania posed, and I had a brainstorm idea. If all data were for sale for 25 cents per record, what about the list of companies who were purchasing the new business formations from the state? That list should also be for sale. I headed for Pennsylvania (actually, I was headed there anyway, courting Debbie Mahoney). I was told that no one had asked for that particular list. "But it is a list," I replied.

I walked out of the Pennsylvania state office building with yet another competitor's complete customer list. This one had 42 names and cost me $10.50. (Even though we ultimately earned several hundred thousand dollars from the names on that list, I will always believe that my most important coup that day was convincing Debbie Mahoney to leave horse country and to move to the sticks of Vermont to be with me.)

One of the names on the list was New England Business Services (NEBS), a publicly traded company selling discount office supplies by mail. I visited them in Groton, Massachusetts. My pitch was that they were paying 25 cents per record and then another 10 cents or so to enter the data from each record. For only 12 cents, or about one-third of their current cost, I would send them a magnetic tape each month. They would save lots of money and not have the hassle of dealing with data entry personnel and paying Pennsylvania in advance each month. While we were at it, we could include similar data for the other 30 states that we were covering at this time.

For a time, this was our biggest sale. NEBS paid us over $3,000 every month—not a bad return on a 25-cent investment (the cost of buying this name from the Commonwealth of Pennsylvania). We eventually sold to many other companies on Pennsylvania's list, using the same pitch.

One company on Pennsylvania's customer list was American Express. Although we had suspected that this company might be interested in our names, we could never find the right person to contact. Now we knew, and American Express eventually became one of our largest customers, several times larger for us than NEBS.

DON'T PAY FOR CALLS TO DIRECTORY ASSISTANCE

As challenging as trade name collecting was, telephone numbers for each new company presented even bigger obstacles (many of our customers wanted a telephone number). Because none of the new companies were listed in any telephone directories, we had to call directory assistance, and this involved a cost of 60 cents, or more than the average cost of the new company name. Clearly, we couldn't afford to pay this fee unless there were no alternatives.

As in most business situations, there are almost always alternatives. Our first choice was pay phones. In almost all states, calls to directory assistance from a pay phone were free. Of course, this was only true for local calls. We would need to hire someone in every area code to make calls to directory assistance from pay phones. And telephone companies were adding on new area codes almost every week.

Our solution was unique. We mailed an offer to every laundromat in the area where we needed phone numbers. Most laundromats have pay phones, as well as customers waiting around for their wash to be finished. We would pay the laundromat owner 25 cents for every phone number that his patrons would get for us from directory assistance. He would offer patrons free washing and drying in exchange for their telephone work while they were waiting. Everyone came out a winner, especially us. We saved 60 cents for every call made at a laundromat.

A savings of 60 cents may not seem like much, but at one time, we were making 120,000 calls to directory assistance each month. That works out to a savings of $72,000 a month—real money, indeed!

The laundromat callers were replaced when we discovered by accident that American Telephone & Telegraph (AT&T), at least in Florida, did not charge blind people for calls to directory assistance. Presumably, these folks could not look the number up in the telephone directory. We found a large group of people who had this exemption from AT&T. Although they were legally blind, they could read large printed letters by holding the pages close to their faces. We wrote a program that printed 2-inch-high letters on a computer screen for them, and they entered the telephone numbers directly into the computer.

For several months, we had a great thing going. More than a dozen legally blind people in Florida earned over $12 per hour working from their home. Everyone was happy, except AT&T when they found out that some blind people were making thousands of calls to directory assistance each month. They closed down our little arrangement, putting all those nice people out of work.

Fortunately for us, at the same time, the North American Free Trade Agreement (NAFTA) was passed. One of the strange provisions of the new law governing trade relations with Mexico and Canada was that telephone calls to directory assistance from Canada were absolutely free. I never could understand why, nor did I seek an answer. Instead, we hired a large crew of callers in Toronto. Once again, we avoided paying long-distance directory assistance calls.

The Canadian callers worked for about two years, and then the NAFTA loophole was suddenly closed. This time, we went to the Internet to find callers who would use pay phones in their area code. In addition, we bought a list of every new business phone listing, a new service offered by most of the Baby Bell phone companies. This gave us a database of our own to find telephone numbers for the new business names that we had collected.

SEEK OUT SYMBIOTIC PARTNERS

One important way in which we gathered new business names, and often telephone numbers as well, was to establish symbiotic relationships with other companies. One important relationship for us was with Homeowners Marketing Service (HMS), in North Hollywood, California. At first, we traded our new homeowner names in six eastern states for HMS's new business names in California. Because we were providing many more names than we were receiving, HMS also paid us about $4,000 per month. On many occasions, this check was the difference between our meeting payroll or not.

The owner of HMS was Barry Weiner, about the most enthusiastic and persuasive salesman I ever met. He offered a simple service (new homeowner names delivered weekly on self-adhesive labels) for a single price ($132 a month) for a limited area (usually two or three adjoining cities) in 27 states. If a customer wanted telephone numbers as well, he or she got two sets of labels, one imprinted with phone numbers.

At one time, I felt that if I went head-to-head with HMS, I would eventually win because I would totally tailor our service to the customer's needs. If the customer wanted a special selection of towns, zip codes, or houses that sold for more than $300,000 on a printed list on paper instead of labels, I would deliver it. Haggling over the details of the service, however, usually ended in fewer sales being made. Furthermore, in my heart I knew that I, or anyone I could hire, could never outsell Barry Weiner. He would simply convince more prospects that the services that he offered were *exactly* what the prospect wanted—even if they weren't. There is still room in our modern world for good salespeople. They will survive and prosper, even if their product is not the best.

Our most important relationship was with Dun & Bradstreet. On one of my courting calls to Pennsylvania, I convinced them to buy every new company name we had for $1.25 each. They had two requirements: (1) The name could not already be in the Dun & Bradstreet database, and (2) we had to telephone each new business and confirm the president's name and the kind of business that they were in.

This sale was significant because it meant that we could expand our coverage to every state in the country, knowing that the data collection cost would be completely covered by selling the names to Dun & Bradstreet. Furthermore, we now had a list of telephone-verified new business names for which we could charge a premium price when we sold it to other customers. Dun & Bradstreet was soon sending us monthly checks in the $40,000 to $60,000 range, and we quickly expanded our coverage to all 50 states.

SELLING IT IS ALWAYS HARDER THAN MAKING IT

So far, I have focused on how The Lead Sheet, under our ownership, used extreme creativity to compile a national list of new businesses (about 125,000 per month) and secure their telephone numbers and business types as well. An equally important feature of our business was how we sold the names.

My bad experience with outside salespeople, especially those paid by straight commission, caused me to seek a way to sell our names with an inside sales force using the mail and telephone. I adopted a system developed by Barry Weiner at HMS. He mailed out 10,000 postcards to prospects every day. (When Barry first told me this on the telephone, I didn't believe him. I flew to California to confirm it.) Each postcard invited the recipient to call an 800-number. The card read, "This may be the wisest marketing decision you ever make."

Each day, about 100 prospects made a call to HMS (that's only 0.1 percent of the postcard recipients). About 10 percent of the callers eventually purchased HMS's list (for $1,584 a year). The postcards cost about $2,500 per day to send out, and resulted in first-year sales of over $15,000 a day. Not bad for a business where the fulfillment cost is about 15 percent of revenue.

HMS experimented with about five new versions of the postcard each month, each with different wording and appeals. Each different version had a code name that could be either a male or female—such as "Ask for Sandy." The telephone operators would compile a daily calculation of which names were asked for, so Barry always knew which postcards were pulling the most leads. Surprising to me, at least, the most successful postcard said little about marketing, but offered three free lottery tickets if the prospect called in. Believe it or not, these prospects ended up buying the service at the same rate as prospects who called in for information about how they could market their business.

I thought that our target market was too sophisticated for post-cards to be the major prospecting tool. More than half of our customers were accountants. Insurance companies were the second largest segment. Four times a year, we sent postcards to every accountant and insurance agent in the country in card decks containing postcards from 30 or more other companies—at a cost of about 2 cents per card. Each lead generated from card decks wound up costing about $20 at our rate of return.

We got a much higher response by mailing a computer-generated first-class single-page letter to our prospects. The letter said a little about the importance of marketing to new businesses and invited the prospect to return the letter in the enclosed postage-paid envelope for full information about our service. These letters cost us about 50 cents each to mail out, and resulted in a 5 percent return rate. Each lead cost us only $10 using these first-class letters, compared with HMS's cost of $25, or the card deck cost of $20.

Once we got a lead, we mailed the prospect a large packet that included a complete description of the service, an order form, and several pages of testimonials from satisfied users of The Lead Sheet.

EVERY MAILING LIST MUST INCLUDE TESTIMONIALS

Testimonials sell. For the most part, they only cost you the effort to compile them. They are worth pure gold in any mailing campaign.

Even if you don't have a single customer, you can find someone to say something nice about your product, service, or even you. Long before you make your first mailing, be ever vigilant for testimonials.

I kept a drawer in my desk with a large sign saying "Testimonials". It was a reminder to always be on the lookout for quotable material. If a customer ever said something nice about our company on the phone to me, I would say my thanks and instantly ask if I could quote them. They almost always said yes.

Our salespeople were offered a $25 bonus if they gathered a testimonial from one of their customers. I know this money was always well spent.

Once, we made a special mailing to our customers offering a free pint of Vermont maple syrup if they said something nice about us or sent us a referral who bought our service. Dozens of customers responded.

Our next mailing had four pages of testimonials. The mailing weighed an extra ounce because of the testimonial pages, but our response rate was the highest ever.

The maple syrup mailing yielded two other bonuses as well. First, we filled an entire bulletin board full of testimonials. This served to inspire morale at our office, especially for the sales team. Everybody likes to read something nice about the company they work for.

Second, we got enough new customer referrals to more than pay for the mailing and the maple syrup. The entire mailing was a total success: We got dozens of testimonials, happier employees, substantial profits on future mailings, and the entire campaign made a profit as well.

The maple syrup mailing was such a winner that we repeated it often. After a year or so, our customers seemed to have run out of maple syrup, and they sent in lots of new testimonials or new referrals. In one year, we sent out more than 2,000 pints of maple syrup—a sweet program in more ways than one.

WOULD YOU PAY $2,000 FOR A ONE-PAGE LETTER?

We were mailing out about 100,000 one-page letters (mostly to accountants) every year and getting about 5,000 new leads. I calculated that if I could increase our response rate by 2 percent, I could afford to pay someone to write a better one-page letter. A copywriter named Linwood Austin promised to increase our response rate by 10 percent, or we would get our money back.

I sent Linwood the $2,000 that he asked for and endured the smirks of my staff (many of whom offered to write a better letter for me at a cost of only $1,000). Several weeks later, Linwood's letter arrived. It was 12 pages long. The text of the letter was full of emotional appeals and overstatements. To me, it exemplified the worst of the get-rich-quick letters that I had often seen. It was pure schmaltzy hucksterism.

NEVER SAY *NEVER* UNTIL YOU TEST

I didn't feel good about sending out this letter under my signature, but Linwood's guarantee was only valid if we sent out his letter without a single alteration. I reluctantly sent out 500 letters so that I would qualify to get my money back.

We got seven responses—a 1.4 percent response rate, not nearly the 5 percent rate we had experienced with our one-page letter. However, these were *orders,* not just leads. Each respondent agreed to pay us for 10 months of service after a 2-month free trial. We got over $5,000 worth of new business from a $300 mailing.

The most important feature of Linwood's letter was that it changed the nature of how we sold our service. Instead of a two-stage effort (the first stage designed just to get a lead), we switched to a one-stage sales process in which we asked for the order in the first mailing. We also provided enough information for the prospect to make the decision in that mailing.

HOW TO ACHIEVE DIRECT MARKETING NIRVANA

We eventually changed Linwood's letter, toned down most of the hype, and condensed it to five pages. Instead of a free trial, we asked for a $50 deposit to start the service. These initial deposits soon covered the entire cost of the mailings. We had achieved direct-mailing nirvana! If you can send out a mailing, and receive enough cash in a couple of weeks to completely cover the cost of the mailing, you have made it. As long as you can deliver what you sell, you can dramatically increase the number of mailings you make, and maintain the eternal happiness of a positive cash flow. (Remember, the variable cost of fulfilling our service was only 15 percent of what we sold it for.)

A UNIQUE CUSTOM PRODUCT ENSURES
CUSTOMER SATISFACTION

About one-half of our sales came from accountants and the small-business service providers who solicited business from newly formed businesses in a local area. For most of these customers, our computer would select the 200 new businesses that opened each month that were physically closest to our customer's office. If two accountants in the same city (but in different zip codes) subscribed to our service, they would receive different lists of new business names each month.

Ultimately, in order to ensure the long-term success of our program, we had to teach our customers how to sell their services to new businesses. This proved to be a difficult task when it came to accountants (whose selling skills usually did not measure up to their analytic skills). We created an 80-page book, entitled *New Business Survival Guide,* which we printed for the accountant (with his or her name as coauthor) to be given away as a premium for new businesses who responded to the accountant's mailing. We also wrote promotional pieces for our other customers to use. The success of our program depended on the success of our customers, and we took extraordinary steps to help our customers become successful.

In addition to local sales, we enjoyed national sales to such companies as America Online (AOL), AT&T, Viking Office Products, and Reliable, as well as American Express. These companies usually purchased a minimum of 10,000 names for a test mailing, and they often bought our entire list of 125,000 names every month. Karen Ramey was our sole national sales representative (although she received much technological and logistic support from her national sales team). Karen was an exceptionally caring and supportive salesperson. She attended direct-mail trade shows, and maintained telephone contact with over 100 customers or prospects every month. Her sales exceeded $1 million a year and represented the most profitable of all of our business lines. We did not have to teach her customers how to sell—they were real pros, and we often learned from them ourselves.

INVEST IN THE HIGHEST-QUALITY PEOPLE—LESSER-QUALITY PEOPLE ARE ULTIMATELY MORE EXPENSIVE

The success of County Data and The Lead Sheet was ultimately determined by some extremely high-quality and hard-working individuals. Some of them had great skills when they came on board, and others grew along with the company. I had a long-standing disdain for employee manuals and job descriptions, but Andrew figured out how to create them without causing problems. He also installed a comprehensive and regular evaluation system whereby every employee was graded (sometimes anonymously) by superiors, coworkers, and subordinates. I was never much good in this area. Andrew was, and the entire team reveled in his leadership.

Two years after County Data closed down, Andrew was interviewing a programmer for a job at his new company. The interview took place in a restaurant. Two former County Data employees approached Andrew and told him what a pleasure it had been working for him—one said that he was the best boss she ever had. After they left the table, Andrew confessed to the programmer that he had fired both of these women. The programmer accepted the job offer. I think the ultimate test of a good manager is how he or she is regarded by people whom he or she had to fire.

Kandi Thermanson, our one-person personnel department, was largely responsible for hiring the high-quality workforce at County Data. Most of all, she was the ultimate gatekeeper. Only the best ever got on board. Every new hire endured a long interview with Kandi and as many as six interviews with potential supervisors or coworkers. One of Kandi's questions was to give three words that best described you as a person. I'm sure I would never have made it through Kandi's gate.

In any small company, every person is really responsible for customer service, but at County Data, Debbie Stearns added new meaning to the concept. Angry customers would call Debbie and, before the conversation ended, would thank her for her help, increase their order with us, refer a potential new customer, or all three.

We rewarded workers better than most companies—after all, they deserved it. Following are the benefits that everyone received:

- One hundred percent of health insurance premiums
- 401(k) retirement contributions matched dollar-for-dollar up to 10 percent of their salary
- Profit sharing (we opened our books to everyone)
- Christmas bonus equal to $10 for every month of service (many earned over $1,000)
- Unlimited sick days
- Birthdays off
- Monthly off-site lunches and games
- Free turkey at Thanksgiving

In early 1996, we seemed to have everything going for us—a $5-million successful growing company and a great team of over 100 workers. Yet, I was unhappy. The company's success depended more on professional management (well provided by my son Andrew and Roland Palmer, our data collection manager) than it did on entrepreneurial skills. I was not a manager and never would be. I felt obsolete. My skills were not needed at the company any longer.

At our annual Christmas party, I had struck up a conversation with one of our new hires. I asked her what she did at County Data. "I'm in data editing," she answered. "And what do you do?" At that moment, I knew the company had grown too large for me.

I was also tired of being broke. Although the company was doing well, there still was not much of a positive cash flow. We still owed over $80,000 on our line of credit at the bank. I was fearful that our cash cow, the County Comps real estate service, would soon disappear. Our only competitor had invested seriously in their service over the past five years (and copied many of our former advantages). In many areas, they now had a better service than we did. We were losing County Comps customers at a fast pace. I was also fearful that all real estate transactions might soon be available for free on the Internet, making our service worthless. (Indeed, within three years, this fear became a reality.) Perhaps new business names would also be posted on the Internet, rendering our entire company worthless.

I decided that it was time for me to sell. I approached ABI and pointed out that their database of 10 million business names, compiled from the Yellow Pages, was missing another 1.5 million names that I had in my computer. Furthermore, list buyers were more interested in my new business names than they were in established business names (which had already been contacted many times). We negotiated a price of $10 million for my company, payable in ABI stock. This price was twice our annual sales of $5 million. On the public market, ABI was valued at four times their sales, so buying us for $10 million in stock would be an immediate gain to them. Although I would be retiring from active participation in the company, my three sons signed five-year employment contracts and were given assurances that the business would continue in Vermont.

IF IT ISN'T IN WRITING, IT ISN'T

Two important considerations of the sale were that (1) that I could sell my ABI stock in six weeks, as soon as quarterly earnings were announced, and (2) ABI would continue to operate our business in Vermont. Vin Gupta, founder and chairman of ABI, said, "We are Wal-Mart and you are a boutique. We would never do anything to upset the magic that you have. There is no way we would ever move your operation to Omaha. In fact we will sign a five-year lease on your building." I was so sure of both of these assurances that I did not ask for them in writing, which was a mistake.

A month after we closed on our deal, ABI bought Database America, a large private competitor. This purchase was so large that, according to Securities and Exchange Commission (SEC) regulations, I could not sell my stock until the new acquisition was completely integrated. The process took almost an entire year. Meanwhile, I still had not collected a nickel from the sale of my company. That was the bad news.

The good news was that the price of ABI stock increased by nearly 50 percent while I was waiting for the opportunity to legally sell some shares. I guess it was worth the wait.

I owned about 50 percent of County Data when we sold out. The other 50 percent was owned by my three sons, my stepson, and my two former wives (at least they got some payoff for enduring the ups and downs of an entrepreneur's life for 14 years each). Ironically, they both bought waterfront condos in the same building in Burlington.

Following the sale, we struggled with trying to integrate a boutique with Wal-Mart. Andrew took most of the static. ABI's first move was to quadruple the prices that we charged for our services. We could not believe it. Surely, everyone would cancel. But they didn't. It became clear that we had been dramatically underpricing our services. Under ABI, we became quite profitable.

Their second move was to reduce the quality of the new business names by compiling them less speedily and far less expensively. I felt there was a great opportunity for someone to go into competition with ABI in this market. It couldn't be me, or my sons, however, as we had all signed five-year noncompete agreements.

I absolutely hated being an employee of ABI. I negotiated a 50 percent cut in my pay for being a half-time employee. Essentially, I did not have to work at all to continue being paid. On three occasions, I typed up a resignation letter. If I weren't paid my salary, maybe ABI would reduce their pressure on Andrew to increase profits. Each time, Andrew refused to pass on my resignation letter to Omaha.

One and a half years after buying my company, ABI decided to close down the Vermont office and move everything to Omaha. To their credit, ABI offered generous severance packages to our people. One hundred people lost their jobs, though, and the County Data dream team was dissolved.

At the time of this writing, only one year remains on our five-year noncompete contracts. Will history repeat itself?

WHAT I LEARNED

Following is 90 percent of everything you will ever need to know about selling by mail. The other 10 percent will take a lifetime to learn.

- *The list rules.* Perhaps 70 percent of a direct-mailing success is due to the *list,* 20 percent is due to the *offer,* and 10 percent can be attributed to the *copy.*
- *Every list should be segmented for higher returns.* At The Lead Sheet, we spent a lot of time selling to accountants. We created entirely different direct-mail programs (varying frequency of mailings, offers, and copy) to 10 segments of the accountant list, as follows:
  1. Current customers
  2. Former customers
  3. Respondents to our earlier mailings
  4. Accountants who had responded to other companies' direct mail
  5. Accountants who had attended marketing seminars

    6. Accountants who were sole practitioners
    7. Accountants who lived in small towns
    8. Female accountants
    9. Newly established accountants
  10. Accountants who had just completed their CPA exam

■ *A good list should be used over and over.* You may even get a higher response from each successive mailing. Your credibility increases every time you contact your prospect.

■ *Your customer is absolutely your best prospect for additional sales.* Some successful direct mailers send mailings to their customer list up to 20 times a year, and they make additional profits with each mailing.

■ *Test, test, test. When you're finished testing, retest!* Direct mail has the potential to be the most scientific of all marketing programs. Every mailing should be coded so that its response rate and profitability can be calculated. Test a new variable every month. Keep testing, and spend your big bucks on the mailings that tested best.

■ *Sell benefits, not features.* The wonderful features of your product or service may have a rational appeal, but purchase decisions are made on the emotional appeal of benefits.

■ *Never underestimate the importance of the offer.* When a recipient opens your package, he or she has one question on his or her mind: What's in it for me? Answer it clearly and soon. An offer can be anything from a discount to a free trial to a free gift. Test a dozen offers and go with the winner.

■ *Include testimonials.* You should *never* make a mailing that doesn't include testimonials from satisfied customers.

■ *Offer a money-back guarantee.* A few people will take advantage of it, but the increased response rate will easily cover the cost of the guarantee.

■ *Every letter should have a postscript (PS).* It is the most read sentence in a direct-mail piece, except for the first sentence. The PS should repeat the major emotional appeal or offer of the letter.

■ *Don't be afraid to copy.*   Keep constant vigilance on the mailings of other companies in your field. If they continue making a particular kind of mailing, it must be working for them (we're assuming that they measure their results). If it works for them, it will probably work for you.

■ *Keep an open mind.*   Sometimes successful mail companies violate many of the aforementioned proven guidelines. If you think that something different, even bizarre, might work in your industry—give it a try. Tests are cheap if you keep them small.

■ *Read* The Complete Direct Mail List Handbook, *by Ed Burnett.*   This is sort of the bible on direct mail. In case I missed something, you will find it in this book.

Chapter 16

Adventures in Russia: Pizza Stores and Ben & Jerry's Ice Cream Shops

How to Achieve Riches behind the Former Iron Curtain

The city of Burlington, Vermont, had established a sister-city relationship with the city of Yaroslavl, Russia, in the early 1990s. Yaroslavl is an industrial city of 600,000 on the Volga River, about 200 miles north of Moscow. It is a beautiful city with many ancient churches.

The locals believe that Yaroslavl's churches survived Stalin's church demolition program because he selected cities in alphabetical order, and *ya* (in Russian, a backward *r*) is the last letter in the Russian alphabet. *Ya* is also the letter for the pronoun *I*, an appropriate indication of where the individual has stood in Russian society for the last 70 years.

Delegations of businesspeople from Yaroslavl and Burlington exchanged visits in 1991. A Russian businessman, Leonid Mozheiko, who headed a sort of private chamber of commerce in Russia, was treated to a weekend of The Accounting Game while visiting the United States.

Leonid asked the owner if The Accounting Game could be presented in Russia as a way of introducing Western accounting standards to Russian accountants. The Accounting Game owner was eager to comply and offered the cut-rate price of $1,000, plus an additional $1,500 or so for traveling expenses. Leonid replied that his salary was $17 per month, and such a sum was totally out of the question. So, he told Leonid that the original author of The Accounting Game happened to live in Burlington. Maybe Terry Allen would do it for less.

In early 1992, several Burlington doctors were collecting medical supplies to donate to Yaroslavl hospitals. Aeroflot airlines offered a free 200-pound freight allowance for humanitarian medical shipments for every paying passenger from the United States. Because there was just over 1 ton of medical supplies, 11 people were needed to buy their own ticket and visit our sister city. Because I had already been asked to perform The Accounting Game in Yaroslavl, I was a natural choice. I accepted, and my experience of business was profoundly altered forever.

CHURCHILL HAD IT RIGHT: RUSSIA IS A RIDDLE WRAPPED IN A MYSTERY INSIDE AN ENIGMA

While teaching The Accounting Game, I learned more about Russian accounting than they did about Western accounting. I have since spent many hours trying to understand their accounting system with little success. They do have a balance sheet, but one side is called *active* and the other *passive,* and as far as I could tell, assets and liabilities appeared on both sides of the balance sheet. However, it did balance, once you adjusted the to-make-it-balance (TMIB) account.

My Russian students were mostly interested in two things: (1) how Americans avoid taxes, and (2) how to get rich fast without working too hard. I didn't figure I could give them much help on either question up to that point in my life. I had never made enough money for tax avoidance to be an issue, and I had spent an entire lifetime working very hard without getting rich.

I was impressed by the Russians' fascination with the free-market system. At the time, anything bought or sold privately was part of the black-market system and was illegal. The rules were just beginning to change—a year later, everything was being publicly offered for sale on every street corner, including salami, vodka, caviar, shoes, tires, puppies, and even books, and a thousand other things as well, like one giant flea market. Russians embraced capitalism with great glee, a welcome change after 70 years of repression.

My Russian accounting students wanted to know if all entrepreneurs were really crooks. Apparently, that had been the official word from the government. In fact, there did not seem to be a word for *entrepreneur* in the Russian language—they used the word *Mafia* to refer to someone who ran his or her own business.

I suggested to Leonid Mozheiko that we start a business together, and open our books to all of the members of the Yaroslavl Business Centre (his private chamber of commerce organization.) We would show all of these budding Russian entrepreneurs that we could run an honest business, pay all of our taxes, and make a profit as well.

DON'T EVER BELIEVE ANY BUSINESS OPPORTUNITY YOU SEE IN RUSSIA

Leonid was excited about starting a business, and I was ecstatic. I saw unbelievable opportunities everywhere! The only question was where to start. Leonid spoke perfect English, as do about 10 percent of Russians. We became instant friends and fellow entrepreneurs. I felt it was a match made in entrepreneurial heaven.

We decided to start with a pizza store. I figured that pizza was relatively cheap, nutritious, and tasty. It appeared that we could purchase all of the ingredients except spices in the local state-owned grocery stores. There were *no* other pizza stores in this city of 600,000. As a special birthday or anniversary treat, people would take the four-hour train ride from Yaroslavl to Moscow to visit Pizza Hut.

We negotiated with the city to lease a huge (11,000 square feet), fully equipped government cafeteria for our pizza store. This cafeteria had nine industrial ovens, 21 refrigerators or freezers, and a fully equipped bakery. It would have cost over $1 million to reproduce the facilities and equipment. The cost to us was $35 per month on a 25-year lease. I thought I had died and gone to heaven.

We were able to secure this facility without going through the auction procedure that was part of the privatization process because the city was eager to encourage American investment. The inexpensive lease was also considered to be a contribution to the sister-city relationship. [Our site, *Café Raduga* (the Rainbow Café), was the 11th state-owned business to be privatized in Yaroslavl.]

I returned home and rushed out to buy two books on how to make pizza. I found books with lots of pictures in case we ran into a translation problem.

Within a month, I was back in Yaroslavl, the proud owner of Café Raduga and beholden to 50 employees who had a long history of stealing food and avoiding work whenever possible. They were good cooks, however.

Less than an hour after arriving with my cookbooks, the entire crew sat down and enjoyed the outcome of their first attempt at making pizza, complete with some Danish smoked meat, which was a fair substitute for pepperoni. Only one employee had eaten a piece of pizza before our party. They loved it. They talked about cooking and selling thousands of pizzas, and some day every cook would marry a rich American.

MOTIVATION APPEALS AREN'T ALWAYS EXPORTABLE

Understanding that my employees were unaccustomed to Western standards of customer service, I devised two motivation schemes. (When customers came into our store, our workers were inclined to disappear into the back room or the bathroom in order to avoid customer contact.) The first was to show them a large bag of Snickers candy bars (a rare delicacy in 1992) and to explain that these were not really Snickers, but customer service awards. If management caught any employee being nice to a customer in any way, such as smiling at them, or saying, "Thank you for coming," that employee would get a Snickers bar. It was three weeks before we gave away our first award. Some habits are hard to change.

My second incentive program was to set a wage budget equal to 35 percent of our gross profit for the prior month. Inflation was raging to such an extent that we had to give everyone a raise every month just to keep up with rising prices for everything. The 35 percent budget established how much we gave out each month. The extreme inflation actually became our greatest friend. Everyone had to get a raise each month, but we did not give everyone an equal increase. The workers who bought our program (e.g., smiling at a customer) got larger raises than the ones who disappeared to a back room when a customer entered the store. In three months, we lost half of our original workers and replaced them with considerably higher-quality people (mostly young women who were unaccustomed to a lifetime of work avoidance).

My entire investment in the pizza operation was $10,000. Most of the money went to dividing the cafeteria into three distinct retail entities with separate entrances and replacing the public bathrooms. Anyone who has not been to Russia cannot imagine how awful most public bathrooms are. Only the most prestigious places offer yesterday's newspaper for toilet paper. Most have nothing.

Once we had built what I'm sure were the cleanest public bathrooms in the city, we applied for a license to open. The city health department refused permission, citing the conditions of our bathrooms. I thought it was a joke until it became clear that they wanted a bribe. I refused to give them a single ruble. For three weeks, instead of making pizza, we remained closed and completely refurbished the interior of our three stores.

Then, I went to the city administration and showed them how much they were losing in taxes because we were not open for business. We got our license within 24 hours without paying any bribes.

Our small retail store offered women's clothes, vodka, and most anything else we could get on consignment. In the other store, we eventually opened a Ben & Jerry's ice cream scoop shop, which became quite successful once our customers discovered that those pieces of chocolate chips and nuts were not impurities that should be spit out.

I calculated that we needed to sell 70 pizzas a day to break even. We accomplished that within three months, and we were already paying more taxes than the city government had enjoyed in gross sales while it was running the cafeteria in the same location. In three months, we had definitively demonstrated to everyone that free enterprise was more productive than government-run business.

I was learning how business was conducted in Russia. One day, I noticed that our sales were more than triple what they were on a typical day. "What happened?" I asked. The answer was that someone with a truck had arrived from a village in the countryside and negotiated to purchase large quantities of everything we used in our pizza and bakery operations.

"You must have given him quite a discount," I said.

My general manager looked perplexed. "Of course not," he ventured. "When we found out how much he wanted, we raised the prices by 10 percent."

An American acquaintance of mine encountered this same pricing phenomenon when he negotiated a large purchase from a state-owned manufacturer of painted wooden toys. The manager wanted a price that was greater than what was being charged in retail stores. "If you buy this many toys," he explained, "we might not be able to get materials to make more, and we will be out of business."

This scarcity mentality had other implications. My general manager once telephoned me excitedly to report that he had successfully purchased two metric tons of tomato sauce. He was pleased with himself because he didn't have to pay a premium. I was appalled. It cost over $4,000, and I had to send more money. I calculated that it would take seven years for us to use that much tomato sauce at our then-current sales volume. In the end, my manager was right—we sold the sauce by the gallon on the sidewalk in front of our store at a nice profit.

Our fifth month was the most profitable in the three-plus years that I owned Café Raduga. We averaged 200 pizzas a day. When I visited the store, my staff proudly presented me with a large plastic bag of rubles, which represented our profit for the month.

I took the bag to Moscow on my way home with the intention of using the contents to buy shares of GUM, a company that owned a

300-store indoor mall next to Red Square, as well as many other retail stores throughout the city. Most of the space was rented to western companies at higher rates than are paid in New York City.

GUM (pronounced "goom") was making a profit of $1.50 per share, and on the market, shares were quoted at $1.50 bid and $2.50 asked. Stock selling at less than two times earnings is a real bargain by Western standards, but there seemed like quite a large spread between the bid and ask, so I suggested that they sell me shares for $2.40 because I was buying 1,500 shares, rather than the 100 shares that the average purchaser bought. "You don't understand the Russian system," the female broker told me. "If you want to buy more than 2,000 shares, the price goes up to $3.00." I understood the concept, but I didn't understand that it applied to security sales as well.

I almost didn't get the shares at any price. The clerk insisted on counting every ruble in my plastic bag with a little machine that manually flipped through every pile of 100 neatly wrapped rubles. Whenever a folded or worn ruble hit the machine, it jammed. The clerk would neatly restack the pile and try it again—over and over again. On one pass, the machine had counted to 98 and the second-from-last ruble jammed. I pleaded that she could easily add 2 to 98 and get 100, but she refused—only the machine could determine that there were 100 bills in the pile.

The counting process had taken more than an hour before some people behind me in line started to grumble. Fortunately for me, I had been the first person in line, securing my place a half hour before the brokerage firm opened at 9:00 A.M. I was becoming a little concerned at the amount of time that it was taking to count the money because I had to leave by 10:30 in order to catch my flight home. I frantically substituted newer rubles for every folded one that I could locate before passing money to the clerk.

Just before the process was completed, the broker stood up and addressed the line (which now stretched out of the brokerage office into the hall). She announced that no more shares would be exchanged that day and if anyone were interested they should return the next day by 9:00 A.M. The Russians in line just shrugged their shoulders and walked away. Americans would never tolerate such treatment. Lawsuits have been filed for less.

My GUM investment eventually increased by over 20 times. When I sold half my shares, I got back all the money I had lost in my pizza store and other Russian ventures (and eventually, indeed, I had lost every penny that I invested).

IN RUSSIA, SALES CAN BE 700 PERCENT HIGHER THAN BREAK-EVEN AND YOU STILL LOSE MONEY

Nine months after opening, we were selling 500 pizzas a day and losing money. So much for my break-even calculation of 70 pizzas a day. Our best customers were Russians having a birthday or American missionaries yearning for a meal that tasted like home.

We weren't losing money because of my Russian workers. They eventually proved to be diligent, hard-working, and resourceful. When I recommended that we hire additional cooks because we were now making 500 pizzas a day with the same number of cooks who were once making 20 a day, the staff said they did not want to hire new people because they would have to share the 35 percent gross profit budget with the new people. Our cooks were earning triple their old wages (after adjusting for inflation), and they loved that aspect of capitalism.

We were selling 500 pizzas a day and losing money because of the regional government's need for cash. They were not getting any revenue from the money-losing behemoth state-owned enterprises (mostly those formerly making war implements). The only source of revenue was from those few small enterprises, like Café Raduga, which had been privatized. And tax they did!

Eighteen different taxes were eventually levied. In addition, the government owned the electricity and heat. (Utility rates were increased by 600 percent in real-dollar terms in the first year.) This explained the inaccuracy of my break-even projections.

The government required that our pizza store hire four bookkeepers and an accountant to make certain that we were paying all of the taxes that were due. In addition, we had to hire a full-time lawyer to keep abreast of the new regulations and taxes that were levied or increased daily. To add insult to injury, we had to pay for a weekly publication put out by the government in which the new taxes (or increases) were documented.

One tax almost amused me. It was called an *income tax.* I noticed that it was paid by the government cafeteria before we took over, even though they were losing tons of money. The income tax was a throwback from the Communist era. It stated that any wages exceeding the minimum wage (about 6 cents an hour) that were paid to workers were not really a wage payment but a distribution of profits and, therefore, taxable at the rate of 25 percent. Because every worker in Russia earns far more than 6 cents an hour (if they are paid), every company pays an income tax, regardless if it ever makes a single ruble of profit or not.

Protection was a particularly unpleasant form of taxation. Although not publicly sanctioned by the government, the Mafia was so inextricably connected that it was difficult to determine with which group you were dealing. The Russian Mafia does not seem to have any family component; rather, it's a loosely organized bunch of thugs working inside, outside, and with the government.

Café Raduga had a uniformed, armed police officer in the store at all times. He remained visible by the front door to let the world know that we had paid for our protection. We paid the salaries of these officers to a government official. The police officers "earned" a salary that was more than double what I had to pay to my general manager, and I'm certain that they actually received only a small portion of this amount.

Speaking of protection, casualty insurance as we know it in the Western world was not available. One block from Café Raduga, the inside of a children's clothing store was completely destroyed by a hand grenade on three separate occasions in the three years that I owned the pizza store. Each time, the hopeful entrepreneur fixed the store up and tried again.

I knew that we were also sitting on a time bomb. At any time, if someone else decided to open a pizza store in Yaroslavl, we might expect to be bombed (hand grenades were available in Moscow for $5). Bombing your competition is apparently a Russian variant of the free-market system.

I think that a basic tenet of communism was that enterprise should be controlled by government because individuals could not be trusted to pay their taxes. For 70 years, entrepreneurs were considered to be criminals. When the Russians decided to try the free-market alternative, they privatized over half of their state-owned businesses, and then taxed these private entities at such an exorbitant rate that the only way to survive was to underreport income and not pay all of the taxes. The end result was that all entrepreneurs became nontaxpaying criminals, exactly what the communist philosophy had predicted.

THERE IS A FINE LINE BETWEEN CREATIVE AND CRIMINAL BEHAVIOR

There were times when I admired how quickly my staff learned to come up with creative business solutions. We had purchased an entire truckload of vodka for the ruble equivalent of 90 cents a bottle. The government passed a decree that no food item (including staples like vodka) could be marked up by more than 10 percent over cost. This meant we could not legally charge more than 99 cents a bottle, even though the going market price was $1.20. Our staff came up with the idea of a combination offer—a bottle of vodka and a plastic bag for only $1.15. We quickly sold out the entire truckload.

A UNIQUE WAY TO SET WAGE RATES

I asked my Russian friends how the government decided how much to pay government workers. In 1992, cafeteria workers were paid $15 a month, doctors earned $18 a month, and assembly-line workers in the tire factory were paid $70 a month. My friends answered that wages were determined by the opportunities for stealing in the various professions. Workers in the restaurant industry were paid the least of all because there was ample food to steal for their families and friends. It was difficult to hide a tire in your clothing, so the factory workers were paid much more.

"But what about the doctors?" I said. "With all their education, why were they paid so little?"

"They get tips," was the only answer I could get.

One day I learned how tips might be paid to a doctor. I was negotiating to buy a dacha from the family of an elderly woman who was living in a nursing home for the mentally insane. We negotiated a price of $1,500 for the little stucco house and one-third of an acre in a small village that was 15 miles outside of Yaroslavl.

The dacha had not been lived in for five years and was in need of considerable repair. I consulted a local carpenter, who made a list of what needed to be done. When I asked him for a price quote, he said, "If you will supply the materials, I'll do the labor for a case of vodka."

That seemed like a reasonable quote. I asked for an estimate of how much the materials might cost. He consulted his list and gave my request several minutes of serious consideration. I will never forget his response. "For another case of vodka, I'll steal the materials."

Satisfied with both the price of the dacha and the projected cost of repairs, I told the family that I would like to buy the dacha. When they went to get their mother's signature on the sales agreement, they learned she had already conveyed the title to her doctor, who had promised her special personal care for the rest of her life in return. At that point, I understood what they meant by *tips*.

In the end, I concluded that the only way to have a successful business in Russia is for it to be owned by someone who was willing to underreport income and not pay all of the taxes due. Because I was not willing to conduct business in this manner, I arranged to sell my business to Russian entrepreneurs who could do what needed to be done to survive. (Ultimately, they couldn't make it either, in spite of a strong local demand for pizza and ice cream.)

WHAT I LEARNED

■ *Russian people are absolutely wonderful in every important way.* However, their system is hopelessly corrupt, making it impossible for the people to enjoy the fruits of the free-market system. If the U.S. political system and financial infrastructure could somehow magically be imposed on Russia, it would quickly become an economic world power. Until something that dramatic occurs, it will continue to be a third-world, essentially bankrupt nation, in spite of its incredible natural and people resources.

■ *Friends are more important than any business success.* All of my Russian business ventures have ended, but I have some great friends who will remain with me for the rest of my life. I wouldn't trade these friends for all the riches I might have made.

■ *What works in the United States does not necessarily work in other cultures (especially Russia).* Everyone should visit Russia at least once. You can't help but return with a great appreciation of our stable political and economic infrastructure that really works.

Chapter 17

Charitable Trusts: Giving Away $1,000 Every Day Forever

How to Give It All Away without Dying First

Once the sale of the business was completed, my lawyer, Jon Eggleston, and accountant, Jeff Small, gave me sound investment advice. Of course, I ignored it. Jon recommended that I become a Florida resident to avoid about $300,000 in Vermont state taxes (enough to buy a luxury condo). All Debbie and I would have to do was stay out of Vermont for six months and a day each year. We sat down and tried to figure out when to leave Vermont. We could identify only two possible months: April (mud season) and November (stick season and deer hunting season). All of the other months we wanted to be in Vermont, either skiing, gardening, or playing tennis. We decided that living here was worth the $300,000 we would lose by staying at home.

BUILD THE HOUSE OF YOUR DREAMS AND YOU MAY NEVER WANT TO LEAVE

The most important reason for not wanting to leave Vermont was our house. Ever since I lost the house of my dreams in South Pomfret, I had longed for a 200-year-old house in the country. When I finally had enough money to afford such a house, Debbie and I couldn't find one that wasn't right on a busy road. (Apparently, that's where they built them 200 years ago.) Our solution was to buy a 226-acre piece of rural Vermont, and design and build our own antique colonial, using recycled materials from several 200-year-old houses. We spent an entire year collecting hand-hewn beams, wide pine floorboards, and slate roofs from Nova Scotia to Pennsylvania.

We ended up with a house that is more than I ever hoped for in my wildest dreams. We fully intend to spend the rest of our lives here. We are in the process of deeding development rights to the Vermont Land Trust to preserve the rural nature of the land forever.

CHARITABLE REMAINDER TRUSTS AREN'T REALLY CHARITABLE UNTIL YOU DIE

Responding to my interest in giving something back for my good fortune, Jeff Small suggested that I set up a charitable remainder trust. This would give me a substantial sum of money every year to live a life of luxury, and when I died, whatever is left would go to charity. "Sounds like the dullest thing I could imagine," I said, "An annuity for life. Why would I want that?"

Jeff seemed perplexed. "Most of my clients work their entire lives to set up an annuity so they will never have financial worries again. You have the chance to do it and you refuse. You must really enjoy living on the edge."

"I must," I responded, "It's the only thing I know."

As soon as I was legally able to transfer my ABI stock, I contributed one-third of my shares to the Terry F. Allen Family Charitable Trust, a 501(c)3 organization. The shares were sold for just over $1.2 million. Not only did I get a deduction for giving away these shares, but I did not have to pay a capital gains tax. It would have been huge. In 1980, I had paid $1 per share for the original shares in my corporation (which eventually became County Data Corporation), and each of these shares were sold for about $100,000 in 1997. I don't think even Warren Buffett has done that well. (If I had known these shares would increase in value by 100,000 times, I would have bought more in 1980.)

The charitable trust is legally required to give away 5 percent of its assets each year, or about $60,000. My goal was to give away much more than this. I set a goal of giving away $1,000 every day for the rest of my life—$365,000 every year—and also of creating enough of a base so that this amount could be given away by the trust forever.

I set these goals to give my investment activities, and my life, some meaning. I had never had much money at any time in my life. I had gained much personal satisfaction by scrambling around to provide a decent lifestyle for my family. Now that I had some money at last, I knew I would not get much satisfaction from just making the numbers larger. I now had enough to live on, and my sons and former wives were secure. I felt that it was the perfect time to use my creative energies to help others.

A wonderful thing about having a family charitable trust is that you get to decide how to give the money away. It is a great opportunity for personal introspection and analysis of your belief systems. With the other trustees (my sons and Debbie), the following seven criteria for our donations were set:

1. The money will be spent entirely in Vermont. (We are a small state without a lot of wealth, and feel that we can do a better job when we stay close to home.)
2. Preference is given to those organizations that have a lot of free contributed labor (a small amount of money combined with donated time can have significant results).
3. Preference is given to those organizations that are primarily serving children and women at risk.
4. Preference is given to those organizations that do not have a development director. (We like to see the bulk of our money going directly to the charity rather than supporting a development team. However, we are sympathetic to groups whose development directors are able to more than cover themselves with grants from other sources.)
5. A maximum of $100 a year is given to any health-related cause. (It seems that every disease and every organ has its own

charity. Much of the money goes to pay for collecting donations, and most of the rest goes to research in far-away states.
We like to see a more immediate and local benefit for our contributions.)

6. Preference is given to those organizations who lack a natural
constituency (most colleges, churches), or who fall through
the cracks in conventional fundraising efforts (e.g., United
Way).

7. The following are excluded from consideration:
   ■ Anything religious
   ■ Capital campaigns (we want to use our limited funds for
   on-going programs)
   ■ Anyone who calls us on the telephone (one call is allowed
   to get our mailing address)

Our first major contribution was $100,000 to build a new outdoor
swimming pool for the Burlington Boys & Girls Club. Debbie and I
got our picture on the front page of the *Burlington Free Press*. This
opened a floodgate of inquiries from charitable groups throughout
the state. Over 50 groups asked us for money.

The phone never seemed to stop ringing. That was when I insti-
tuted the injunction against phone calls. Every letter we send out
reminds the charity that a phone call automatically eliminates them
from consideration that year. (We have already withheld money
from some who called and had been slated to receive money.) If the
phone continued to ring, I would have no time left to earn money to
give away.

In our first 2½ years of existence, we have given away over
$800,000, and the $1.2 million has grown to over $2 million in
value. A healthy stock market has helped (although the year 2000
was a difficult one). We have contributed to over 60 Vermont organizations, including food shelves, homeless programs, rape crisis
centers, playground groups, environmental groups, land trusts, and
dozens of others. Now that the telephone has stopped ringing, it has
really been fun.

The trust's largest commitment came about from my involvement
as a trustee of Champlain College. A small Burlington-based college, Champlain has remarkable success in preparing young people

for well-paying, technologically advanced jobs. It was one of the first colleges to offer a major in website design, for example. My family trust had given a $5,000 scholarship to the college, and half of it was given to a freshman accounting major named Sonia Kemp.

Sonia wrote me a thank-you letter that will ultimately affect hundreds of Vermont young people. She told me about her life with a dysfunctional biological family, drug and alcohol addiction, domestic violence and jail, and that she was shunted from one foster home to another.

In her sophomore year in high school, she was getting low grades, and in many respects was carrying on the family traditions. One of her teachers got through to her, asking if that was the kind of life she wanted to live. Sonia resolved to turn her life around, and did. She graduated near the top of her class and got a full scholarship in the accounting program at Champlain. Next year, she will be the first person in her biological family to graduate from college.

Sonia's letter inspired me to support others like her who attend Champlain College. If this was the kind of person my money was helping, I wanted it to be there. The trust has committed $150,000 every year for 10 years for fifty $3,000 scholarships to needy Vermonters. I receive 50 thank-you letters each year from the scholarship recipients. They are wonderful reminders for me that I did the right thing with this money.

BIOGRAPHIES PROVIDE INSPIRATION

Other than maintaining a passing average in school, there are two stipulations for these scholarship recipients. First, each student must read a biography or autobiography of his or her own choosing. I believe that we can all learn many valuable things from every person's life. Most successful people had to endure substantial obstacles to achieve whatever they accomplished. Struggling to get through school and pay for it as well is one of those obstacles.

As a young teenager, I had read Andrew Carnegie's biography. He had spent the first half of his life amassing a fortune in the steel industry, and the second half of his life in what he called the more difficult task of giving it away responsibly. I thought this was a great life to emulate, and wrote down a goal for myself of giving away a million dollars in my lifetime. I feel blessed to have been able to reach this goal.

The second requirement of my scholarship recipients is to spend an hour with me (as a group) each September. In this hour, we work on creating a list of personal goals for each student. I have long believed that the process of writing down goals has an almost mystical quality that causes you to move in the direction of achieving them. It is perhaps an unconscious attempt on your part, but writing them down and reviewing them often somehow helps make them come true.

I have written down a list of 10 goals for every year of the last 45 years. I still have every goals list I ever made. This may sound a little neurotic, but I clearly believe that it is a helpful exercise that results in higher levels of achievement and satisfaction. Now, if I could only lose those 10 pounds. (That has been 1 of my 10 yearly goals at least 30 times.)

The second largest charity that our trust has supported is Debbie's project—the Ferrisburgh Artisans Guild. At an auction, we bought an interesting 16-acre property on Route 7 in Ferrisburgh. In addition to an 1810 brick colonial, the property had six other structures, including the second oldest covered bridge in Vermont, a train depot (now home to fine furniture makers), a large gift shop (now a pottery studio and art education center), a cider mill (now a gourmet restaurant—the Starry Night Cafe), a smokehouse, and several barns. The main building serves as a gallery for over 150 juried Vermont artists.

For the first two years, the Guild required almost $150,000 of the trust's money each year to remain afloat. Artists' sales increased by 77 percent in the year 2000, however, and we hope that the Guild will become self-sufficient in less than five years. That will free up lots of money to give to other worthy efforts in Vermont.

ANGEL INVESTORS DESERVE A SPECIAL PLACE IN HEAVEN

Another form of charity (some would say) is my other major endeavor right now—angel investing. I am a member of the Angel

Investors Group, a loosely affiliated group of mostly former entrepreneurs who get together once a month to hear two presentations from would-be entrepreneurs seeking money. [I understand that there is another company with our initials: AIG (an insurance company, I think). We have decided not to contest their use of our initials.] I have made private angel investments between $25,000 and $100,000 in more than a dozen companies in Vermont in the last four years. So far, four have gone belly-up, but it's still early. That's why I call these investments another form of charity.

UNIQUE ANGEL INVESTMENT MODEL

Rather than owning 5 percent or 10 percent of a start-up company, there is another form of angel investing that I think offers a greater chance of ultimate success. The downside is that you will inevitably get more involved. In this model, a corporation is set up with the investor and the entrepreneur as directors. The investor owns 100 percent of the stock. The entrepreneur and investor create a business plan that makes sense to both of them, and the entrepreneur goes to work. Each month, the investor puts in enough cash to pay all the unpaid bills. The entrepreneur draws a fixed salary until the investor's money is paid back.

As soon as the company makes a profit, the investor starts getting his money back. He does not receive any interest on his investment. Once he has been paid back in full for his principal, the investor transfers 70 percent of the company stock to the entrepreneur, who now controls the company.

The investor then starts earning a yearly salary that is equal to 30 percent of the maximum amount of money that he loaned to the company. This salary continues as long as the entrepreneur has any interest in the company.

I used this formula with Chris Hallowell to set up a credit card processing company. Chris had worked at County Data, so I knew his work ethic, and I liked the business idea. At first, Chris focused on setting up credit card payment systems for new businesses (buying names from The Lead Sheet, then owned by ABI). Soon, he discovered that a more lucrative market was to offer much lower rates than local banks were charging retail stores to process credit cards. (Many banks charged a 3.5 percent processing fee for credit card sales, whereas our company could do it for less than 2 percent.) Each month, Chris would call and tell me how much money he would need to get through the month. He wanted to take as little as possible, because my payback was determined by the maximum loan I extended.

I liked the arrangement because I controlled the corporation until I got my money back. At any time, if Chris did not perform according to the business plan, I could fire him and hire someone else to run the company. Of course, we often negotiated around the business plan specifications—neither of us really wanted anyone else to be running the company.

The most I had to loan to this business was $80,000. Chris is now successful and has almost as many merchant credit card accounts as the largest bank in Vermont. The loan is being repaid to me at about $5,000 per month out of profits. (It would have been paid off in full long ago if Chris had not been the victim of some outrageous credit card fraud, a risk he is now insured against). In mid-2001, I will convey 70 percent of the company stock to Chris, and enjoy a $24,000 annual salary from then on. It has been four years since I have received a salary from anyone. It will feel good.

Finally, I am involved in one investment activity that actually makes good money. A younger and much smarter friend of mine, John Fife, and I own a small-business investment company (SBIC) called Chicago Venture Partners, L.P. I am a minority partner, owning 27 percent. Together, we pledged to invest $10 million in the SBIC, and the SBA (Small Business Administration) will loan us another $20 million to invest in small businesses.

Most of our investments are in early-stage high-tech companies with at least $1 million in sales and a proven business model. Our average investment is $2 million. So far, we have invested in nine such companies, and every company but one is doing very well. In five cases, other venture capital money has come into the company at a much higher valuation than ours, suggesting that our investment has increased in value. Our second investment was in Open Orders, a Boston software company. We invested $3.2 million for 40 percent of the company. In less than two years, IBM bought the company for $18 million, giving us about a $4-million profit.

Another of our companies, Alert Cellular in Salt Lake City, is making a profit of about $2 million a year. We own 49 percent of Alert, and my share of the profits comes to over $250,000 a year. Not bad, considering my share of the investment was only $270,000. Having some real capital of your own really does make it easier.

Ironically, the only investment that is not looking good is the only company that has gone public. We bought about 400,000 shares of Caldera (a Linux company) for $6 a share. Two months later, the company went public at $14 and the stock soared to $33. We were jumping up and down in glee. The stock later crashed to less than $2, and we were prohibited from selling our shares until February 2001. (We believe that we will eventually make a profit on Caldera, but everyone knows that there is nothing predictable about the stock market.)

WHAT I LEARNED

- *Giving it away is more fun than making it.*
- *There is great satisfaction in giving away money to worthy causes while you are still alive.* Surely, it's more fun giving it away while you're around to see the results of your generosity. Why do so many people wait until they're dead before they give it away?
- *The best angel investments are larger ones in which the investor retains a large-equity interest.* As Andrew Carnegie said, put all your eggs in one basket and watch the basket.
- *Whatever you do, do it with passion.* Life is too short to waste your time doing things half-heartedly.

Chapter 18

Looking Back

How to Turn $10 into $10 Million in Ten Easy Steps

When I look back over my life, I realize that one business inevitably led to another one, and there was a natural progression from one to the next. Even though there were many distractions and chasing after rabbits instead of hunting the elephant, the journey was not haphazard. Every business naturally evolved from an earlier one. Here is how the progression went:

1. Bought a book for $10 entitled *How I Turned $1,000 into a Million in Real Estate in My Spare Time,* by William Nickerson.

2. Bought all the real estate I could get my hands on with no money down.

3. Converted several large single-family houses into apartments using rented tools. Became the largest customer of the local equipment rental dealer.

4. Bought the local rental business with no money down, and expanded it to a six-store chain using bank financing.

5. Tried to find a book about how to advertise and promote an equipment rental business. Couldn't find one, so wrote it myself.

6. While writing the book, came up with the idea of mailing a coupon to new homeowners. Tried it and it worked.
7. Offered the coupon-mailing service to other merchants, creating a new business—Merchants Welcome Service.
8. Tried to sell the list of new homeowners we were compiling. It worked, and *Real Estate Transfer Directory* became a reality.
9. Discovered that a neat way to sell real estate data was to compile a list of newly formed real estate agencies. Started compiling a list of real estate agencies as well as all new companies and selling the list to many businesses, mostly to accountants.
10. Expanded the new-business-formations list compilation business to a national level and sold the company to a public company for more than $10,000,000.

See how easy it can be?

THE HIERARCHY OF CAPITAL SOURCES

Looking back at my fund-raising activity, I realize that I used a great variety of different sources. All capital is not equal. Some capital requires high-interest payments or giving away ownership of your company, whereas other capital does not entail such encumbrances.

The most expensive sources of capital are the easiest to locate. Getting the money from them is not easy, however. For a wonderful description of the emotional effort and agony of seeking capital from venture capital firms, a must-read is *The Leap,* by Tom Ashbrook (New York, Houghton Mifflin, 2000).

Many entrepreneurs knock themselves out chasing after the most expensive sources of capital. With a little imagination and effort directed in other areas, they might be able to find less expensive, or even free, capital to start their business.

I have created the Hierarchy of Capital Sources (Fig. 18.1) as a rough guide to looking for the highest-quality capital (i.e., least expensive in the obligations that it entails). Generally, you should start at the top and only work down the hierarchy when you have fully explored opportunities at the upper levels. With luck and hard

> ## Creativity
> ## Customers
> ## Suppliers
> ## Personal Resources
> ## Angels
> ## Local Development Organizations
> ## Banks
> ## Friends and Relatives
> ## Strangers
> ## Venture Capital
> ## Secured Lenders

Figure 18.1   The Hierarchy of Capital Sources.

work, you may never have to resort to sources lower than the top four (all of which require no interest or equity dilution).

This hierarchy may not be appropriate for all businesses, and the precise order of the sources may vary by individual situations. However, no matter what kind of business you are contemplating, you can benefit by giving serious consideration to every single source, starting at the top. Don't overlook a single opportunity.

Creativity

Every new business is essentially a marketing research experiment. You create a product or service and then go out and see if enough people will buy your offering to make it a viable business.

If you think of what you are doing as a market test rather than the building of a business, you can come up with all sorts of creative ideas to spend less (i.e., require less capital) to achieve your objective. Once you have run a successful market test, finding all sorts of capital will be a cinch.

The first step in using your creativity as a substitute for costly capital is to use the 10 percent rule: "How can I test this product and use only 10 percent of the capital I originally intended?" Spend time brainstorming this idea, and you can save yourself tens of thousands of dollars.

Some ideas you might come up with include the following:

■ Do your market research with an order form (and maybe ask for cash in advance).

■ Rent, don't buy, every tangible asset possible.

■ Rent, don't employ, people—subcontract everything possible to other people or companies.

■ Share retail or office space with someone else in a related industry.

■ Limit your market area to a precise geographical area (you can always expand once the test is successful).

■ Keep your day job (or teach school at night, or wait on tables weekends) so you don't have to draw a salary at first.

Your own creativity is the most important of all capital sources— you find capital by figuring out how you can meet your objectives with less of it. You will also make the best of your most scarce resource—your time—by avoiding the all-encompassing search for outside capital. Many companies have fallen by the wayside because the entrepreneur spent too much time trying to raise money and not enough time running the business.

Customers

If you can collect money in advance from your customers, even if it's just a deposit, you have uncovered the second best source of capital. There is no interest for you to pay, and you make a sale at the same time that you receive money. Repayment to your customer involves delivery of goods or services on which you should be making a fair profit. Best of all, when a customer gives you money in advance, you have proved that there is really a market for your product or service.

Suppliers

Negotiate extended payment terms with your suppliers, and you have discovered a wonderful source of capital for your business. Again, there is usually no interest to pay. If you sell your inventory for cash (collecting cash or a credit card payment), you have free cash in the bank, which may be used for many business purposes. Suppliers may also be eager enough for your business to loan you money to help you get started.

Bob Harnish, an old and dear friend of mine, owned the Cortina ski lodge at Killington. After two consecutive winters of little snow, his business had suffered, and he faced a liquidity crunch. He approached his suppliers (e.g., linen service, fuel oil dealer, food and wine suppliers, etc.), and almost every supplier made him unsecured short-term loans to retain his business. Snow finally came, Bob repaid his suppliers, and Cortina has been a great success ever since.

A special kind of supplier is the person who wants to sell you his or her business. By accepting extended payment terms, the seller of a business could easily become your most important source of capital. I have used sellers as willing sources of capital more than a dozen times. They liked it because they can get a higher price for their business, and I liked it because I needed little or no cash.

Personal Resources

Presumably, you have some of your own money to put into your business. If you don't, get as many credit cards as you possibly can while you still have a paying job. Then you will have a source of funds.

If you are expecting to get money from any outside sources, it will be far easier if you have put your own money into the business. *Sweat equity* (i.e., working real hard with little or no pay) is important, but investors like to see that you have real money on the line as well.

Angels

There are two categories of angel investors. The first I call *eagles*. They have usually earned their money through a successful business of their own, although a few have inherited money. Eagles are generally financially astute. They have probably read hundreds of business plans and invested in dozens of companies. Oftentimes, they serve on many boards of directors or provide valuable consulting advice for entrepreneurs. Eagles are the best variety of angels to get money from because they can also be a source of free consulting advice and outside business contacts.

Until recently, angel investors worked by themselves, and were often difficult to find. Some maintained loose informal ties with other angels. Now, they are organized. They regularly get together and meet as a group to consider investments. Usually, they share the cost and the time of conducting due diligence on proposed investment opportunities.

The bottom line is that angel investors are easier to find than ever (we even have an active angel investing group here in Vermont). You can find them by asking lawyers, accountants, bankers, business schools (entrepreneurship professors), or anyone who has a business financed with angel money.

A second variety of angel investor exists. I call them the *pigeon* variety. They have saved up a little money, but they are not rich. They might make a single angel investment in their lifetime. They usually fall blindly in love with a product or service idea, or a friend or relative's scheme, and plunk down their money with little or no investigation of the industry, the likely success of the business, or the skills of management. In the end, almost all pigeons lose every penny they invest.

The moral of this story is that if you are planning to start a business of your own, you must be nice to everyone. You never know when you might be talking to an angel investor—pigeon variety.

Local Development Organization

More and more government agencies at the local, county, and state levels are getting into the venture capital business. Often, they make investments (usually loans) primarily to stimulate the local economy rather than to earn a big return on their investment. Accordingly, this money comes with a lower interest rate and no request for equity. Even more important, many of these loans are made with less scrutiny of the financial statements than more sophisticated sources of money might employ.

Banks

Remember, banks don't loan money, but bankers do. It is a good idea to develop a personal relationship with a banker, or two or three, well before you actually need money. Once a banker has confidence in you and your business acumen, you may be able to get money that you never thought possible. I recommend getting to know several commercial lending officers because they often change jobs inside and outside of the bank, and you have to start all over again with a new person.

Even though banks are not in the venture capital business, they do make loans to companies whose business is seasonal, or where there is a lag between when a sale is made and cash is received. Accounts receivable financing is a popular form of getting capital from banks.

A good business plan can demonstrate to your banker why you need money for the slow months of the years, and how and when you will repay the loan. If you can make a reasonable case that you will need the money for less than a year, you have a good chance of getting an unsecured loan from a banker (be prepared to co-sign the loan as an individual, however).

Friends and Relatives

If there is any way of skipping over friends and relatives as sources of capital, by all means, do it. Borrowing money from friends and relatives is tainted by the personal relationship that you have with these people. You will probably overpromise when you can repay their loans, and this will be a source of anguish and unhappiness for both parties. It gets even worse if you can't repay the loan at all (this possibility must be considered, in spite of how certain your business idea seems). In reality, probably at least half of all personal loans to start a business are *never* repaid.

The good thing about borrowing from friends and relatives (and the reason I suggest that you get all the money you can from all the other sources before you approach those who are closest to you) is that they will probably advance you the money no matter how bad your balance sheet looks. In fact, friends and relatives probably won't even ask to see your balance sheet. All other types of capital sources will check it out thoroughly. As an alternative to getting cash from friends or relatives, you might consider asking them to co-sign a note from some other source, such as a bank. Of course, you will be taking all of the psychic and personal risks that you would incur if you had borrowed the money directly from your friend or relative.

Strangers

The best thing about strangers is that there are so many of them. No matter how hard you try, you will never run out of strangers to ask for money. Most Americans have credit cards, a fact which makes all of them a source of capital.

Two guys whom I once knew rode the trains from Darien, Connecticut, to New York City back and forth all day long, selecting seats next to prosperous-looking commuters. They struck up conversations with each traveling companion, and always ended up talking about the business they were contemplating. They raised $200,000 of start-up capital in less than a month.

Use your creativity to find strangers to ask for money. Expand your network and ask people whom you know for the names of people whom you don't know. There is no stigma to asking for money. Most people will be flattered to think you believed they looked prosperous enough to invest in your business.

In every case, if you ask someone for money and they decline your request, you don't lose anything. In the worst case, you end up just where you started. Nothing lost, little gained. (I believe there is almost always something gained in every unsuccessful encounter: You learn about objections people might have, or how you could have made a more effective presentation of your ideas.)

Every person who turns you down should be asked for a referral. "If this investment is not good for you, whom else do you know to whom I should speak?" you should ask. Having just turned you down, they may feel good about giving you a good referral. This is an excellent way of expanding your list of strangers to speak with.

Venture Capital

If you have an idea that could turn into a really big business, you might be of interest to a venture capital company. Most of these firms expect to invest $2 million or more, but there are some small-business investment companies (SBICs) that might prefer smaller amounts. Be prepared to give up a large percentage of your company to get this kind of money. Venture capital firms expect to see a detailed business plan that outlines a sound business model, a competent management team, and a reasonable exit strategy (i.e., how they will get their money back, either through an IPO or sale of the company).

Secured Lenders

Like death and taxes, secured lenders will always be there. They are the least imaginative or interesting of all of the sources of capital. They are unwilling to take a risk.

Unsecured lenders are not your friends. They don't care if your business succeeds or not. (In fact, they may be hoping that you will fail so they can seize your collateral, which might be worth more than the money they loaned to you.) All of the other sources of capital will be rooting for you to succeed. They'll give you leads for possible new customers, and they'll buy your product or service themselves if they need it.

You don't have to be nice to secured lenders. All they care about is the value of your collateral and how high an interest rate they can extract from you. If any of the higher-level sources of capital brings up the subject of collateral for their loan, instantly shift them to the lowest-ranking category where they belong, groveling around with the other low-lying snakes. Most start-ups don't have a lot of collateral to borrow against, so this level of lender is irrelevant anyway.

FEEL POSITIVE ABOUT ASKING FOR MONEY

While seeking money from any potential source of capital (and virtually anyone is truly a potential source), it is important to maintain a healthy psychological attitude about what you are doing. In no way should you feel embarrassed or consider your search for money as an indication of personal weakness.

On the contrary, you are offering people the opportunity to participate in the creation of something beautiful. There is romance and excitement in the transition of a unique idea into a business reality. (Every business transaction, unless fraud is involved, is a win-win situation for both parties.)

When you invite someone to invest in your idea, you are offering them something they could never find for sale in the Yellow Pages. There will never again be an offer exactly like yours. Isn't that an exhilarating thought? They can vicariously participate in the success of your dream, and they won't have to bother with the minutiae of actually making the business work.

Not only are you flattering your prospective investor by asking them for money, you are offering them a unique opportunity that they won't be able to find anywhere else. They should be grateful to you for making your offer.

ONE FINAL BIT OF ADVICE—WHAT TO DO
WITH THE FIRST $1,000 THAT YOU SAVE

In the first half of our adult life, most of us do not accumulate much in the way of hard cash. For some of us, the first half stretches to become the first 80 or 90 percent of our adult lives. Because you are reading this book, I guess you are most likely in that earlier stage when you are not living off your accumulated savings.

So, what do you do when you save your first $1,000 or $2,000? Put it in a savings account for a rainy day? Buy a hot high-tech stock? Or blow it on a vacation? Financial advisors would recommend savings or investing. I would suggest checking travel destinations on the Internet.

Saving for a rainy day seems like such good practical advice. To me, it's a waste of hard-earned money. As long as you have a credit card (or better, two or more credit cards) with unused credit, you have perpetual protection against that rainy day that probably will never come anyway. And you don't have your hard-earned cash tied up wastefully earning 5 percent interest.

Investing in a hot tech stock can be exciting. You get to feel that you're part of the new economy, and you have something to look for in the financial pages. You can groan in anguish or cry out in delight every time you see your stock symbol crawling along the C-SPAN screen. What do you really get, though, even if you are lucky enough to pick the right stock? Your investment may double or triple in a year, so now you have $2,000 or $4,000 or so. Has your life really changed? Not really. Maybe you have two or three stock symbols to watch, but your financial situation is still essentially worthless.

Taking the vacation is surely the wisest long-term financial decision. Take along a book to read that will make you a better or smarter person. Open your eyes to things that are different in your strange new surroundings. Maybe you'll discover a business idea that you can take home and put to use. While you're away from your at-home routine, write down your goals or plan your future.

In short, the best way to spend the first few dollars that you accumulate is to invest in yourself. Read a book every week. (You can read books like newspapers, skimming for a few good ideas).

You might consider reading *How to Get Control of Your Time and Your Life,* by Alan Lakein, the best book I have found on time management, or *Looking Out for Number One,* by Robert J. Ringer, an entertaining reminder that you can probably achieve much more than you ever thought possible.

Take an evening course at a local college. Learn a new language (perhaps a computer language). Buy a computer, and discover the world of the Internet.

One wonderful way to invest in yourself is to start your own business, even if it's part-time. That's what I did for my entire life. Having your own business is an accelerated learning experience, and it pays great dividends (in the form of lessons), even if you never make a nickel of real money.

I told you the story of how I set up my most successful corporation by issuing 100 shares of stock to myself and my family at $1 each. Sixteen years later, I sold these shares for $100,000 each, netting over $10 million on a $100 investment. These kinds of returns are only possible if you invest in yourself rather than someone else's company.

WHAT TO DO WITH THE FIRST MILLION DOLLARS YOU SAVE

In my experience, when the big money comes, you may be shocked at how you spend it. I had spent a lifetime of hanging on the edge, owing the bank and creditors more than I could pay, and worrying about meeting payrolls. Surely, when my ship came in, I would pay off all of my mortgages; invest my money in fixed-income instruments; and live the easy, stress-free life that I deserved.

Today, in spite of my business successes, I have the biggest mortgage in my life, and I still don't have a savings account, certificates of deposit, or a bond. I am still living on the edge, although not quite as close to it as in my earlier days. It's nice to have a little cushion and to continue to scratch my entrepreneurial itch by investing in other people's growing businesses.

Clearly, my active participation in charitable giving is personally more rewarding than anything I have done in my life. I just love it. And I want to do more, which gives meaning to all of my investment activities. The more money I can make, the more I will have to give away.

What you do with your first million is really up to you. From personal experience, it's nice to have the choice. I feel strongly that you should invest your first $1,000 in yourself, whatever form that investment might take. I cannot give you any advice on what to do with your first million. I can only tell you what I did with mine, much to my own surprise.

NOTHING EVER WORKS OUT THE WAY YOU EXPECT

I started a ski lodge as a way to meet women and found a wife before the first ski bunny arrived.

I had a loyal employee who had five children and a horrible credit history. I found her a below-market house in an estate sale, co-signed a loan for her down payment, and convinced my bank to bend its rules and grant her a mortgage. Over the next two years, she embezzled from me every month.

After many years of teaching, I returned to school to earn a Ph.D. so that I could get a tenure-track teaching position. Once I got the degree, I never taught full-time again.

Most entrepreneurs live for the day when they finally have their own IPO. My only company that had an IPO resulted in my losing every dollar that I had invested. The trick is to be prepared for anything—and you won't be surprised when everything works out exactly opposite to what you had originally expected.

CONCLUSION

This book was designed to be a model of the life of an entrepreneur. I hope it caught the spirit of this life choice, especially the vicissitudes of every conceivable kind—the exhilaration of success and the agony of defeat. A model can be helpful to persuade or dissuade us to pursue a similar path. I have shown you what this kind of life is like; only you can decide whether it's for you.

If you choose this kind of life for yourself, I wish you happy entrepreneuring. The journey will always be more important than the destination. That said, I hope your ship comes in before your dock rots.

BIBLIOGRAPHY

Allen, Archie P. *Coach's Guide to Defensive Baseball.* Englewood Cliffs, NJ: Prentice-Hall, 1960.

Ashbrook, Tom. *The Leap.* New York: Houghton Mifflin, 2000.

Books in Print. New Providence, NJ: R.R. Bowker, annual publication.

Burnett, Ed. *The Complete Direct Mail List Handbook.* Englewood Cliffs, NJ: Prentice-Hall, 1988.

Carnegie, Andrew. *Autobiography of Andrew Carnegie.* Garden City, NY: Doubleday, Doran, 1933.

Charrell, Ralph. *A Great New Way to Make Money.* New York: Stein and Day, 1976.

The Direct Marketing Handbook. New York: McGraw-Hill, 1984.

Dyer, Wayne W. *Your Erroneous Zones.* New York: Funk & Wagnalls Book Publishing, 1976.

Editor & Publisher. New York: Editor & Publisher Co., 1966.

Garn, Roy. *The Magic Power of Emotional Appeal.* Englewood Cliffs, NJ: Prentice-Hall, 1960.

Hill, Napoleon. *Think and Grow Rich.* New York: Hawthorn Books, 1966.

Klauser, Henriette Anne. *Write It Down, Make It Happen.* New York: Scribner, 2000.

Lakein, Alan. *How to Get Control of Your Time and Your Life.* New York: New American Library, 1974.

Lerner, Max. *Thomas Jefferson: America's Philosopher-King.* New Brunswick, NJ: Transaction Publishers, 1996.

McWilliams, Peter and John-Roger *Do It!* Los Angeles: Prelude Press, 1991.

Needleman, Jacob. *Money and the Meaning of Life.* New York: Currency Doubleday, 1991.

Nickerson, William. *How I Turned $1,000 into a Million in Real Estate.* New York: Simon & Shuster, 1959.

Rackham, Neil. *SPIN Selling.* New York: McGraw-Hill, 1988.

Rand, Ayn. *Atlas Shrugged.* New York: Random House, 1957.

Rand, Ayn. *The Fountainhead.* Philadelphia: The Blakiston Company, 1943.

Ray, Sondra. *Rebirthing.* Berkeley, CA: Celestial Arts, 1978.

Ringer, Robert J. *Looking Out for Number One.* Beverly Hills, CA: Los Angeles Book Corp., 1977.

Schwartz, David Joseph. *The Magic of Thinking Big.* New York: Simon & Schuster, 1987.

INDEX

■ Index ■

▪ Index ▪

■ Index ■